The Witness
Who Spoke with God

The Witness
Who Spoke with God

---

and Other Tales
from the Courthouse

MILTON S. GOULD

The Viking Press • *New York*

First published in 1979 by the Viking Press
625 Madison Avenue, New York, N.Y. 10022
Published simultaneously in Canada by
Penguin Books Canada Limited

LIBRARY OF CONGRESS CATALOGING IN PUBLICATION DATA
Gould, Milton S
The witness who spoke with God
and other tales from the courthouse.

Includes index.
1. Gould, Milton S.   2. Lawyers—United States—
Biography.   3. Law—United States—Anecdotes,
facetiae, satire, etc.   I. Title.
KF373.G64A35   340'.092'4 [B]   79–10038
ISBN 0–670–69158–5

Most of these stories originally appeared in the *New York Law Journal*
Printed in the United States of America
Set in Video Janson

DEDICATION

This book is dedicated with affection and respect to the lawyers and judges of New York, past and present. They have been my friends, good companions, and honored adversaries for more than forty years. To have been of their goodly company is one of the chief rewards of an active professional life. In this book they appear as Cromwell had wanted his portrait to appear: "roughnesses, pimples, warts and everything." Surely, we have had our Wanderers who have erred and strayed from the Way. You will read of some of them in this book. But it should gleam from these pages that New York's lawyers and judges are a tried and valiant fellowship, hardy and courageous professionals devoted to the common good and to the discharge of their traditional obligations.

INTRODUCTION

When a book is completed, the author looks back to recall the moment of its birth. This book is the result of an accident. In the fall of 1976, the publisher of *The New York Law Journal* gave his annual dinner for the board of editors of that publication. After dinner, methods and ideas for broadening the compass of the *Law Journal* were discussed, for we were all interested in leavening the daily loaf of technical articles, calendars, and decisions. Even lawyers and judges, we agreed, are entitled to one sweetmeat a day. It was suggested that among us were lawyers and judges with memoirs, recollections, souvenirs of their professional lives, that would provide entertaining reading. The story about Hymie Schorenstein that you will find in the early part of this book was the first one of these legal memoirs published in the paper. It attracted attention among lawyers and came to the notice of Elisabeth Sifton, of The Viking Press. She not only enjoyed it but wrote me a letter suggesting that a collection of such pieces might be the basis for a book of general interest. I regaled her with some of the yarns with which I had bored countless dinner tables for almost half a century. To my delight, she was enthusiastic, and encouraged me to produce a few more stories. Gradually the form of a book began to appear. It is designed as an entertainment, not as a memoir.

There is one problem with such a book. Every active trial lawyer has a treasure house of reminiscences that make good stories and merit preservation. But most of us are incurable hams, and the books that lawyers turn out about themselves are often self-adulatory. Criminal lawyers shamelessly trumpet their sleaziest skills; negligence lawyers display *their* aptitudes; corporate lawyers, political lawyers, labor lawyers, judges (high and low), have all produced memoirs with the air of Little Jack Horner. And, indeed, they are usually very smart, very skillful, and very successful people. But vanity and bombast overlay the riches; the horn is tooted so loudly it drowns out the other music.

I resolved that this would not be a book about *me.* It is a book about the practice of law in New York City in other times. Mostly, I have tried to write as an observer and to describe my own part without bluster. In my own work, I have often felt ridiculous. High in value among our prizes should be the ability to laugh at ourselves. I hope you will find that quality here.

Then there is the subject of privileged communications. Many of the cases I have worked on and situations I have lived through would make interesting stories. But they cannot be told without violating the client-lawyer relationship, with its seal of confidentiality, no different from that which attaches to conversations between a priest and his communicants or a doctor and his patients. We lawyers are forbidden to make capital from what our clients tell us, no

matter how entertaining or novel or dramatic those communications may be.

The New York bar of fifty years ago was divided by two
great gulfs: geographical and ethnic. Geographically, the
bar was divided between "downtown" and "uptown."
"Downtown" was a tight little area of a few acres around
Wall Street, bounded on the south by Exchange Place, on
the north by Cedar Street, on the east by Pearl Street, and
on the west by Broadway. In this compact little enclave,
much smaller than the nodal "City" of London, were almost all of the top-flight "elite" law firms and a few *ar-
rivistes*—predominantly Jewish and Irish firms that hoped
some of the prestige of the locale would rub off on them.
"Uptown lawyer" was virtually a term of opprobrium.
Fifty-one Chambers Street, 2 Lafayette Street, 270 Broadway, are all certainly places in downtown New York; but
such an address automatically stigmatized a law firm as
second class. Even the Woolworth Building, across the
park from City Hall, was a professional demimonde, inhabited by patent and bankruptcy lawyers. An address on
Forty Second Street, or in midtown Manhattan, stamped a
firm as professional *canaille.* The lawyers who inhabited
these offices were criminal lawyers or negligence lawyers
or labor lawyers, or they served the needs of the despised
garment industry.

Brooklyn, the Bronx, Queens, and Staten Island are all
parts of New York City. But in the legal world of the 1930s,
they might have been in Ultima Thule. Brooklyn, it is true,
had two or three substantial and prestigious firms, but they
served mostly the banks and real-estate interests of the
borough. The large office buildings around Borough Hall
were warrens infested with a swarm of negligence and
criminal lawyers of dubious bloodlines. "Court Street lawyer" was even more a term of contempt than "uptown

lawyer." As for the Bronx and Queens, the only lawyers in those ultramundane outstations practiced in street-level storefront offices (sometimes shared with bail bondsmen and city marshals) nestling around the local municipal and magistrate courts, and served only the needs of the local peasantry. Staten Island was a shore dimly seen from Battery Park. As far as we knew, if there were any lawyers out there, their offices were in caves shared with penguins.

The downtown blue bloods clustered tightly around the big banks and the investment-banking and stock-brokerage firms that provided them with their lucrative no-risk legal monopoly: most of America's corporate and financial law business. Fifteen Broad Street was the center of this oligarchy; in that building were the *crème de la crème* of the group. Not far behind were 14 Wall Street and 48 Wall Street. Ancillary to these bastions of pride and prestige were the luncheon clubs that served their members. Needless to say, the standards of admission to the clubs were substantially those of admission to partnership in the elitist firms.

But the really great gulf that divided the New York bar was the prevailing ethnic and religious bigotry and prejudice. I emphasize this because it was a pervasive fact of life, and its diurnal presence permeated our thoughts and our lives. It may seem an intrusion at this point, but my readers will not understand the times of which I write unless the subject is addressed bluntly and honestly.

Today, social equality and civil rights have become comparative truisms. The need to honor such principles is taken for granted. But those of us who came to the New York bar a half-century ago found ourselves in a microcosm in which racial and religious bigotry, xenophobia, anti-Semitism, and every other form of "elitism" were openly practiced and generally accepted as immutable facts of life. The most desirable and lucrative corporate law business was concentrated in the hands of approximately twenty Wall Street law firms, and until about 1940, they successfully resisted all attempts at democratizing their offices. The lawyers in these firms were almost all white and Anglo-Saxon. They constituted an "ascendancy" as oppressive as that of the Anglo-Irish landlords, and the effect was just as evil.

Tension between such elitism and democracy in the legal profession was not new. It had manifested itself as early as the time of Andrew Jackson. As the self-taught young men of the frontier society aspired to the bar and even to the bench, it was inevitable that such rivalries should emerge between them and the university scholars of the effete East. But they were all drawn from the same ethnic stock, and as the frontiers became "civilized" both groups coalesced into a solid, unitary Anglo-Saxon bloc. But elitism in the American bar did not flower and become poisonous until the elitists realized that their comfortable and profitable ascendancy was threatened by the sons of immigrants, first from Ireland and then from Eastern and Southern Europe. By the end of the century the Anglo-Saxon American bar understood that it was engaged in a struggle that turned openly on ethnicity and class. Their antagonists were the progeny of those immigrants who toiled in the sweatshops to finance the education of sons and daughters.*

The effects of ethnic discrimination were felt most keenly in New York because Jewish lawyers were a formidable fraction of the New York bar. The ugly fact is that until the coming of the New Deal and World War II, the

---

*There is a powerful description of this conflict in *Unequal Justice*, by Professor Jerrold S. Auerbach. He tells the story of how the American bar mobilized to meet the threat of these *Niedermenschen*.

doors of prestigious law firms in New York were virtually closed to Jews and other minorities. Of course, there were a few exceptions: in New York these were drawn almost entirely from "Our Crowd," the prosperous German-Jewish banking and commercial families. In those rare instances when the barriers dropped to admit such Jews, individual conformity and urbanity were usually coupled with control of lucrative family law business. Almost universally, the elitists protected their preserves, and the young hotshots of immigrant Irish, Jewish, and (much later) Italian origin were rigidly excluded from corporate and financial work in the law and were channeled into negligence, criminal, and bankruptcy work. In these fields they prospered because of their talent and industry.

The depth of prejudice in the New York bar produced some grotesque malignancies in the ascendancy, and some startling expressions, comparable to the racial theorizing of Goebbels, Rosenberg, and Streicher. Harlan Stone, later dean of the Columbia Law School and still later Chief Justice of the U.S. Supreme Court, spoke of Jewish and other immigrant lawyers who "exhibit racial tendencies toward study by memorization," and he characterized their intellectual quality as "almost Oriental in fidelity to the minutiae of the subject without regard to any controlling rule or reason." The chairman of the American Bar Association's Committee on Ethics in the early 1900s wrote piously of his revulsion at the legal ethics of "Russian Jew boys who come up out of the gutter [and are] merely following the methods their fathers had been using in selling shoe strings and other merchandise."

In the minds of the Establishment lawyers then, the assumed "racial traits" of Jews were equated with unethical behavior. A famous constitutional lawyer, James M. Beck, former Solicitor General of the United States, could bring himself to write, in 1922: "If the old American stock can be organized, we can still avert the threatened decay of constitutionalism in this country." To such minds did the American bar entrust the task of effecting "equal justice under law."

An amusing and ironic instance of prejudice against Jewish lawyers in New York is offered by the experience of Max D. Steuer, whose name became a synonym for excellence in advocacy. When Steuer was admitted to the New York bar, in 1893, he could not find a job in a law office. "The final blow came when Nadal Jones & Moulton, a large firm specializing in the defense of claims for injury, rejected an application for a position at the salary of six dollars a week. If [Steuer] wanted to be a lawyer, he had to be his own employer."*

There is no more sordid chapter in the history of bigotry in the American bar than the lynching party organized by the leaders of the profession against the elevation of Louis Brandeis to the Supreme Court in 1916. The Brandeis case is historically important to any study of the birth of decency and equal opportunity in the profession of law because it was the most conspicuous, although far from the last, rear-guard action of the elitist bar to keep "foreigners" off its sacred turf. It is ironical that the saintly Brandeis was attacked not in his professional attainments—which were virtually conceded—but in his *character*, by the hired hacks of an industrial and commercial system just beginning to emerge from its most predatory and antisocial period.

Those Jews who entered the legal system in New York half a century ago encountered this kind of prejudice and bigotry at the threshold. We were given polite interviews,

*Aaron Steuer, *Max D. Steuer—Trial Lawyer* (New York: Random House, 1950), p. 13.

but no jobs. We found jobs with "Jewish" law firms, or we resigned ourselves to negligence work, criminal work, or bankruptcy work—all of which were despised by the Establishment law firms. Of course, here and there an accident occurred, and one of us got a position with one of the "white-shoe" firms.

On balance, I must say that those who were turned away probably fared better than those who were admitted. Of course, a few outcasts fought their way to the top in the Establishment law firms. But, generally, the Jews, the Irish, and the Italians who were employed by the Establishment firms became their managing clerks (after all, someone had to deal with all those characters in the courthouses) or "bankruptcy specialists." For some strange reason, the big Wall Street firms, even those that had big banks as important clients, did not do their own bankruptcy work but farmed it out to small, highly specialized, mostly "Jewish" firms, which throve on it. Still, it was desirable to have in each of the big firms at least one lawyer who could supervise the relationship with the bankruptcy specialists. Since they were mostly Jewish, these overseers were also mostly Jewish. It was like having a conscientious mulatto to watch over the field hands. These "overseers" developed into lawyers of enormous expertise and judgment in bankruptcy and corporate reorganization, but they seldom became partners in the firms they worked for. They were made "senior associates"; they were well-paid and highly respected employees, treated with great consideration, and their offices enjoyed the same views of New York harbor. But they never became partners. Even after World War II, when the barriers were smashed and talented associates of Jewish, Italian, even Polish derivation were admitted to partnerships, these oldsters, born a generation too soon, remained senior associates.

The intransigence of the Old Guard of the white-shoe bar about admitting the *Niedermenschen* to their sacred society is illustrated by the experience of a friend of this writer. I met Gerald Coogan* in 1934 when we were adversaries in an unfair-competition case. He was an associate in one of the oldest, best-known, and most snobbish of the Wall Street law firms. He was an Irish American—big, strong, handsome, and personable. He was also capable, intelligent and dignified. In 1939 we were both at the stage of professional growth where we should either become partners in our respective firms or move on. My partnership was secure; I knew that my friend Gerald was in competition with at least two other men in his firm, both Anglo-Saxons who conformed far more closely to the firm's partnership pattern than Gerald did. They came from the right families, they had gone to the right schools, and they worshiped at the right altars.

The senior partner in the firm that employed Gerald was a legend at the New York bar. If his ancestors did not arrive on the *Mayflower*, they were on the next boat; he had followed the Groton–Yale–Harvard Law School route; his clubs were the most rigidly exclusive; he served as a trustee of both Mets: art and opera. Now in his middle sixties, he practiced both law and snobbery with the air of a magnifico.

At about the time when this mogul was to announce which of the three candidates would be admitted to part-

---

*In this anecdote I have altered the names to protect both the innocent and the guilty. The innocent have survived and are happy. The guilty have gone to their own rewards. The firm of which I write also survives as an important and respected entity. Its partners are predominantly Anglo-Saxon, but the associates constitute a fair cross section of New York's ethnic rainbow. At least three of the senior partners, all admitted long after the departure of the execrable Mr. Butt, are Jewish.

nership, I encountered Gerald in the Long Island Railroad Terminal. We both lived in the same suburb, and we spent many hours together traveling back and forth from our modest homes on the North Shore to our equally modest jobs on Wall Street. On this Saturday afternoon, my friend's round Celtic countenance did not show its usual good cheer. He would not at first tell me what was disturbing him, although I pressed him. Our train was rattling past Flushing Meadow before a distracted Gerald looked up from the newspaper he was pretending to read. "I'll tell you what's wrong," he said. "I think I am finished in my law firm. I'm going to look for something else."

Since friend Gerald had a wife and three kids, a mortgage, and about ninety dollars in the bank, this was desperate talk. Jobs were very scarce. I am writing of a time when the median income of Manhattan lawyers was below $3,000; when almost half the members of the metropolitan bar earned less than the minimum subsistence level for American families; when in a period of about three months 1,500 New York lawyers had filed paupers' oaths in order to qualify for WPA work relief.

"Are you nuts?" I said. "You are a fine lawyer, with a great firm, making a good living. What do you want to do, starve to death?"

"Well," said my friend Gerald, "listen to this story and then tell me if you think I can stay in that firm. As you know, almost all of my work is done for Mr. Tutt."* Mr. Tutt was known to me as a former U.S. attorney, a widely respected litigator, and a lawyer whose insistence on professional excellence was a byword. He was then in his late sixties.

---

*His name was not Tutt. I call him "Mr. Tutt" because he had many of the qualities of Arthur Train's unforgettable old lawyer.

Gerald went on: "About a month ago, Mr. Tutt invited me to lunch at his club. He told me that he was delighted with my work, he thought I had the makings of a fine trial lawyer, and he was vigorously recommending to Mr. Butt that I should be made a partner. As you know, there are three of us who joined the firm about the same time. Mr. Butt has a practice of never making more than two partners in a single year. You know my two competitors: Albert is a moron, who got a job with us because his uncle is the president of an insurance company that is one of our principal clients; Bertram's wife is the daughter of a man who roomed with our senior partner at law school. He is a bright fellow, but his chief ambition is to be America's amateur-golf champion. So when Mr. Tutt told me he was going to recommend me so highly for partnership, I thought it was in the bag. Not so.

"Yesterday afternoon, Mr. Butt announced that Albert and Bertram are to become partners. No mention of me. I went in to Mr. Tutt. I asked him why I had been passed over. The old man was brokenhearted. He told me he had done everything he could; he could not understand it. He urged me to speak with Mr. Butt. I went to Butt's office but he was too busy to see me. He told me to come in this morning.

"When I went in to him this morning, he was talking with one of the older partners. He looked up at me. He did not invite me to sit down. He asked, 'Yes, Mr. Coogan, you wanted to see me? What about?'

"I described my discomfiture, stammering, 'Mr. Butt, I cannot understand why I have not been made a partner. Mr. Tutt, who knows most about me, says he recommended me very highly. Certainly my work compares favorably with that of the two men who have been named. I should like to know why.'

"Butt's expression did not change. He asked me, 'Mr. Coogan, what college did you attend?'

" 'Holy Cross.'

" 'And what law school did you attend?'

" 'Notre Dame.'

" 'And to what clubs do you belong?'

" 'None.'

"And then he blandly smiled, and purred at me, 'Mr. Coogan, do you need any further explanation? Now, please excuse me. As you can see, I am engaged in something important.' "

By the time he reached this point in his narrative Gerald was almost in tears from chagrin and disappointment. But he did *not* leave the firm; he remained as an associate, then as a senior associate, doing the most important litigation in the office. Not until Mr. Butt died did the firm confer a partnership on him.

Many gifted lawyers who were excluded by lineage from substantial corporate law business found a medium even more exciting and lucrative than accident cases and criminal work: the field of stockholder litigation. When I began to practice law in New York, in 1933, a handful of lawyers specialized in bringing stockholder-derivative suits here and in Delaware. Of course, they were regarded by the respectable bar as pariahs. Of course, they were mostly Jewish lawyers, some of whom have now become respected, even legendary figures—accepted, admired, and even feared in all strata of the profession. In those days, and for many years thereafter, they were despised as "strike suitors," probably the least pungent of the epithets applied to them. But the evidence is unmistakable that these professional outcasts, by their diligence, imagination, courage, and skill, evolved into one of the most powerful and dynamic forces for corporate decency at work in our system.

Any historian of the development of our profession in the twentieth century should recognize that it was the very exclusion of these men from the ranks of the Establishment lawyers that transformed them into the skilled and intrepid *condottieri* who have done so much to keep American business on the level.

What changed the situation? What trampled down the professional infamy? I believe there were two factors: the coming of the New Deal and then World War II. When Mr. Roosevelt began his process of changing the social and economic face of America, he stimulated events that were to alter the misshapen social structure of the American bar, which was divided into what Professor Karl Llewellyn has described, with accuracy and felicity, as the "blue-stocking, respectable bar" and the "catch-as-catch-can bar." The New Deal erected a scaling ladder for those excluded by ethnic and religious prejudice. The government needed lawyers, and for the most part it found them among the disinherited, who desperately needed jobs. And in the course of doing those jobs, many of them developed such skills, expertise, reputation, and prestige that when they were ready to leave government, they were snapped up by the elitist firms. Why not? The very presence of these luminaries, with their special know-how and their government connections, attracted new corporate clients and reassured the old ones. Then came World War II, and as the associates and young partners departed for the OTCs and the boot camps, the big firms needed hands, any hands. It mattered little, in that emergency, in the big firms as in the infantry, whether the hands were Jewish, Italian, Irish, or Greek, as long as they could do the work. So a second crack opened in the barrier. And some of these substitutes proved so useful that they stayed in place even when the old boys drifted back from the war.

Even today, when those of us who succeeded in the game of the law look back on the old days, we are sickened by the bigotry and prejudice that were accepted precepts of that world. We would be much sicker if we were not so satisfied with the way things turned out.

Some of my tales derive from my association with Judge Samuel H. Kaufman, and he does emerge as a kind of hero. He was my first boss, my first mentor, and my first model. I owe so much to his concern, his tutelage, and his example that my readers will understand the evidences of my affection for him and my admiration for his talents and qualities. The first part of this book is entitled "The Old Firm." Almost every mature lawyer has his "old firm"—the little community of lawyers in which he was first exposed to our craft. The mind of a novitiate lawyer is like a sensitized photographic plate; the early impressions endure. My old firm left me with many happy memories and also with recollections of some of my youthful *gaucheries,* which, almost fifty years later, make me squirm with embarrassment.

Lawyers have the same penchant as fishermen for telling their tales. Some remember only the cases they won. We tend to remember our cases and the parts we played in heroic terms. Often our tales have the flavor of Aeneas' famous lines: *Quaeque ipse miserrima vidi et quorum pars magna fui* ("All the deeds of woe mine eyes have beheld, and those whereof I was no small part").

ACKNOWLEDGMENTS

Inevitably the author of a book such as this is indebted to many people. Jerry Finkelstein, publisher of the *New York Law Journal*, and James Finkelstein, president of the *Law Journal*, encouraged me to write the early stories that appeared in that publication and that led to the writing of this book; the editor-in-chief of the *Law Journal*, Charles F. Kiley, furnished helpful editorial guidance, as did Nelson Seitel, of the same publication. I am indebted to Congressman Emanuel Celler for the "Ferryboat" story, which makes Hymie Schorenstein a part of the political folklore of America. Rose Hettich told the story of my first interview with Weitzner, which you will find in "The Old Firm." Judge Edward Weinfeld, of the federal court in New York, first suggested that I should recall in print our happy memories of Sam Kaufman. My lifelong friend Raphael L. Elias reminded me of some of the qualities of "Mr. Fearless," embodied in the tale of his misadventures. My brother, Walter I. Gould, who was an involuntary actor in the battle of Pitkin Avenue, helped me recall some of the details of that escapade.

Charles Trynin, Bert Berri's neighbor in Brooklyn, gave me useful recollections of the recluse's way of life. Junius P. Wilson, Jr., of Mineola, who worked with us in "The Investigation," remembered some forgotten details of that experience. Several lawyers helped to reconstruct the personality of Judge Bondy, the judicial hero of "The Witness Who Spoke with God." I must particularly thank Mark Kaplan, who once served as Bondy's law clerk.

Some of the details of Brien McMahon's personality came from my partner Jesse Climenko, who shared my long friendship with McMahon, and from John Lane, of Washington, who was the senator's administrative assistant. Some of the details of McMahon's trip to Nevada recounted in "The Fatal Photograph" come from Judge John Sirica, who was his companion on that expedition.

Many lawyers and judges contributed to the collage of "The Golden Age of Gasner's." Jack Gasner provided the history of that great institution. Former judge Saul S. Streit, one of the companions of my professioanl life, furnished numberless recollections. The story about Judge Dawson come from that inimitable raconteur Frank Raichle. Judge Kevin Duffy, of the Southern District, gave me the story about the Muslim defendant who appeared before Tom Murphy. Bernard D. Fischman is the source of the Archie Palmer story. Robert Markewich, of one of New York's best-known legal families, told me the anecdote about Max D. Steuer in Poughkeepsie. Judge Aron Steuer's affectionate memoir of his famous father was most helpful.

I could not have written the Mandelbaum story without the help of several people. Saul Streit served with Mandelbaum in Roosevelt's "Turkey Cabinet" and gave me important details; he also imparted some facts about Mandelbaum's appointment to the bench. My interest in Mandelbaum and his career was stimulated by several conversations with the late Samuel I. Rosenman, a fine judge, intimate of governors and presidents, and an honored colleague of mine in the rehabilitation of one of America's great motion-picture companies. Other stories come from Charles L. Sylvester, Bethuel M. Webster, James G. Foley, Thomas F. Reddy, Jr., Judge Raphael P. Koenig, and Samuel M. Koenigsberg. The discovery of Mandelbaum's handwritten marginal note on *Erie* v. *Tompkins* in Volume 304 of the Supreme Court Reports was reported to me by Judge Edward J. Ryan, of the Southern District. Louis Perlmutter, who served as Mandelbaum's law secretary, recalled some of the history of that lovable man.

In writing the Manton story, I drew on the recollections of Robert L. Werner, who was a member of the prosecuting team. Harold A. Lynton, who worked on the Prudence Company reorganization, helped me recall many details of that complex litigation. Judge Herbert Stern, of the federal court in New Jersey, is an expert in the history of the New York Bar and directed my attention to some important background material.

Daniel Fusaro, clerk of the U. S. Court of Appeals, was most helpful in directing me to materials on Manton and the Werblows.

I must thank Professor Gray Thoron, of the Cornell Law School, for his useful suggestions in organizing the materials. My partner Bernard D. Fischman was my chief sounding-board during the composition of this book; his judgments are reflected on almost every page. To Elisabeth Sifton, of The Viking Press, I owe thanks not only for encouragement and guidance but for her fastidious editing.

Most of all, I acknowledge the contributions of my wife, Eleanor, who has endured the retelling of stories she has heard a hundred times and provided throughout the composing and word-shaping an invaluable sense of taste and restraint.

CONTENTS

PART I

The Old Firm

In September 1933 I went to inquire about a job at the small Wall Street law firm of Kaufman Weitzner and Celler. An old lawyer, a family friend, had arranged an interview with Sam Kaufman. But when I arrived at the office, Kaufman was "not available." No explanation was offered, and I was turned over to the number-two partner, Emil Weitzner. Weitzner showed little enthusiasm about my qualifications. He asked for "references" other than the veteran who had sent me to the firm. I explained that I had been away from New York, at Cornell and its law school, for seven years, and knew almost no one in New York. I suggested that I could get references from some of the university officials in Ithaca. I named the president of the university, the dean of the law school, the dean of the college of arts and sciences, the director of public information. That I really knew these people well enough to give them as references was not the result of any scholarly accomplishments. In 1930, when I was graduated from college, my family was broke. So I went to work. I worked for the *Cornell Daily Sun,* for the *Ithaca Journal,* for the *Cornell Alumni News,* and for the university administration. In my spare time I attended the law school. I did not learn much law, but I did get to know the local big shots. When I mentioned these names, Weitzner's lip curled in a sneer, which I later came to know only too well. As I explained that these people were friends who would be glad to supply information about me, he was visibly unimpressed. He took note of the names and gave me the usual "Don't call us, we'll call you." I left him convinced I would never hear from him again.

I learned later from Weitzner's then secretary (who became a lawyer and spent the next thirty years working with me in successor firms) what happened when I left. Weitzner had told her, "I'm going to teach that young man a lesson." He was sure the dignitaries at Cornell I had named as references did not even know of my existence. He dictated a letter to each of them. This was the Weitzner that I later came to know so well: a lawyer of considerable attainments but an old-maidish pietist, who lost no chance to parade his own righteousness.

About two weeks later, I received a telephone call. I was to go to see Kaufman, who happened to be at the Presbyterian Hospital, up at 168th Street. I was still plodding from law office to law office seeking employment that would get me into court, and I was getting to the end of the money I had saved in my last summer in Ithaca. This was the Depression year 1933, and I was beginning to pay fresh attention to the apple vendors in the streets. So I was eager to see Sam Kaufman.

I found him in a private hospital room, one arm and one leg suspended from the ceiling in traction, surrounded by piles of letters and legal papers. Timidly, I announced my presence. The apparition in the bed, swathed in dressings, encased in plaster, turned toward me, and for the first time I saw that warm smile that was to illumine our lives for many years.

"Gould," I said. "You sent for me?"

"Oh," said Kaufman, "you're the young man I've been reading about." His one good arm waved at some letters. "I've got some fine letters about you from people in Ithaca. I've got to give you a try."

He explained that he had been thrown from a horse and badly injured, and Weitzner was running the office in his absence. "Go down to Weitzner and tell him I said to give you a job!" That is how I became the managing attorney at

Kaufman Weitzner & Celler, for twenty-five dollars a week. (If I had not been admitted to the bar a few weeks earlier, I would have been the managing clerk.)

The term "managing attorney" is misleading. In the big law firms of today, it is a highly responsible position, usually held by a lawyer of great sophistication. But in the small law offices of that age, the job was usually filled by the youngest and least important lawyer in the office. To him was assigned the dry, thankless, and unremunerative task of following the court calendars, checking for judicial decisions, filing and serving papers, and doing all those countless legal chores that require more physical than intellectual vigor. The job had one great advantage: it afforded its occupant a panorama of what was happening in the office. It was an ideal position in which to learn the pragmatics of the law practice. I found myself soaking up information about the courts, the clients, the partners, the associates.

Samuel Kaufman was the senior partner. He was a dynamic trial lawyer, then in his early forties, who was the undisputed potentate of the establishment. Although he was generally thoughtful, even genial, he had an imperious quality about him, and when he snapped his fingers, we all jumped. There were two other partners: Emil Weitzner and Emanuel Celler. Celler was then a fairly young congressman from Brooklyn. As the longtime chairman of the Judiciary Committee of the House, he was to make many important contributions to federal law and procedure, and became the venerated Nestor of the House of Representatives. Weitzner was the bookish backup scholar for Kaufman, but he was a formidable litigator in his own right. There were about ten or twelve associates who worked chiefly under his tutelary direction, but everybody deferred to Kaufman, who ruled the roost with a quick mind, a quick tongue, and a quick temper.

Kaufman had a special quality that endeared him to the young men in the office. It was not only that he was warm, friendly, and thoughtful; most of all, he was devoted to the process of developing the professional skills of those who worked for him. He had no children of his own, and he became a surrogate father to us, demanding and receiving hard work, intelligence, and loyalty.

Since Sam Kaufman plays an important part in some of the stories that follow, I should tell you something about him. He was a New Yorker, born and bred, educated in the city's public schools. He studied law at New York University Law School before World War I (long before it attained the great academic eminence it enjoys today) and then became a great advocate in an era that was a Golden Age of trial lawyers. They were a gifted and glittering company who lit up the courts in the quarter century before World War II.

In 1948 Kaufman was appointed by President Truman to the U.S. District Court for the Southern District of New York. He served as a judge of that court for only four years, then he suffered a stroke that left him helplessly disabled until he died, in 1960. Today, he is recalled as the judge who presided at the first trial of Alger Hiss and who (when he exercised judicial control over the reorganization of the Third Avenue transit system) defied the truculent Mike Quill to avert a crippling transportation strike in New York in 1950.

1

THE BASHAW OF BROWNSVILLE

I had been in the office only a few weeks when Emil Weitzner instructed me to accompany him to court in a case that was my introduction to Brownsville and its *grand seigneur*, Hymie Schorenstein.

"Brownsville" is the name given to the eastern *banlieue* of Brooklyn. Today, it is a typical urban slum, a place of moldering tenements and run-down retail stores. Decay and neglect scream out at the passerby. The inhabitants who occupy this rubble-filled desert live like refugees in a battle area. Pitkin Avenue, the main artery of the area, seems a path cut by bulldozers through the urban debris.

It was not so fifty years ago. Then Brownsville was a pulsing, vibrant community, filled with first- and second-generation Jewish immigrants throbbing with upward mobility. The uncrowned king of this way station to assimilation and prosperity was Hyman Schorenstein. There were probably thousands of Hymies in Brownsville—but when you said "Hymie" to the natives, people knew you meant Schorenstein.

Nominally, Hymie was the Democratic district leader in Brownsville; in fact, he was its undisputed overlord. He ruled his district like Kublai Khan, and his writ ran to every candy store, every floating pinochle game, every Turkish bath and pickle factory. Should hot knishes be sold from a pushcart in front of Liebowitz's Delicatessen? It was Hymie who decreed that the pushcart had to go to another location. It was Hymie who ordained that the pool parlor remain closed on the Sabbath but that a shoe-shine parlor (operated, of course, by a Calabrian heretic) should remain open.

Hymie's appearance and demeanor were in keeping with his imperial role. Pitkin Avenue's tailors and haberdashers dressed him so that his sartorial splendor matched his portliness. To his constituents, the face he presented was one of self-assured benevolence. He dispensed condolences, comforts, favors, and advice with a manner appropriate to Andrew Carnegie, Pope Pius, and Marcus Aurelius. He was the friend, confidant, and trusted ally of every significant political leader of his time, from John McCooey to Herbert Lehman. Though his Yiddish was fluent, his fractured "English" would have served as a model for the characters of Milt Gross or Leo Rosten's *H*Y*M*A*N   K*A*P*L*A*N*. But what he lacked in syntax, he made up for in decisiveness.

There was one tragic flaw in the effulgent personality of this municipal monarch: he was completely illiterate. The printed word was to him a mystery as deep as the runes of the Celts or the hieroglyphs of the pharaohs. This was his secret, known to all his associates and jealously guarded by them. Hymie could not read or write, but woe to the clubhouse captain who ever dropped the pretense that Hymie was a literary adept. His illiteracy was never, never mentioned.

Schorenstein's dread "secret" was so widely known and so carefully respected that it engendered many anecdotes. It is told that when he was being questioned by Samuel Seabury before the famous Hofstadter Committee, the majestic Seabury asked Hymie to examine a document and "interpret" it. "Objection sustained!" thundered Senator Hofstadter. "Please do not give Commissioner Schorenstein any documents, sir. Read them yourself."

Despite his handicap, Hymie Schorenstein was a director of an investment company, an officer and director of a bank, a deputy U.S. Marshal, Deputy Register of Kings County, a member of the Executive Committee of the Democratic Party of Kings County, a member of the Democratic State Committee, and a delegate to the Electoral College. There is no indication that his tragic flaw affected the discharge of his duties.

In 1931 James A. McQuade, then Register of Kings County, appointed Schorenstein Commissioner of Records of Kings County. (Both positions have long since been abolished.) The office of Commissioner of Records of Kings County had been created by the legislature of New York in 1904. The legislative purpose was stated to be "the completion and care of the block indexes and reindexing plant, and for the care and preservation of the County records, old town and other records." To perform this task the Register of Kings County was directed to appoint "a suitable person," and it is probable that in selecting Hymie for this sensitive post, Mr. McQuade was actuated by qualities other than the new commissioner's literary gifts.

To the end of his days Hymie exulted in the honorific "Commissioner." He was seldom addressed or referred to by any other title. But before long, Hymie was to pay a price for his honor.

Into the placid tranquillity of Schorenstein's reign over
Brownsville there crept a dangerous insurgent, one Murray M. Pomeranz. Pomeranz, it is said, nursed a deep
grudge against Schorenstein.

Two explanations have been offered for Pomeranz's
assumption of the role of David against this political
Goliath. First, we are told that he was one of the victims of a successful purge that Schorenstein had carried
out against the Socialists, who at one time were important in Brownsville politics. Hymie had a strong prejudice against "Bolsheviks." Loudly and often he proclaimed his contempt for all persons who failed to
perceive that the American political system was the best
in the world. It has also been suggested that Pomeranz
had been unsuccessful in obtaining Schorenstein's support for some political job. But there is no doubt that
Pomeranz was motivated more by a personal vendetta
against Schorenstein than by any high-minded civic im-
pulses. Whatever his motive, in 1933 Pomeranz declared
unremitting war on Hymie Schorenstein. His first on-
slaught was to apply by letter and in person to the governor for Schorenstein's removal. This produced no result. His next move was in the courts.

The year 1933 was the beginning of the New Deal. It was
a year for insurgents. While Roosevelt was skinning the fat
cats all over the land, in New York, La Guardia, the Little
Flower, was mounting his attack on Tammany. A thorough dismantling of "machine politics" was being orches-
trated by Samuel Seabury, and self-appointed reformers
like Pomeranz made the voice of the snapping turtle heard
in our land. In the prevailing atmosphere of political reform, where could one find a more rewarding target than
an illiterate political pro, functioning as Commissioner of
Records, no less? So Pomeranz brought a mandamus pro-

ceeding* in Supreme Court, Kings County (against Aaron
L. Jacoby, McQuade's successor as Register of Kings
County), to remove Schorenstein from his commissioner-
ship on the ground that he was not a "suitable person"
within the meaning of the statute. The petition alleged that
"the said Hyman Schorenstein is unable to read or write
the English language or any language," and besought the
court to determine whether the legislature intended that
"an appointee who is unable to read or write the English
language or any language" is "a suitable person," to remove
Schorenstein, et cetera.

Word of Pomeranz's impiety quickly spread through
Brooklyn. When it reached the *sanctum* of John McCooey,
Democratic czar of Brooklyn, he assembled his troops for
the defense of his beleaguered lieutenant. Among the myr-
midons was Emanuel Celler, whose congressional district
included Schorenstein's 23rd Assembly District. Mannie
Celler assumed overall responsibility for the defense, but
the actual strategy and tactics were the work of Celler's
litigating partners, Sam Kaufman and Emil Weitzner.
These two brought their devastating talents in the courts
to bear on the hapless Pomeranz.

I was recruited for the "research." Since I had been
admitted to the bar only a month before, I was plainly the
associate who could most easily be spared from other, more
lucrative tasks. My job was easy: first, I carried Weitzner's
bag to the courthouse; second, because Schorenstein hardly
satisfied Weitzner's fastidious social sense, I was the chosen
messenger between lawyer and client.

The matter came on before the Honorable George H.
Furman in Supreme Court in Brooklyn in October 1933.

---

*"Mandamus" is legalese for a court proceeding to compel an official to
act.

Pomeranz, appearing *pro se,** made the ceiling reverberate with his oratory; it was clear that the stability and safety of the Republic depended on Hymie's removal. The closing of banks, the bread lines, and the repudiation of the gold standard were all somehow related to Hymie's tenure as Commissioner of Records.

Weitzner's response on behalf of Schorenstein was short, crisp, and to the point. He argued simply that there was no statutory or legal definition of "a suitable person"; that if the legislature had intended a test of literacy for the commissioner it would have said so; and that the only qualifications for holding office in New York State were full age, citizenship, and residence. Nothing about literacy.

Judge Furman adopted Weitzner's argument. His decision rejecting Pomeranz's crusade recounted Schorenstein's accomplishments *in extenso;* he defined "suitability"; and he concluded that there was no requirement that the commissioner of records know how to read and write.†

After Judge Furman's decision, Pomeranz appealed to the Appellate Division, Second Department. Weitzner instructed me to prepare a brief in response to the appellant's diatribe against Schorenstein. As I worked one night in the library on this task it occurred to me that in the hearing below, there had been no proof that Schorenstein could not read or write any particular language; the emphasis had been on his inability to read or write *English*. Well, I reasoned, Aristotle could not read or write English. Nor could Tolstoy! Nor Spinoza! Maybe, I thought, Schorenstein is an expert in both oral and written Yiddish! This is the kind of lucubration that has a wild appeal for young lawyers. But

---

*The legal term for a fool who acts as his own lawyer.
†The case is reported in the books as *Matter of Pomeranz (Jacoby)*, 199 Misc. 99; 266 N.Y.S. 691 (1933).

some vague impulse suggested caution. I reached for the telephone, to call Schorenstein at The Club, to check my brilliant thought. The conversation went like this:

"Commissioner, this is Mr. Gould."

"Who-o-o?"

"Gould," I said. "You know, the young man from Mannie Celler's office, the one that worked with Mr. Weitzner on your case."

"Oh," said Hymie in his most sugary political accents. *"That* Mr. Gould! How are you, sonny? What can I do for you?"

"Commissioner," I said, "I would like to ask you a question."

"Anything, sonny, anything! You done for me such a fine job, you can ask anything." His tones were those of the omnipotent political boss, ready to bestow some boon on a deserving supplicant.

"Commissioner," I said, "can you read and write Yiddish?"

There was a pregnant silence. When Hymie next spoke, his tone was different. The honey had disappeared from his voice; now he was the rugged street fighter, ready to repel any attack on his scholarship. "Vat are you doing, sonny?" he inquired, wariness and suspicion in every syllable. "You're writing the brief?"

"Yes, Commissioner," I said. "I'm writing the brief in the Appellate Division."

"Sonny," he said, and now there was a firm, steely edge to his voice, "you are a very nice *boychick.* And someday maybe you are going to be a smart lawyer. So maybe you shouldn't mind taking a little advice from an old man to a young man. Do you mind?"

"No, Commissioner," I said. "I'll be happy to get your advice."

"My Ed Weiss, young man," said the sage, "my Ed Weiss is you should write your brief, and mind your business, and don't ask no damn-fool questions." There was a click; the conversation was over.

I wrote the brief. Weitzner argued the appeal, and the Appellate Division, Second Department, unanimously affirmed Judge Furman's opinion, adding its authority to the doctrine that the Commissioner of Records of Kings County was not required by law to be literate.* The Court of Appeals denied Pomeranz's motion for leave to appeal, adding its *imprimatur* to this useful precept. At this point, Murray Pomeranz sinks into the shadows.

Hymie emerged from his humiliating ordeal inwardly shaken but outwardly imperturbable. For the next twenty years, until he died, in 1953, he presided over the teeming life of Brownsville. Each night he sat in a leather chair on an elevated dais in the clubhouse. Constituents, each with a plea for help, sat in ranks before him. He dispensed favors, justice, relief, and occasional scorn. And when he was given papers to read, he would hand them to one of the literate henchmen at his elbow, with the words "Read 'em to me. Mine eyes is getting bad and the light is no good."

Hymie is long since gone but not forgotten, for he made an immortal contribution to the folklore of American politics. The following story was first told to this writer in 1934 or 1935 by that ageless political savant Mannie Celler and was enshrined by Theodore White in his *Making of the President, 1960.*

In the early 1920s Hymie "arranged" for a young lawyer in his district to be the Democratic nominee for the state assembly. Once the nomination was announced, the eager young aspirant was ignored. He was not asked to make any

*241 App. Div. 739; 270 N.Y.S. 948 (1934).

speeches or kiss any babies. Night after night he came to the clubhouse and was ignored. Finally he protested to Hymie; he insisted that as a candidate for office he should be exposed to the electorate. Hymie listened patiently.

Then he said, "Young feller, let me explain to you something about politics. Did you ever go down to the river and watch the ferryboats come in? And when the ferryboat comes in, all the *dreck*, all the garbage that is floating in the water, comes in with the ferryboat. Well, young feller, Al Smith is the ferryboat. You are the garbage. You do nothing!"

2

HOW SAM KAUFMAN LOST AND REGAINED HIS BEST CLIENT

A half-century ago, the island of Manhattan still harbored some large industrial establishments. One of the most impressive was the big printing and binding establishment J. J. Little & Ives, at Twenty-third Street and First Avenue, near the East River. Little & Ives was one of the two or three most substantial clients of Sam Kaufman's bustling law office, at 60 Wall Street. Kaufman treasured his professional relationship with Little & Ives and his personal intimacy with its owner, Arthur W. Little, always known as "the Colonel."

Little once told me that the foundation of Little & Ives had been laid by profits from printing the memoirs of Ulysses S. Grant. As the Colonel told the story, when Grant left the presidency, in the spring of 1877, he was America's greatest hero, but he was almost broke. Not even the scandals of his second administration—the Crédit Mobilier, the Whiskey Ring, the bribery of his Secretary of War—could diminish the affection of Americans for the great hero of the Civil War. But even heroes must eat, and

Grant had staked everything on an investment in a New York banking house, Grant and Ward, which went bankrupt in 1884, amid charges of fraud. Grant was humiliated, and penniless. Even worse, he learned that he was suffering from cancer of the throat and that he had little more than a year of life left.

At this desperate moment, he was approached by an enterprising printer in New York City, J. J. Little. Little proposed to advance funds to Grant and his family while Grant composed his *Personal Memoirs*. Little also undertook to print and distribute the finished work, for a share of the profits. The work required the same degree of heroism Grant had shown when, as a young captain, he had dragged a light howitzer into a belfry at San Cosme in the final storming of Mexico's defenses. But Grant's fortitude was rewarded. He finished the manuscript in 1885, only four days before he died. The sales earned for his family more than $500,000, a vast sum, especially for that time. And it earned about as much for the enterprising printer, who plowed his profits into the impressive book manufactory at First Avenue and Twenty-third Street.

At the turn of the century J. J. Little & Ives was said to be the largest and most complete printing and binding establishment in the nation. By the year 1933 it was a seemingly prosperous enterprise, sprawling along the East River, humming with activity, employing hundreds of laborers, and turning out an enormous number of books. But, in truth, the Depression had caught up with Little & Ives. People who lacked bread had little money for books. The publishers for whom Little & Ives manufactured books could not pay their bills. And much of the legal work Kaufman's office performed for Little & Ives concerned ways in which to turn stacks of unwanted books into money for the payroll.

The law firm was pulsing with profitable activity, and

there were clients by the score. But in Sam Kaufman's mind, the work for Little & Ives took precedence over everything else, and the work was always entrusted to the most skillful hands in the office. There was a reason for this.

Before Kaufman came out of the army, in 1918, his commanding officer had been Colonel Little, heir to the benefactor of the Grant family and sole proprietor of J. J. Little & Ives. The Colonel had befriended the young Captain Kaufman. He introduced Kaufman to his wealthy and influential friends in New York's commercial establishment. The Colonel trumpeted Kaufman's talents to the world, and his influence had contributed vastly to Sam Kaufman's ascent to professional success. Kaufman tried in every way to repay the help he had received from the Colonel. And in those Depression days, with book publishers collapsing like pricked balloons all over New York, the Colonel and Little & Ives needed all the help Kaufman could give.

It was not easy to serve Colonel Little. He was an autocrat, a snob, and a bigot. His sales manager, Pete Mallon, was usually called "the Mick." The principal financial aide was John J. A. Hosenlopp (whom we knew as "Gus"), a delightful philosopher whose forebears had fought with Molly Pitcher at Monmouth. But to Colonel Little he was always "that dumb Kraut." The Colonel's attitudes toward the immigrant Italians and Jews who worked in his plant can be easily imagined.

As a combat officer Arthur Little had commanded the famous New York regiment of Negro troops in France, the "Men of Bronze," When I learned this, I expected him to show some special affection for that race. But as far as I can recall, blacks were employed at Little & Ives in only the most poorly paid and servile positions, and the good Colonel invariably referred to them by the usual nasty epithets. His greatest aversion was to professional labor leaders, whom he normally described as "Reds," "Bolsheviks," "foreign agitators." Indeed, it was the threat of unionization at the East Side plant that had led the Colonel to set up a runaway printing and binding establishment in Kingsport, Tennessee. (He sold it when the threat passed, and it grew, under more flexible leadership, into The Kingsport Press, one of America's greatest *unionized* typographical plants.)

It was remarkable that the Colonel maintained such a close personal and professional relationship with Sam Kaufman. He knew that Kaufman had been born in New York of Jewish immigrant parents, although Kaufman had successfully cultivated the manners, appearance, and diction of a patrician American. Mysteriously, the Colonel's blatant chauvinism and xenophobia remained in check when he dealt with Kaufman, and their friendship was serene, rewarding, and profitable. Until Mr. Fearless* came along.

Fearless was one of about ten young lawyers who worked for Kaufman's firm as associates. When I came to the firm, he had been out of law school for about five or six years. It did not take me long to discover that everyone regarded him as the "star" of the young men, obviously destined for greatness in the law. The reasons were plain. In all those attributes that are sought in a young lawyer he excelled. Indeed, he shone, he glittered. Not only that, but

---

*I have altered Fearless' name because he is long dead, and it is entirely possible that his children, who, I believe, are still living in New York, have never heard this tale. Any readers consumed with curiosity will find the stark outline of my tale in *The New York Times,* issues of December 8, 1937 (p. 12, col. 1), February 3, 1938 (p. 9, col. 1), and March 5, 1938 (p. 21, col. 6). The truly inquisitive will find nourishment at page 286 of the Criminal Docket of the United States District Court for the Southern District of New York for the year 1937.

he was above average in height, strongly built, handsome of countenance. His dental perfection was displayed with great frequency in a smile that was winning and infectious. His manner was a balanced masterpiece of measured modesty and self-confidence, of humility and authority. To us, the youngsters, he was Beau Geste, and in his legal pronouncements and judgments he was Sir Oracle.

I had been in the office only a few weeks when I had the good fortune to carry Kaufman's bag to the courthouse. En route, the great man asked the usual questions about my progress and offered some fatherly advice. "Keep your eye on Fearless," he told me. "That young man will go far. He has everything. Model your behavior after his." Long after, when I knew both men better and many things had happened, I understood that in Fearless, Sam Kaufman saw himself as a young lawyer; maybe he even saw the son he never had. Both men had great ambition, dynamism, and captivating personalities. There were some important differences.

Fearless excelled especially in his uncanny ability to capture the confidence of clients. He was an adept in nurturing that communion of *trust* that is the indispensable ingredient of a happy relationship between lawyer and client. His virtuoso display of this felicitous quality had persuaded Kaufman to entrust Fearless with the affairs of Arthur W. Little and J. J. Little & Ives. Moreover, Fearless kindled some vague paternal flickers in the breast of that old bear Arthur Little, for with Fearless he showed none of the savage irascibility that made others fear him. (His own son and his stepson were active in his business, and the Colonel brutalized both young men, as he did all his employees.) Fearless became a regular caller at the Colonel's home, a privilege rarely extended even to Kaufman. And when Fearless was absent from our office, it was understood that he was "with the Colonel," a blanket excuse that covered many varied activities.

As I have related, the book-publishing industry was hard hit in those Depression years. Little & Ives kept several of its more viable accounts afloat by making generous extensions of credit. Among the beneficiaries of this policy was Ray Long & Richard R. Smith. The two eponyms of the firm had established their company in the 1920s, when a prosperous America hungered for literature. Ray Long had been editor of *Cosmopolitan* when it competed with the *Saturday Evening Post* for the affection of readers and advertisers. Dick Smith was a legendary adviser to the great literary figures of the era. Together they prospered. For three years after the Great Crash they were sustained by extensions of credit from Little & Ives, but in 1934 the credit ran out, and Long & Smith filed a petition in bankruptcy in the United States District Court for the Southern District of New York. Since Little & Ives was by far its largest creditor, it was in a position to dominate the administration of the bankrupt estate, including the designation of the trustee. Fearless was, of course, in command.

My only direct concern with the matter was that in my capacity as managing attorney, there came to me a copy of a memorandum from Kaufman to Fearless advising that Kaufman wanted to be named as trustee in bankruptcy and directing that when the order of appointment (of Kaufman) was filed, the Boss was to be told immediately. Of course, I paid special heed and asked daily of Fearless, "Where is the Long and Smith order?"

The only response was the flash of that captivating million-dollar smile, the gleam of those pearly teeth, and the breezy assurance that all was well. "Don't worry, sport," said our young meteor, "the situation is well in hand."

But Kaufman's daily importunities about the order appointing a trustee troubled me. After a week or more of being whipsawed between the Big Boss and Young Lochinvar, I stopped at the office of the referee in bankruptcy and inquired about the status of the order in *Long & Smith*. Within minutes I had a copy of the order in my hand. It named as the trustee not Kaufman but *Fearless*. There was no mistake; the order resulted from an application submitted by Fearless in the conventional form, for our firm, requesting that *he* be named trustee.

I went back to the office, clutching in my hand copies of the order and of the application on which it was based. I made first for the office of Mr. Fearless; he was "out." I then went to Kaufman's office and showed him the order and the application.

In the few months in which I had been in his firm, I had seen little of Sam Kaufman. To me he was as remote as the Dalai Lama. What I had seen was calm, genial, amiable. Now the man was transformed into a raging demon. His features were contorted by fury; he used expletives he must have learned in the AEF; he stormed out of his office in search of the errant star, brandishing the legal papers like a tomahawk. I trembled lest I be caught up in the tempest of Kaufman's rage. I had read of the execution of messengers who brought the tidings of calamity to a potentate. Well, I was a messenger, Kaufman was a potentate (to me, at least), and plainly the tidings were sufficiently calamitous to transform this amiable patron into Caliban.

The next few hours in that office were like life in a bomb shelter. Fearless was tracked down and brought back. There was a tempestuous meeting in Kaufman's room. We underlings heard only slamming of doors, occasional shouts of fury that penetrated the walls. At length, Fearless emerged. His face no longer bore the radiant, confident smile; it bore an expression of grim martyrdom. He spoke no words but went directly to his own office and started cleaning out his desk. Within an hour he was gone into ignominious exile, nevermore to darken the doors of Kaufman, Weitzner & Celler—or so we thought.

Fearless, in fact, went directly from the law office to the Colonel. Gus Hosenlopp told me years later of the scene, which he had witnessed. Fearless explained to the Colonel that Kaufman's personal ambition to be trustee for the bankrupt Long & Smith was inimical to Little & Ives; that he, Fearless, had jeopardized his career to serve the ends of the Colonel and the company. He improvised a few comments on Kaufman's alleged observations on the character and personality of the Colonel. He told the Colonel how his own loyalty and devotion had been rewarded by Kaufman's abuse, how he had been thrust into the darkness by Sam the Savage. What a touching scene!

Within days Fearless was established in his own office, at 2 Lafayette Street, under the patronage of the Colonel, and the law business of J. J. Little & Ives was being transferred from our office to Fearless'. Indeed, as managing attorney, I was an actor in the physical task of arranging for Fearless to be substituted for our firm in a score of pending matters, and in delivering many files. A curtain of barbed wire descended between Arthur Little and Sam Kaufman. There were no more jolly visits to the magnificent Victorian residence on Lexington Avenue; the two friends were effectively estranged. To Arthur Little, Kaufman had become an ingrate who valued vanity and ambition above the interests of his benefactor. To Kaufman, Fearless was Iago, a vicious knave who had betrayed him, stolen his best client, and poisoned a treasured friendship with the Colonel. The name of the Amalekite was spoken no more in our precincts.

But there soon came to our ears some strange reports.

You must remember, these were the darkest days of the Great Depression. My salary was twenty-five dollars a week. While the partners dwelt in marble halls and gave off an aura of opulence, the young lawyers of that era, unless they had well-to-do families, lived in chronic penury. We ate forty-cent lunches; the purchase of a suit of clothes was a major economic event. The ownership of a motorcar was a luxury only to be dreamed about. Now we began to hear that Fearless had established his young family in a Park Avenue apartment—a *duplex*, yet. Next came the report that he had a limousine that rivaled Sam Kaufman's in splendor—chauffeur-driven, yet. Then came the news that the exile had purchased a sumptuous summer place in Southampton—not the Rockaways, but *Southampton*, summer abode of magnificos. As we chomped our hamburgers in the hash joints and beaneries of Wall Street's back alleys, we spoke of almost nothing else. The Fallen Angel, the Betrayer of the Faith, expelled from our ranks for perfidy and insubordination, had risen to wealth and power. The peasants heard the sounds of revelry from the castle, but of Mr. Big himself we caught no glimpse.

In the next few years I made a little professional progress on my own. Nothing, of course, to compare with our Lucifer's. I was given some little cases to try; I carried Kaufman's bag to court in some real cases; I did a stint for a couple of years as a prosecutor, from which I returned to Sam Kaufman's firm. The only news of Fearless that reached me was consistent with what we had already heard: he was living in great style; not only was he the lawyer for Little & Ives (*our* Little & Ives), but he had replaced Kaufman as guide, philosopher, and friend of that Prince of Printers, Arthur W. Little, and the patronage and favor of the Colonel had brought many new clients to his doors. He had become a personage. Our own little accomplishments paled in his brilliant glow.

One day in the late fall of 1937, our telephone operator advised me that Mr. Fearless was in the reception room, asking to see me. "Fearless?" I asked. *"Our* Mr. Fearless?"

"The same," she answered.

I recall that there flashed through my mind the ugly scene that would ensue if Kaufman were to encounter this miscreant on our own turf. On the few occasions when the name of the maligant had been uttered in Sam Kaufman's hearing, his eyes had narrowed into ominous slits; his chest had heaved in frustrated ferocity. His fingers itched for the feel of Fearless' jugular. I had visions of physical violence, in which the diminutive Sam would be no match for the heavy-muscled athlete. I rushed to the reception room and breathlessly brought Fearless to the privacy and security of my own little office, trembling that my door would open to reveal the presence of the Boss. As I write these words I realize that I can remember the ensuing conversation so clearly over the span of four decades. But then, in almost half a century of turbulent lawyering, I have had only one or two such conversations.

There sat Fearless, expensively tailored, with the same old infectious smile, the same old sangfroid. "My God," I said, "what are you doing here? If the Boss sees you, there will be murder."

"Easy, sport," said Lucifer. "When you hear what I have to say, you will go in and tell him I am here and why. And all will be well. Trust me, I know what I'm doing." I could still fall under the spell of that captivating personality; somehow, I *did* trust him.

"Do you remember," he asked, "a bankruptcy case called Long & Smith?" Remember? How could I forget the early trauma of that experience? You might as well ask Bloody Mary if she remembered Calais!

"Well," he continued, "you'll remember I was the trustee of Long & Smith. I've been running the estate for the last four years. *In those four years I have stolen about four hundred and fifty thousand dollars from the estate. The FBI fellows are up in my office now, checking the books. By tomorrow afternoon they will know that I have forged the signature of the referee on four hundred and fifty thousand dollars' worth of checks.* I'm here because I want you to be my lawyer. I've been hearing a few things about you, and I want you to handle this for me."

My reaction was one of incredulity mixed with terror. As he told me this fearsome tale he reached into his pocket and extracted a check in a respectable sum, as a retainer for my services. He explained that the check was from his mother-in-law; it was not part of the money he had stolen from the creditors of Long & Smith.

When I had recovered from the shock of the revelation, I explained to Fearless that I could not act for him without Kaufman's approval.

"Of course," said Fearless. "Go in and tell him the story. Show him the check. I'll bet he lets you take the case."

I pointed out that Kaufman would certainly not let me take the matter on unless the full facts were exposed to the Colonel. After all, I observed, Little & Ives owned most of the claims against the bankrupt Long & Smith. That made the Colonel's company the principal victim of Fearless' larceny.

"Of course," said Fearless. "The Colonel has to learn about it sooner or later. He may as well hear it from you as from the FBI."

I was not quite ready to go to Kaufman; first, I had to recover my mental equilibrium. I was still reeling from the enormity of Fearless' revelation.

"Why?" I asked, much in the manner of the law students

and dinner-table companions who were to press this sort of question on me for the next thirty or forty years as I told the story. "Why?" With success and prosperity in his grasp, why had Fearless done these heinous things?

"Pure greed, pure stupidity," said the onetime prodigy. "The money was there, and I simply borrowed it. I meant to repay it from stock-market transactions, trading in commodity futures, even from some hot tips on horses." And the Park Avenue duplex, the chauffeur-driven limousine, the summer place in Southampton? All, all, had come from the stolen money. In that moment my admiration for the man, my secret envy of his accomplishments, was transformed into ashes and funeral meats.

I went into Kaufman's room with the retainer check in my hand, still slightly dazed. When I told him who was in my office, he almost exploded. His usually benign smile melted into an expression of rage. "Throw the bum out," he shrieked. "I'll kill him if I see him."

"Wait, wait," I urged. I told him the story as related by Fearless.

Incredulity was succeeded by horror. Then came some pardonable expressions of the "I knew it—I could have told you so" family.

As I explained that Fearless had authorized me to disclose the full turpitude of his acts to the Colonel, a strange brightness came into Kaufman's eyes. "You know," he said, "the last time I spoke to Arthur Little, it was to tell him that Fearless was a liar, an ingrate, and a thief." He reached for the telephone. Within minutes the Colonel had learned the extent of Fearless' offenses.

What followed is somewhat blurred in my memory. In a short time the Colonel and Gus Hosenlopp sat in Sam Kaufman's office. While Kaufman and the Colonel figuratively fell into each other's arms in fervent reconciliation,

I was on my way to the U.S. Attorney's office in Foley Square with the repentant Fearless in tow. Of course, he was "cooperative." Within days he was indicted for "misappropriation of monies from an estate in bankruptcy, and forgery of the signature of an officer of the U. S. District Court, S.D. of N.Y." So saith the clerk's docket notes of December 16, 1937. And on February 2, 1938, the erstwhile hero was sentenced by Judge Robert P. Patterson to serve two years in the penitentiary.

But it was not the end of the story.

The relationship of trust between the Colonel and Sam Kaufman was reestablished on a new basis: they had suffered together at the hands of the same betrayer. Kaufman remained the Colonel's lawyer and friend until Kaufman became a federal judge, in 1948. It would be neat and fitting if I could tell you that Fearless' life was cut off in conventional classic style by the conventional divine vengeance for the conventional Greek sin of insolence against the gods. But somehow the theme of the morality plays does not work out in real life.

Fearless earned an early parole; he charmed his jailers, as he did everyone else. He got a job in an upstate factory. When World War II came, he led the conversion of the plant to military production. He earned a substantial proprietary interest in the company. When he died, some years ago, he left a large fortune and a host of admirers. I concede that this dénouement detracts from the moral value of my story. The "happy" ending would have disqualified Fearless as a fitting subject for the Greek dramatists of the Golden Age. Yet, to Sam Kaufman, who suffered much from his misplaced confidence, Fearless was the most notable example of the golden youths, the happy warriors, who fell victim to that dreadful lawyers' malady, *hubris*.

3

THE MOUSE-GRAY EMINENCE

Behind every fine trial lawyer there is usually at least one expert in the preparation of cases. Often these assistants go on to become eminent trial lawyers on their own. Indeed, the best education for the arena is the task of preparing the gladiator for battle.

Sam Kaufman exacted meticulous care from his helpers in the preparation of trials. In many of his early major contests, that function had been discharged by Emil Weitzner. I never learned how Kaufman and Weitzner came to know each other, and I do not think the two men became real friends. Their relationship was rooted in mutual need. When that vanished, the relationship foundered. But I did learn that Kaufman had developed a deep respect for Weitzner's talents in preparing and organizing complex litigation.

By the time I came to the firm, in 1933, Weitzner had outgrown the task of preparation. Though he remained the *fidus Achates* to the more lustrous Kaufman, the job was now generally assigned to one of the younger men. While Kaufman was off on his glamorous trials, and Celler was laying the foundations of his great legislative career, Weitzner really ran the office.

Weitzner ran it with a fanatical devotion to excellence. He trained us to write clear, compact prose; he drilled us in the need for thoroughness in research. On the whole, no law office ever had a better teacher than Emil Weitzner. The true scholars among the young lawyers who served under Weitzner came to admire and even love him. The less disciplined, the free spirits among us, resented his didactic stringency and came to loathe him. I certainly fell into the second group. At the distance of forty-five years, I know now that I was unfair and even cruel to this devoted pietist. But in those days I chafed at Weitzner's emphasis on petty details, his impatience with any deviation from orthodoxy. While I became a warm admirer of the spectacular Kaufman, Weitzner was my *bête noire*. He must have become aware of my hostility; he grew to distrust my professional methods—and, as you shall see, with good reason.

Like Kaufman, Weitzner was a child of Jewish immigrant parents. As did so many others of his generation, he not only survived the milieu of New York's teeming East Side but rose high above it. In appearance and manner he was a cultured gentleman with a fastidious care for the English language. He was capable of icy *hauteur* as well as amiability; intellectually, he was the stuff of which chess champions and atomic physicists are made. Emotionally, he was a mess. His father had died early, and Weitzner was reared by a mother and three older sisters, none of whom ever married. This female gaggle hovered over him, doted on him, spoiled him. Even when I first knew him, when he was married and had two children, the solicitude of the three spinsters was visited on him daily. Life with that sterile harem had left its marks on Weitzner. He was soft, sensitive, delicate, and one of his chief characteristics was an abhorrence of physical violence. I was to learn that he had a deep revulsion to the sight of blood. It was this trait that eventually poisoned our relationship and made him my "enemy"—at least in my mind.

In 1934 the firm was engaged by the Wise Shoe Company to guide that retail chain in its guerrilla war with the Retail Shoe Salesmen's Union. The union, fighting for recognition by the company, began to picket the company's stores in the metropolitan area. The picketing at the company's Pitkin Avenue store, in Brooklyn (in the heart of Hymie Schorenstein's political satrapy), erupted into some turbulent conflicts between pickets and nonunion employees. This was in the early days of the New Deal, when the right of labor unions to organize employees was still developing. I assisted Weitzner in obtaining a broad injunction in Supreme Court, Kings County, against picketing at the Pitkin Avenue store. The Appellate Division, Second Department, had affirmed the injunction as it applied to the Pitkin Avenue store on a brief that Weitzner and I wrote.* The injunction was in full effect, certified copies had been served on the union, and for a short while there was no picketing. All was quiet on the pavement in front of the Wise shoe store on Pitkin Avenue.

But on one Friday evening in early October 1934, events exploded. The union's officials, thwarted by the injunction against picketing, had enlisted the aid of the Young People's Socialist League, known in an early manifestation of the left-wing propensity for acronyms as the "YPSLs." The heavily Jewish population of Brownsville in that era harbored many "socialists" and labor sympathizers. This

---

*242 App. Div. 660; modified, 266 N.Y. 264.

was the era in which the International Ladies Garment
Workers Union and the Amalgamated Clothing Workers
of America were in the forefront of labor's crusade, and the
folk heroes of the Jewish working class were Hillquit, Barondess, Dubinsky, Hillman, et al. So the YPSLs who were
marching up and down in front of the shoe store, carrying
their signs and shouting imprecations against the bosses
and the capitalist bloodsuckers, did not lack for sympathizers. Friday nights on Pitkin Avenue were like Sundays on
the Via Veneto; the world of Brownsville spilled into the
main shopping street. On this Friday night the sidewalk in
front of the store was packed with highly vocal supporters
of the union's aspirations. The employees of Wise Shoe
were beleaguered behind their plate-glass battlements.

We were informed of the sabbatical siege by a frantic
telephone call from the manager of the store. Weitzner and
I met at his uptown apartment to plan a relief expedition
to raise the siege. While we were planning, Celler called
Weitzner from Washington to urge some action. He had
been aroused by a telephone call from Hymie Schorenstein, who regarded any public gathering on Pitkin Avenue
(unless he had organized it himself) as a revolt against law,
order, and Schorenstein. To him the union officials, the
YPSLs, and their sympathizers were a bunch of Bolsheviks
who were defiling American institutions and who should
be sent back where they came from. Though Hymie was a
New Deal Democrat, he was no liberal—unless FDR or
Lehman or John McCooey told him to be a liberal. Also he
felt, as did Celler, that the rioting on his own territory
could be politically damaging to Celler, who relied heavily
on that assembly district for support in the congressional
election to be held in November, only about a month off.
If things got out of hand, Brownsville might go Republican, or even—God forbid!—Socialist.

The terms of the injunction against picketing by the union applied, of course, to persons acting in concert with the union officials. An obvious prerequisite to a contempt proceeding against the union and its YPSL minions was to serve the injunction on the young firebrands. Weitzner instructed me that on the next day, Saturday, I should dispatch one Leo Meehan, a brawny and agile messenger in our office, to Pitkin Avenue to serve certified copies of the injunction on the YPSLs. Then, on Sunday, I would prepare an application for an order to show cause why the union and the YPSLs should not be held in contempt. Weitzner knew that I had a long-standing date to attend a Cornell-Columbia football game on that Saturday. It was agreed that I should come to the office on Sunday, draft the papers, and submit them to Weitzner on Sunday evening, so that they could be presented to the court on Monday morning. I called Meehan and gave him Weitzner's order.

On Saturday I went to the football game with my friend and former roommate in Ithaca, John Walker. Walker was then a reporter on the *Herald Tribune;* he was a sturdy youth, with a certain often-demonstrated weakness for barroom pugilism. We were accompanied by two well-bred young ladies who did not know that they were about to be introduced to a world they had never dreamed of and of which their equally well bred mothers would never have approved. Nor did I know that while I was enjoying the football game, the society of the two belles, and a number of libations at Baker Field, there were being enacted on Pitkin Avenue scenes reminiscent of Eisenstein's *Potemkin.*

When the game ended, our party stopped at my parents' apartment in Washington Heights, about midway between Baker Field and a postgame party we were to attend near Columbia. On arrival, I learned that there was an urgent telephone message for me from a Mr. Meehan, who wanted me to call him at the Cumberland Hospital in Brooklyn. I called Meehan. He reported that he was being treated for lacerations and abrasions of the head incurred while he was engaged in carrying out the order to serve the injunction on the YPSL pickets. He would have to remain in the hospital overnight because of a suspected concussion. He had *not* been able to effect service on the YPSL pickets. He made it clear that he would have preferred the normal Saturday-night brawls on his native heath—Amsterdam Avenue—to becoming embroiled with a gang of wild, revolutionary Maccabees on Pitkin Avenue.

At this point I committed the blunder that was to begin the alienation between Weitzner and me. I did *not* call Weitzner; I did *not* seek advice from older and wiser heads. Instead, I saw myself as some kind of legal paladin who would himself go in harm's way against the Brownsville insurgents. Plans to attend the postgame party were canceled. Walker and I, accompanied by the unsuspecting damsels, set out by car for Pitkin Avenue. How much of our boldness was pot-valor, derived from the frequent potations at the football game, how much was a need to display our virile intrepidity before the young ladies, how much was plain youthful stupidity, I cannot now say. I can only say that the doomed expedition reached Brownsville about dusk; the transport that carried us there was parked on a quiet street, a block or two from Pitkin Avenue. The two young ladies were instructed to wait for us in the car while the assault force, Walker and Gould, approached the combat area: the Wise shoe store on Pitkin Avenue.

In those days, on a Saturday night, when the Jewish Sabbath ended at sunset, Pitkin Avenue would normally be thronged, especially on a pleasant day in early autumn. On this evening, the street was carrying its usual post-Sabbath traffic; but for about fifty or one hundred feet in front of the store the sidewalk was packed with hundreds of union sympathizers. A narrow lane was kept open immediately in front of the store; in this lane four or five wild-eyed youths, aflame with revolutionary zeal, marched back and forth carrying signs blazoned with such slogans as DOWN WITH THE WISE SHOE COMPANY AND ITS BLOODSUCKING WALL STREET LAWYERS! DON'T PATRONIZE THIS STORE! IT IS OWNED BY CAPITALIST LEECHES WHO HIRE WALL STREET COSSACKS TO STARVE THE WORKERS! Similar battle cries issued from the mouths of the pickets and were echoed by their supporters in the crowd. On the fringes of the crowd were a few of New York's finest, whose only concern was to keep the vehicular traffic moving.

Walker and I pushed our way through the crowd into the store. There were no customers. It was as easy for the housewife of Brownsville to get into the Wise shoe store as it was for Joan of Arc to get into Orléans. A panic-stricken manager and a few terrified clerks had remained in the store because it was safer than trying to escape. From the manager I obtained the certified copies of the injunction left with him. A copy had been affixed to the door of the shop, but it drew only sneers. Armed with the certified copies, and brandishing them as if they were Excalibur, Walker and I shoved through the crowd to the pickets. I planted myself in front of one of these chanting, frenzied dervishes and began to intone the formula of legal service, with the solemnity of a cleric pronouncing excommunication on a heretic.

"I hereby serve upon you"—someone punched me in the back—"an order of the Supreme Court"—a kick in the shins—"of Kings County"—an arm around my neck—"gurgle, gurgle, gurgle." The paper I was waving in front of the picket was torn from my hand. Walker (to whom I had imparted the ritual of legal service on the way to the fray) fared little better. Two or three wiry YPSLs were swarming over him. When Walker told the tale in later years, he would affirm that the calves of his legs bore the marks of one of the YPSLs' teeth. I can only affirm that there was a wild melee out of which a few solid facts emerge:

1. Walker knocked one picket to the ground.
2. I struck a few ineffectual blows at unidentified targets.
3. The cops who were on the outskirts of the crowd moved in with their nightsticks to rescue Walker and me from the impassioned revolutionary horde. (In court, next morning, the pickets averred that the cops rescued *them* from Walker and me. Since we were outnumbered by a hundred to one, this testimony was understandably unimpressive.)

The brief battle of Pitkin Avenue was over. When the fog of carnage had cleared, Walker and I charged the pickets with assault and demanded that they be arrested by the cops. The pickets charged Walker and me with assault and demanded that *we* be arrested by the cops. The cops were only too happy to comply with *both* demands. As all of the arrested combatants were being conducted in police cars to the Pennsylvania Avenue police station, I remembered the two innocent nymphs who had been left behind in the parked car. I persuaded the police sergeant to let us stop en route to instruct these poor camp followers to join us at the precinct.

At the police station things began to sort out. Formal charges were entered against Walker and me for assault and battery on the pickets. We, in turn, lodged charges of mayhem and riot, among others, against two or three of the pickets. Next it occurred to me that my generalissimo, Weitzner, sitting back in his command post on West End

Avenue, should be informed that the course of the campaign had changed. I remember speaking with him on the telephone. He was a member of a string quartet that assembled at his home every Saturday night. When I called, he was wrenched from the tranquil beauties of Brahms or Mozart. He was not in a very receptive mood for my narrative.

"Mr. Weitzner," I said, "I am at the Pennsylvania Avenue police station in Brooklyn."

"What the devil are you doing there," he asked, "and what has it to do with me?"

Slowly I imparted to him the saga of the day, starting with the attack on Leo Meehan. When I got to the part about coming out to Brownsville to effect personal service on the pickets, he began to tell me in his most pungent prose how many kinds of a damned fool I was. His voice got shriller and shriller, and when I told him of the battle of the Pitkin Avenue sidewalk, he began to scream. The words are not recallable, but they were pithy and denunciatory, and generally conveyed the idea that he never wanted to see me again. At that point I think his wife (or the second violinist) picked him off the floor. Somehow he was restored to sanity, because I was to learn that he called Hymie Schorenstein, who showed up at the police station in about an hour, accompanied by a clubhouse lawyer who was an expert in such legal imbroglios. Walker and I were locked up in a cell with a seatless toilet. The pickets were confined in a similarly luxurious *oubliette* across from us. Between the two cells there passed a stream of taunts, threats, and sneers. I think both Dickens and Trollope have noted the talent of adolescents for this type of cultural exchange in confined quarters.

Just before the key turned on us, and thinking myself abandoned by all mankind, I had telephoned my brother in

Manhattan, who arrived almost simultaneously with Schorenstein. He brought no bail money, but he did have the Sunday-morning papers and a corned-beef sandwich for each of us. Sustenance, he thought, for the minds and bodies of the imprisoned.

Hymie saved the night. He arranged somehow for Walker and me to be released for appearance in the magistrate's court, somewhere on the eastern boundaries of transfluvial Kings County on Sunday morning. Walker and I spent the night in a Turkish bath on Pitkin Avenue, where, under Hymie's imperial aegis, we were treated like visiting royalty. The pickets spent the night in the local hoosegow. My brother conducted the two frightened fillies back to their homes in civilized Manhattan.

Next morning, Walker and I appeared before a magistrate, accompanied by a confident, smiling Schorenstein and his oily, self-possessed clubhouse attorney. The magistrate seemed to have a passing acquaintance with Hymie and his henchman. He scornfully dismissed the charges against Walker and me, contriving to make a few remarks about his devotion to those great public servants Congressman Emanuel Celler and Commissioner Schorenstein. Walker and I were just a couple of decent citizens, "officers of the court," trying to carry out lawful processes, and the magistrate had his eye on a nomination to the City Court.

As to the pickets, the indignant magistrate had no trouble finding them guilty of disorderly conduct. He fined them ten dollars each, and the fine was paid immediately by a foreign-looking figure who, Hymie assured us, was an emissary of the Bolsheviks. Justice had prevailed. Walker and I expressed our thanks to Schorenstein and his clubhouse familiar, and returned to Manhattan. The Battle of Pitkin Avenue was indeed at an end. But not for me.

I went to the office and prepared an affidavit and order

to show cause why the YPSLs should not be held in contempt of the court's injunction. Later in the day, I brought the papers up to Weitzner's apartment for his editing and approval. He received me with the icy chill of which he was a master. I gave him a slightly expurgated version of the passage-at-arms on Pitkin Avenue. He told me that he had already been fully informed by Mr. Schorenstein. He then launched into a careful and incisive recital of my deficiencies of judgment and character. At this distance, I must concede that he was accurate and just. At that time, I was outraged that heroism should be rewarded with such ingratitude. Weitzner must have been storing up for a long time his scornful evaluation of my talents—or lack thereof. He discoursed at length on violence, on his aversion to physical combat. "You are supposed to be a lawyer, not a thug" was the theme of his homily. I know now that all the time he was talking to me, he was saying to himself, "This crazy kid must go."

For a few weeks I went about my tasks, ignored by Weitzner. Gradually his bitterness toward me seemed to thaw and I began to hope that we could live in peace and amity. Then, a few days before Christmas, I accompanied Weitzner to Washington for a hearing before one of the transient New Deal agencies, the Federal Alcohol Control Administration. The firm represented the Allied Brewing & Distilling Company, and in its behalf, under Weitzner's direction, I had prepared an application to that agency for a new distillery license. In Washington we joined Louis Bernstein, the company's president. We worked with Bernstein, who was the chief witness in support of the application, until late in the night. Next morning we appeared before the agency. The hearing was concluded just in time for us to board the *Congressional Limited*, which left Washington at four o'clock in the afternoon. We sat in three seats in a parlor car, Bernstein between Weitzner and me.

Bernstein was a pleasant, amiable man, very small, very slight, with a tendency to shyness. His profile plainly announced his Semitic origin. When we settled in our seats, all three of us showed signs of fatigue. I know I pretended to read for a while and then dozed off.

When the train stopped at Baltimore, the empty seat across from Bernstein was filled by a florid, middle-aged man whose manner proclaimed that he had more than a drop taken before boarding the train. As we pulled out of Baltimore he noisily instructed the porter to bring him a drink. He was loud, he was brash, he was offensive. The sober passengers buried their noses in magazines and ignored him; Bernstein appeared to shrink into his parlor seat. I snoozed on, waking once to hear the ribald lush across the aisle invite Bernstein to join him in a drink and Bernstein refuse with studied civility. I was awakened again to hear this drunken fool direct taunts and vicious anti-Semitic remarks at Bernstein. To me, at that age and in that era, this was a tocsin to battle. I became fully awake. I began to remonstrate. The man now made some offensive remark to me, touching on my own origin and ancestry. Then he placed his thumb over the top of a ginger-ale bottle and squirted it at Bernstein, accompanying this gesture with some further insufferable racial slurs. Feral youthful passion took command. I sprang across the aisle and struck the man; I hit him again in the face with my left hand, on which I had a ring with a chipped stone. The ring caught him under his right eye, and as he fell back into the Pullman chair a small curtain of blood began to trickle down from the cut.

I cannot recall the precise sequence of events after that. I know that the man was revived, that ice was applied to the cut, and somehow peace was restored. At that point I remembered Weitzner.

Weitzner had collapsed in his seat, completely unconscious, in a dead faint. Now we all ministered to him. By the time we reached Philadelphia he had recovered sufficiently to go to the men's room, where he spent the next hour gasping and retching. At Manhattan Transfer he returned to his seat. He sat in stony silence, gazing out of the car window through heavily lidded eyes at the Jersey Meadows. He would neither look at me nor speak to me.

At Pennsylvania Station I offered to help him back to his home. He shook his head from side to side; he pointed a quavering finger at me. "I never want to see you again. I'll deal with you in the morning."

Next morning I went to the office prepared to be fired. I was sure that my tenure at Kaufman Weitzner & Celler could not survive both battles: Pitkin Avenue and the *Congressional Limited*. I waited all morning, but no word came from Weitzner. Toward noon I received a summons from the Big Boss, Kaufman.

When I entered his room, he looked at me quizzically. "Well?" he asked.

"Mr. Kaufman," I said, "I suppose you have heard what happened last night?"

"I have heard," said Kaufman.

"Mr. Kaufman," I said, "I am very sorry it happened. I am very sorry Mr. Weitzner took it so hard. But I can't promise it won't happen again. Nobody can stand for that sort of thing."

"Enough," said Kaufman. "I talked with Bernstein as well as Weitzner. I think you should have killed the son of a bitch. As for him"—beckoning toward Weitzner's room —"he's always had a very weak stomach. Let's forget all about it."

So I stayed with the firm. But I had little to do with Weitzner, who regarded me with fresh distrust. He manifested his appraisal of my professional reliability by assigning to me only the most trifling tasks. In a few months Sam Kaufman rescued me from purgatory by taking me with him into an important new government job.

4

INNOCENTS AFLOAT:
SAM KAUFMAN TAKES
A SHORT CRUISE

Sam Kaufman had a passion for neatness. In dress he was fastidious. In his taste for food he was a delicate gourmet. He made it a point to introduce us to New York's best restaurants. As you worked with him you began to be familiar with some of the city's finest eating places, resorts that were beyond our ken and our means. It was a great treat to stay in the evening, assisting Sam in preparing a case for trial and then to dine with him in Lucullan splendor at Sweet's or Cavanaugh's or Le Chambord. One of his special favorites was Villepigue's, in Sheepshead Bay. Five or six times a year, Kaufman would make the long ride to Sheepshead Bay with one or two of his "boys" to regale himself and his guests with Villepigue's sumptuous shore dinners, the climax of which was always a large broiled lobster.

Kaufman insisted that his close associates dress with neatness and with dignity. No shirt sleeves in the office. When you went to court, you wore a hat. If you accompanied him to court, your shoes were shined, your shirt was white, and your suit (vested, of course) was of a dark hue that, to him, bespoke dignity. He had a special contempt for "slobs." He even discriminated among clients; those who did not conform with Sam's standards as to appearance and personal habits were soon relegated to the attention of partners and associates who could not afford to be so squeamish. I recall a single, conspicuous exception.

One Saturday afternoon in 1934, I was working in the library of Kaufman Weitzner & Celler. The entire office reflected Sam Kaufman's deep care for dignity and decorum—the reception room was paneled in chaste white; the style was stately Colonial—and the tone carried over into the library, which expressed solid dignity. In that time, law offices were open and active on Saturday until about four P.M., when the weekend officially began. As a group of young associates sat in that austere library, waiting for four o'clock to happen, the doors swung open to reveal a corpulent, middle-aged ragamuffin. Remember that this was a time when people were judged at first glance by their dress. A gentleman was attired like a gentleman; a vagabond wore the uniform of that class. What stood in the doorway of the library was Weary Willie—ragged, unkempt, and unmistakably unwashed. It was the kind of figure that in those Depression years sidled up to the comparatively affluent in the street and besought a nickel for a cup of coffee. Plainly, here was a panhandler who had somehow found his way up to the firm's offices. His very presence was a profanity.

The intruder spoke. "Where the hell is Sam Kaufman?" he demanded in a surly, peremptory voice. His tone implied that the Great Kaufman had nothing better to do on a Saturday afternoon than to sit in his office waiting for the appearance of a street Arab.

The very use of Kaufman's first name by this tatterdema-

lion character shocked us. And the use of a tone and manner that bespoke familiarity—even social equality—with
our chief, that exemplar of punctilio in dress and manner,
was a shock. But one among us, a year or two more advanced in experience than the rest, apparently *knew* something; he reacted electrically to the appearance of the hob-
goblin. He rushed out and in a moment returned with Emil
Weitzner.

Weitzner was no less fastidious in manner and dress than
Sam Kaufman. As I have told you, he was a crisp scholar
with a passion for precision and the coolest of social manners, especially in his dealings with the young lawyers.
With Kaufman we were always at ease; with Weitzner we
trembled over a split infinitive. To our amazement,
Weitzner all but embraced the gamy villein. "Bert!" he
exclaimed. "How good to see you. Too bad Sam didn't
know you were coming. Please come into my office."

There was no sign of Weitzner's normal social chill. He
was almost obsequious toward this ragged bum, whom he
gently drew into his office. Our more experienced brother
told us that he recognized the vagabond and he imparted
what he knew about him.

Herbert Berri was the only son (and heir) of William
Berri, one of the great men of Brooklyn in the nineteenth
century. The father had been a successful industrialist,
publisher, and civic leader, acclaimed for his leadership in
effecting civic and political reforms in that mysterious
transpontine borough. When William Berri died, his millions passed to "Bert." Bert was weak, idle, unsuccessful in
every enterprise save one: he had contrived to retain William Berri's fortune intact. This he accomplished by prac-
ticing a kind of savage parsimony, and in this process he
had sunk lower and lower into the life of a hermit.

Bert lived in the kitchen of a large mansion on one of

Brooklyn's most beautiful tree-lined streets; all the other rooms were closed off. The palatial salons in which William Berri had once entertained the borough's social and political elite had now fallen into ruin, through neglect and disuse. Water, gas, and electricity had been cut off for nonpayment of bills. Heat came only from a wood stove, fueled by sticks and branches picked up in the streets. Discarded newspapers were an auxiliary source of energy. Bert had become a local character, shunned by his respectable neighbors and taunted by neighborhood children. The single room in which this pitiful recluse lived was littered with filth. His millions were safely harbored in banks, but he would not indulge himself in the barest amenities.

I learned that in the dim past Berri had a wife and two sons. He had encountered Sam Kaufman when it became necessary to employ trial counsel because his wife had sued for a separation.

Kaufman later told us about the trial of that matrimonial dispute. According to Kaufman, Mrs. Berri, who had been a domestic in the home of Bert's father, was annexed by Bert and bore him two sons before Bert's brutish habits drove her to the courts for protection. Kaufman told me that Bert Berri wanted to challenge the paternity of his younger son, hinting darkly that his father, William Berri, was the child's sire. But Kaufman talked Bert out of this defense, and the trial was for separation.

The hapless Mrs. Berri was on the witness stand recounting instances of Bert's cruel treatment. She was a slight, timid woman; Bert was a burly two-hundred-pounder who looked and sounded like a filthy grizzly bear. She testified tearfully that in addition to his other brutalities, Bert made bizarre sexual demands on her. When the terrified, exhausted woman could no longer endure these excesses, she claimed, he would lie in bed and masturbate.

When this testimony was related to a shocked court, Bert turned to Kaufman and spluttered in an outraged voice, audible throughout the room: "She's a goddamn liar! I haven't done that in three years!" At this stage, Kaufman worked out a settlement.

By the time of that Saturday afternoon the wife was dead, the two sons were completely alienated from their father and off in the mists, and Kaufman was established as Bert's only friend and his counselor. He was also established as Bert's executor and as trustee for the two sons, which probably explains the delicacy with which he was treated by the principal partners in the firm.

I heard Berri's name mentioned in the office from time to time, but I cannot recall seeing him again until sometime in the latter part of 1937. About that time, Kaufman called me into his office. There sat Berri, still looking like an oversized scarecrow, and smelling like the Canarsie dumps. I marveled that the finicky Kaufman would breathe the same air. Berri accepted my presence with open suspicion. He wanted his trusted friend and counselor, Sam Kaufman, to advise him, not some unknown, supercilious novice. Kaufman persuaded him that I was at most a "helper" to him, and Berri grudgingly consented to my attendance.

Sam handed me a libel in admiralty* in the U.S. District Court in Brooklyn. The document alleged that the libelant (the claimant), one Jens Huntze, had been employed to make certain repairs on a "yacht" owned by Berri; that in the course of carrying out his duties, he had fallen from the mast because the ropes securing a bos'n's chair were defective; that he had sustained serious injuries; and now he demanded that the vessel, i.e., Berri, pay him a large sum

---

*A "libel" is the jargon of admiralty lawyers for what landlubbers call a "complaint." It is the original pleading in a lawsuit.

in damages. My first reaction was one of surprise that Berri owned a yacht. The image of this fetid hulk clad in rags, topped by a yachtsman's cap, facing the Atlantic breezes, was just too incongruous. But I learned that Berri did indeed own a powerboat, his only extravagance. He had hired the libelant, a seaman of German birth, to repair the mast. Berri told us that a rope had indeed parted, hurling the seaman to the deck and causing injuries. Since I was the only associate in the office with any experience in admiralty matters, Kaufman assigned the case to me for preparation. Berri insisted, of course, that Kaufman should himself conduct the trial. There was no insurance; that would have been an incredible luxury for Berri.

Berri's boat was berthed at a small yacht club in the Flatlands section of Brooklyn, where the accident had occurred. The yacht club should not be confused with the luxurious marinas of this day. It was a primitive structure on Gerritsen Inlet, just north of Sheepshead Bay. From Gerritsen Inlet to the big, broad Atlantic Ocean is little more than a nautical mile. Berri made some noises about the desirability of inspecting the boat. As I recall, I made arrangements for photographs to be taken, and in due course I received some glossy prints of an ordinary cabin cruiser with a stumpy mast. The photographs showed the little vessel to be in a somewhat disorderly condition, but there was nothing to suggest that it was a floating garbage dump.

As the day of trial drew near I approached Kaufman to discuss the case and prepare him for the trial. Kaufman told me that Berri was insistent that both he and I actually inspect the boat, the scene of the accident. When I signified some reluctance to make the long trek down to South Brooklyn, Kaufman smiled his irresistible smile. "Tell you what, son," he said. "We'll go down late tomorrow after-

noon and look at Berri's boat. That should take about ten
minutes. Then we'll go over to Villepigue's and eat a couple of their lobsters. How does that strike you?"

I was utterly seduced. I would have agreed to inspect
Charon's ferryboat for one of Villepigue's lobsters.

Late the next afternoon, we set out for the Flatlands in
Kaufman's impressive, chauffeur-driven Pierce-Arrow. In
that age a man's opulence was measured in direct ratio to
the wheelbase length of his car. And Sam's car was long
and luxurious. It stood out in contrast to the drab, weather-
beaten little yacht club at which Berri kept his boat. When
we arrived, there stood the skipper on the dock, smiling in
hospitality and happiness, clad as usual in his grease-
stained tatters, giving off his normal aroma. His ridiculous
appearance was accentuated by a grimy, battered yachtsman's cap that might have been discarded by Magellan.
Proudly, he led us to his argosy. It made a comic scene: two
lawyers, clad in the formal Wall Street fashion of their day,
marching behind this ragged, evil-smelling Scaramouche
to his equally malodorous boat.

I had seen the photographs of Berri's bark, but no picture could convey the filth and disorder that prevailed. The
paint was peeling; there were a few shreds of a tattered
awning; ropes, cans, and nautical gear were strewn about.
And there arose from the wreckage a smell compounded of
petrol, garbage, and ordure. Berri's normal odor was per-
fume compared to the cloacal fumes that emanated from
this yacht. Berri muttered that he had been engaged in
repairing a clogged "head" when we arrived. That was to
explain the smell, of which even Berri was aware.

Kaufman became pale; his nostrils began to twitch.
Bravely, he followed Berri over the side; I followed them.
For the next few minutes Berri pointed out to us the details
of the accident. He showed us the mast where the ropes

were secured. Then he turned away from us, toward the stern of the boat.

Kaufman and I were fighting for air when we heard the engine start. Before he or I could act, the bow of the little boat swung away from the dock, and we were chugging off into the little estuary that led to Sheepshead Bay. Kaufman began to expostulate with Berri, but the helmsman was laughing the crazed laughter of the Flying Dutchman. The little trick he had played on Kaufman filled him with delight. "Gonna take you fellows for a little spin," he shouted.

We stood helplessly as the chortling boob at the wheel turned the boat into Sheepshead Bay. In a few minutes we were rounding Rockaway Point and heading into the vast Atlantic. The wind thundered around us; the ocean swells struck us. We pitched and tossed, and Sam Kaufman began to turn green. Berri headed the little boat into the wind and insisted that I take the wheel. In a daze, I complied with our skipper's orders: "Keep her headed this way," shouted Berri over the roar of the wind. I think "this way" was the coast of Portugal.

Berri disappeared into the cabin. In a few moments he emerged with a collapsible table; he opened the legs, set it down, and dived back into the cabin. Now he brought out some greasy brown-paper bags, from which he drew paper plates and some of the worst-looking food I have ever seen in my life. I can remember only potato salad and cold cuts. Now he was setting up chairs and with the air of Sardanapalus inviting his courtiers to some new thrills in gastronomy, Berri gestured toward the table. "Gonna treat you guys to a little feed," he said.

At the sight of the rancid mess displayed on the table, even my youthful viscera began to churn. But the revolting display pushed Kaufman over the edge of mere nausea. His face was a greenish-yellow mask of anguish and terror. Yet he was a legal warrior of an ancient breed. He kept on trying; and I followed the lead of my chief. When Berri's attention was on me, Kaufman surreptitiously tossed his food over his shoulder and into the Atlantic. When Berri turned to Kaufman, I played the same game. I began to hope that we would make it through the meal.

But now Herbert Berri contributed his final savage thrust at our composure. His mouth crammed with the revolting stuff, he jabbed a dirty finger at Sam Kaufman. "I want you guys to know that I don't eat this fancy every day," he shouted over the din. "This is a special treat." Something snapped inside Sam Kaufman. He rushed to the side and surrendered to the horrors of seasickness.

I besought Berri to turn back, to bring us to land. As I ministered to my stricken chief Berri grudgingly turned the boat landward, muttering all the time about wasting the fine food he had offered us. Kaufman was semiconscious when we reached the dock, where his devoted chauffeur, Tom, anxiously awaited us. Tom and I carried him over the side and into the car. Plainly, any thought of Villepigue's and its succulent lobsters was out of the question. We streaked to Manhattan, leaving the bewildered Berri on the dock, shaking his head in disbelief that we should have rejected the feast he had spread before us.

About halfway to the Brooklyn Bridge, Sam recovered consciousness long enough to instruct me to telephone his wife and arrange for his physician to be at his apartment. I spent the rest of the evening consoling Anne Kaufman while the doctor addressed himself to the recumbent Sam.

By the following afternoon, Kaufman had recovered sufficiently to come to the office. I looked in to inquire about his condition. He was still pale, but his eyes twinkled. "Son," he said, "I owe you one lobster."

About the case: we went to trial, and at the point where

we had to exhibit Bert to the jury, Kaufman persuaded him to shell out a few thousand dollars for a settlement. The settlement was reached late one afternoon in the old federal courthouse in Brooklyn. As we stood on the sidewalk outside, bidding adieu to our client, the Aromatic Mariner, Kaufman said to me, "Well, son, how do you feel about a little trip to Sheepshead Bay?" I finally *did* get my lobster.

PART II

The Investigation

In 1935 Sam Kaufman was in his middle forties. He was not only a first-class trial lawyer, but he had important connections in the Democratic Party, both in New York and in Washington. Mannie Celler, his law partner, was one of Roosevelt's principal lieutenants in the House of Representatives. Kaufman was on terms of intimacy with some of the great figures of the New Deal. Attorney General Cummings was a close friend. Joseph E. Davies, later famous for his *Mission to Moscow* and one of Roosevelt's pundits on matters foreign and domestic, was Sam's friend and fishing-cum-poker-companion (at the celebrated Jefferson Island Club, the New Deal sodality whose virile social rites were attended even by the Chief), and he entrusted much of the substantial litigation of the Davies law firm in Washington to Sam. There were others: Donald Richberg, Seth Richardson, Samuel I. Rosenman, powerful personalities in the years when the New Deal was coming of age, were all friends and fans of Sam Kaufman.

By 1935 Sam had accumulated a respectable financial competence out of his successful law practice and from an interest in a solidly lucrative family business. In his mind, the time had come to realize the two major ambitions of his life: he wanted to be U.S. Attorney in the Southern District of New York and then to be a judge in that district court. It was almost a foregone conclusion that he would attain both goals. He had the ability, the connections, and the itch.

One day Joe Davies, Sam's chief sponsor on matters political, told Kaufman that Martin Conboy, a close friend of FDR and the incumbent U.S. Attorney in New York, was talking about leaving that office. He suggested that Kaufman send to the White House a local emissary who could sing his praises to the President. Kaufman and his kitchen cabinet selected a distinguished New York lawyer for this errand, Lamar Hardy, who enjoyed the President's friendship and confidence. Hardy was a courtly Southerner whose charm and accent came straight from his antebellum Cavalier ancestors. Hardy went to Washington, met with Roosevelt, and returned to inform a stricken Kaufman that he, Hardy, had been selected as Conboy's successor. There was no articulated bitterness; there were a few arch allusions to John Alden's courtship of the maiden Priscilla, and the matter was dropped. This was the way things happened in that Imperial Age, and nobody with good sense and political ambitions wanted to be tagged as a bad sport. Hardy *did* tell Kaufman that he intended to leave the office early in 1937. So Kaufman bowed to the will of Roosevelt (as who did not?) and bided his time.

Joe Davies persisted in Kaufman's cause. He assured Sam that he needed only some additional "exposure" and he would be a "shoo-in" to be U.S. Attorney in succession to the lucky Lamar Hardy. The opportunity for "exposure" came very quickly.

In that day there was a scandal over the prevalent abuses in the operation of the laws controlling immigration in the United States and the naturalization of aliens. The Immigration Acts of 1921 and of 1924, with their harsh exclusionary quotas, made it difficult for Poles, Yugoslavs, and most of all Italians to enter the United States legally. Despite the vast number of Italian Americans then living in the United States, the derivation of the "quotas" from years when European immigration was largely from England, Ireland, and Germany militated against Italians. So the cousins from Calabria trying to escape from the harsh poverty of the Mezzogiorno found it difficult to get visas. As a result, hundreds of thousands came in by clandestine means. Once here, these unfortunates were preyed upon and exploited by extortioners, racketeers, and con men. The most tragic flimflam played on these hapless men and women was to sell them bogus certificates of naturalization to "make them legal."

The Immigration and Naturalization Service had conducted a massive investigation into the frauds practiced on these aliens, and by 1935 a number of important criminal cases were ready to be prosecuted, chiefly in the Southern and Eastern districts of New York. (These two federal judicial districts embrace New York City.) The alien victims of these frauds were spread over the country, but the crooked "brokers" and racketeers were concentrated in New York. More importantly, for decades New York's Ellis Island had been the chief port of entry for the masses of immigrants who came from Europe. As a result, the records involved in the frauds were concentrated at Ellis Island, and the corrupt employees of the Immigration and Naturalization Service who were seduced into falsifying and manipulating these records were almost all in the New York area.

Many cases involving these frauds were in the process of investigation, and about ten or twenty were ready for presentation to grand juries. The principal investigation unit had been set up in New York, under the direction of W. Frank Watkins and Charles P. Muller. Both men were Civil Service zealots. Watkins was in his late forties; his hair was iron-gray, his eyes were steely-blue, and his heart was like flint. His entire career had been in the Immigration Service, most of it in pursuing the wayward and corrupt. His vocabulary was heavily larded with words like "skulduggery," "rapscallions," and "hanky-panky." He was all cop. When he talked of snaring some delinquent or dishonest officer, his ample chest filled and his eyes glowed. As to his own integrity—well, he lived at the YMCA and every five years he ordered from Montgomery Ward a blue serge suit of a fabric made specially for railroad conductors. When you took it off, you could lean it against the wall. These were Watkins' luxuries.

Charley Muller knew more about naturalization law than any other man in the land. He had used his discharge money from the Spanish-American War to pay his law-school tuition. Muller had been one of the few men wounded at the Battle of Santiago Bay. He was serving as a seaman on the USS *Brooklyn* when a Spanish projectile, one of the few that found a target that day, struck the steel plating, about ten feet from Muller. Of course, it did not explode; but the concussion affected the hearing of one ear for life. It had one other effect. Muller became one of the few passionate patriots this writer has ever encountered. He spoke of his country as most men speak of wives and sweethearts. He had neither of these; the USA was Charley's mistress.

The number and complexity of these cases taxed the resources of the local U.S. Attorneys. So Daniel W. McCormack, then Commissioner of Immigration and Naturalization, requested the Attorney General to set up a "Special Unit" in New York with its own investigators and prosecutors to continue the work, under the direction of Watkins and Muller. In April 1935 Sam Kaufman was chosen by Homer Cummings, the Attorney General, to head the Special Unit, with the title of Special Assistant to the Attorney General. In later years this sort of investigative and prosecutorial group was known more dramatically as a "Strike Force," but in the drab, bureaucratic nomenclature of that era it was simply a "Special Unit."

Kaufman chose as his chief assistant a burly, determined, myopic scholar named Sylvester Pindyck. Pindyck was a no-nonsense character, addicted to hard and thorough work. His father had died when he was quite young, leaving him well endowed with money and female relatives. Pindyck had worked at Kaufman's law office after graduating from Columbia Law School in the 1920s. He had left to handle family affairs, but when Kaufman was chosen as chief prosecutor of the investigation, he recruited Pindyck to organize and administer the office. Pindyck lived with his mother and three sisters in a Flatbush mansion. To him the office was a quiet refuge, and he was always there— nights and weekends, Sundays and holidays.

There were four other aides, of whom I was the youngest, the most callow, and probably the most self-important.

Our job was to prosecute the racketeers and corrupt officers of the Immigration and Naturalization Service who preyed on the unfortunate aliens who had entered the United States illegally. There were several networks of those rascals who furnished the spurious certificates of naturalization to the many thousands of illegal entrants who paid huge sums to be "legal," as they thought. In fact, the citizenship certificates peddled by the racketeers, with the help of faithless government officers, were worthless. Though the certificates were actually issued by federal courts all over the country, their issuance was based on one of several techniques of fraud, all of which involved the subversion and corruption of employees of the Immigration and Naturalization Service.

The crudest method was the "match" case. Let us suppose that Gaetano Porcupino entered the United States illegally in 1924 by deserting from the crew of an Italian vessel in a U.S. port. He is now working as a busboy in Peoria, and he trembles every time he glimpses a badge on a blue tunic. He arranges through one of the ethnic networks to have the manifests at Ellis Island examined by one of the crooked clerks. It is found that one Giulio Porcupino arrived lawfully on the *Giuseppe Verdi* in 1919. Giulio's physical description, place of birth, and other details are not too different from Gaetano's. Gaetano is furnished with Giulio's details. He applies for naturalization, alleging that he was admitted lawfully at New York in 1919 as Giulio—but he now prefers to be called Gaetano, after his wife's dead brother. His application is sent to Ellis Island for checking. Sure enough, there on the passenger manifest of the SS *Giuseppe Verdi* appear all the facts: date of birth, birthplace, names of parents, even "scar on left hand." Presto, the naturalization court gets an official certificate of arrival attesting to Gaetano's lawful admission for permanent residence. He becomes a citizen. He no longer fears the law. And all for about one thousand dollars.

But this type of fraud was easily detected. When the certificate of arrival was issued, there was supposed to be a notation of its issuance placed on the manifest. And when the true Giulio applied for naturalization, it was plain that some impostor had already used his lawful entry for an unlawful purpose. Result: Watkins' agents were picking up thousands of Gaetanos all over the country and deporting them to Italy. Their papers were worthless. And the word was soon broadcast that the match case did not work.

A refinement was needed, and it was found. By the late 1920s racketeers were arranging with crooked clerks at Ellis Island to remove entire *pages* from the bound volumes of the manifests; these clerks even used the specially constructed typewriters of the Immigration Service to type in the names of the unlawful entrants and all the required biographical data. These fake additions were perforce made at the top or bottom of the manifest pages, and the fact that the pages had been neatly sliced out was detectable. Many thousands of such spurious insertions were made on the third-class-passenger manifests of ships that arrived from Naples and Trieste. This method was far more expensive than matching and exposed the corrupted clerks to more danger. The removal of the sheet, the insertion of the names, and the careful replacement of the sheet in the bound manifest volumes required skills that were almost surgical. The clerks actually used scalpels borrowed from Ellis Island's Hospital.

But Watkins' sleuths learned from one of their informers about this new and improved method. Teams were dispatched to Ellis Island to examine the suspected manifest volumes. Before long, the hapless beneficiaries of naturalization papers based on these faked manifest entries were being picked up in droves by immigration inspectors and herded up the gangplanks for deportation.

As these methods were exposed and their victims identified, their exploiters—the racketeers, intermediaries, and crooked immigration and naturalization officers—were being convicted in batches, and that did great credit to Watkins and his bloodhounds and to the prosecuting skills of Kaufman, Pindyck, and the other members of the Special Unit.*

There was one other method the racketeers used, far more sophisticated than the match cases or the faked manifest entries. But we did not learn about this technique until

---

*There were a number of federal criminal statutes under which these wretches could be prosecuted, but the Congress had provided us with a simple catchall: under the provisions of Title 8, Section 414 of the U.S. Code (as it then existed) any person who made a false statement in a naturalization proceeding or any person who aided or abetted him was guilty of a felony with big penalties. Our arsenal also included the conventional perjury and conspiracy statutes.

more than a year after April 1935, when we started our work.

We started on the wrong foot, with a case that embarrassed Sam Kaufman, frustrated Pindyck, and gave me a swelled head.

5

JUDICIAL REBUKE

As a general rule Kaufman insisted on careful and conscientious preparation of every legal case. He, himself, had neither the patience nor the aptitude for the hard work of preparation, so he chose his assistants with great care and held them to a high standard of thoroughness. He came to rely so heavily on them that he would, from time to time, lapse into a cavalier indifference to the details of a case he was about to try. I never saw this attitude manifested while I worked at Kaufman Weitzner & Celler from 1933 to 1935; but, then, I had little contact with Kaufman in that time. When he took me along to the immigration investigation, I saw that Kaufman's reluctance to immerse himself in the minutiae of preparation for trials became a vexing problem to his staff, especially to his chief assistant, Sylvester Pindyck. Pindyck's meticulous attention to every detail of a lawsuit was recognized by all of us. We even made jokes about his diligence. Sam Kaufman leaned so heavily on Pindyck that we had difficulty making him participate in the actual preparation. He seemed to feel that if Pindyck was satisfied, there was no need for more preparation. This led to some serious lapses and mistakes—most of which we managed to overcome. Kaufman's fierce pride and enormous self-confidence were almost always justified. But one such lapse led to a judicial rebuke that Kaufman pretended to overlook. I know that it nettled him for the rest of his life.

Judicial rebukes vary from the absurd to the devastating. When the late Judge Irving Saypol in New York State Supreme Court censured one lawyer for wearing a bow tie in his courtroom and a lady lawyer for the grandeur of her millinery, everybody had a good laugh, and the incidents were dismissed as personal conceits by a crotchety fellow who was a pretty good judge in spite of these silly foibles. But there are instances when judicial rebukes, usually unjustified, swell up into dangerous clashes between judges and lawyers, and have a destructive impact on either or both. In the English courts a single bitter exchange between judge and barrister can devastate a lawyer's career. Such advocates as Erskine, Carson, and Marshall Hall were the recipients of such reprimands. Marshall Hall's treatment by an irate judge almost wrecked his career.

I have witnessed such incidents, although I don't recall that I have ever been the recipient of any serious wigging from the bench. But one such experience in a trial in which I participated is worth recounting, although it interrupts our story. In 1971 I defended a stockbroker charged in federal court in New York with conspiring to violate the Interest Equalization Tax Law (since repealed). It was the first (and perhaps the only) prosecution under that arcane statute, and a serious one, because the claim was that the United States had been defrauded out of some twenty million dollars in taxes. A conviction would have meant not only a substantial prison term but the virtual extinction of the broker's firm, a hitherto respected member of the New York Stock Exchange. The prosecutor was an able and diligent young man who had made an intensive study of the statute but who had little or no experience in the courtroom. The federal judge before whom the case was tried was (and is) one of the brightest stars of the Southern District bench. He had a gift for sorting out the issues and for moving a complex case to conclusion with a minimum of courtroom nonsense. He also had a very short fuse, a loud and commanding voice, and a fierce impatience with incompetent lawyers.

Our trial was in its earliest stages when the judge sustained my objections to the form of a number of the young prosecutor's questions. It was plain that however erudite he was in income-tax law, he knew little about framing questions to conform with the rules of evidence. Bench conferences in which the judge, outside the jury's hearing, sought to instruct him in the proper formulation of questions proved unavailing. The luckless youth kept relapsing into insufferable technical solecisms, which led to objections that were sustained by the judge with an increasing level of impatience, scorn, and remonstrance. After an hour or two, the judge exploded. He excused the jury from the room; he excoriated the prosecutor for his lack of elementary courtroom skills; finally he sent for the Chief Assistant U.S. Attorney, the ashen-faced young prosecutor's immediate superior. The time was about noon. When the Chief Assistant arrived, the judge informed him that he had until two o'clock to replace our fumbling novice with an Assistant U.S. Attorney of acceptable competence. Otherwise, said the judge, he would dismiss the indictment.

One can only guess at the feverish activities of the next two hours in the offices of the U.S. Attorney while the crestfallen young prosecutor briefed his designated successor. At two o'clock a new prosecutor appeared before the judge and jury. He knew little about the Interest Equalization Tax Law, but he did know how to ask questions that would survive my objections. The young man who had been replaced sat at the counsel table, prompting and abetting his successor. To no avail. The case was lost to the government, and I am told that though he has become a useful and successful tax lawyer, the first fellow has not set foot in a courtroom since his doleful experience.

A few weeks after Kaufman had set up his staff for the immigration and naturalization investigation, we filed our first indictment. The defendant was Umberto Migliacci, an utterly unimportant figure who had violated the immigration laws in a minor way. But he was the defendant in our first case, and it was thought that this had some public-relations importance to the future of the investigation. The case had been worked up by Watkins' highly competent bloodhounds. Pindyck directed me to interview the witnesses and get the case ready for Kaufman to try. "Take this one," said Pindyck. "It's like shooting fish in a barrel. You'll get some experience. This one is so easy, even a novice like you couldn't fuck it up." This was a characteristically encouraging *exordium* from Pindyck. But he was right. It was an easy case: simple issue, few witnesses, overwhelming proof of guilt.

The indictment had been filed in the U.S. District Court for the Eastern District. The case was assigned to the Honorable Clarence G. Galston, a flinty little judicial adept with a scholar's mind, a glittering command of language, and the acerbity of a Marine drill sergeant. (I once heard Galston engage in substantially the following colloquy with a lawyer who appeared before him:

"Are you ready for trial, Mr. Jones?" asked the judge.

"Ready, Your Honor," answered Mr. Jones.

"I trust, Mr. Jones, you are not answering 'ready' in the Pickwickian sense."

"I'm not sure I understand, Your Honor. What is Pickwickian?"

The judge: "Mr. Jones, have you never heard of Mr. Pickwick?"

Jones: "I'm not sure, Your Honor. Is he somebody here in Brooklyn? Is he in our case?"

The judge: "Mr. Jones, Mr. Pickwick is a character in Dickens who did not always mean exactly what he said. I merely hope you mean what you say when you answer 'ready.' "

Jones: "Oh, I am ready, all right. But who is the other man you mentioned—Mr. Dickens?"

Galston: "Let's drop it, Mr. Jones. Just be here tomorrow morning with your witnesses ready for trial. And, Mr. Jones, if you will stop at my chambers, my secretary will lend you a book. You will find it is in the English language, but I trust that will not prove an insuperable impediment.")

Early in the day before we were to appear before Judge Galston in *United States* v. *Migliacci*, I went into Kaufman's office to prepare him. "Mr. Kaufman," I said, "I have in my office Mr. Caruso, who is our principal witness in the Migliacci case. I think you ought to hear what he says."

"Migliacci?" asked Kaufman. "I never heard of it. What's that all about?"

I was appalled. I had prepared and delivered to Kaufman about a week earlier a folder containing the indictment, digests of the testimony of the witnesses, copies of the chief exhibits, memoranda of law—all meticulously prepared under the watchful eye of Pindyck. Plainly, Kaufman had not even heard of it. "Migliacci," I cried. "The case you are supposed to try tomorrow over in Brooklyn. Didn't you see the folder I left for you?"

"Oh," said Kaufman, "that case. I never read the folder. Pindyck told me it was an easy one."

"Mr. Kaufman," I pleaded, "let me go over it with you. Come inside and listen to this witness, Caruso."

"No," said Kaufman. "I have something else to do. I'll try to read the folder tonight. Just meet me in court tomorrow morning, ready to go."

"Mr. Kaufman," I begged. "At least listen to this witness, Caruso."

"No," said Kaufman, "just meet me in court tomorrow."

Next morning I went over to court in Brooklyn. I made sure that Watkins' well-trained sheep dogs had herded the witnesses into their pen. Then I walked into the courtroom to meet Kaufman. He was not there. I was in a telephone booth calling the office to learn his whereabouts when one of the agents tapped on the glass. The judge was on the bench, ready to call the calendar. As I came into the room the clerk intoned, "United States versus Umberto Migliacci."

"Ready for the defendant," said Migliacci's lawyer.

"How about the government?" asked the judge. "Where is Mr. Kaufman?"

"Your Honor—" I got no further.

"Who are you?" asked the judge. "Where is Mr. Kaufman?"

I explained that I was one of Kaufman's assistants, that Mr. Kaufman was delayed, presumably by traffic. Could we not hold things up for a short while?

"Nonsense," said the judge. "Aren't you the young man who appeared before me last week and told me the government was ready? Did you not ask me to set this case down for trial this morning? Are you not authorized by the Attorney General to try this case?"

The answer to every question had to be yes.

"Then," said the judge, "this case is ready on both sides. Let us pick a jury."

"But Mr. Kaufman—" I stuttered.

"Never mind Mr. Kaufman," said the judge, with pardonable asperity. "Pick a jury."

I trembled as we went through the ritual of jury selection. Should I tell the judge I was only a year and a half out of law school? My trial experience only a few pushovers in the municipal court? Should I tell him I had been admitted to the bar of the federal court only a few months back? I conducted the jury selection for the government by feel and touch, with one eye cocked over my left shoulder at the back door, hoping Kaufman would appear over the horizon and rescue me from the dim mystery in which I was immersed. Halfway through, one of Watkins' agents handed me a message from Pindyck: Kaufman was delayed in another court; I was admonished to carry on as best I could.

The jury was completed. Still no Kaufman. "You may open to the jury, Mr. Gould," said the judge. By now he at least knew my name.

I had observed other lawyers. I doubt I had ever addressed a jury before this. But I got through the opening presentation of the prosecution's case without notable event. The defendant's lawyer asked and obtained from the judge the right to reserve his opening until after our case was completed.

"Call your first witness," directed his honor. Again I looked to the back of the courtroom, for Kaufman, for relief. The agent I had stationed at the door shook his head. Negative. No Kaufman.

"The government calls Mr. Caruso," I announced over the thumping of my heart. Within moments, Mr. Caruso was on the witness stand, duly sworn, and had embarked

on his description of the felonious conduct of the defendant, Migliacci. Fortified with the fact sheet, the summary
of Caruso's testimony that I had prepared for Kaufman, I
was managing to elicit a few preliminary answers from
Caruso. The time was about noon; Kaufman was two hours
late. The judge smiled down at me benignly; I even suspected some compassion in his manner.

At about this point, the back doors opened and Kaufman
appeared. He treated Judge Galston to his most ingratiating smile, nodded in civility to defense counsel, and turned
to me, as if nothing unusual had occurred. "Okay, son,"
said Kaufman. "I'll take over now." He took the fact sheet
from my hand. I dumbly indicated the point I had reached
with the witness, Caruso. The jury seemed to give as much
attention to the switch from Young Novice Gould to Old
Master Kaufman as they would have given if the bottle on
the water cooler had been replaced.

Kaufman exuded poise and self-confidence. He turned to
the witness. "Now, Mr. Migliacci . . ." he began.

"Mr. Kaufman," I said in a fierce whisper that must have
been audible a block away. "Mr. Kaufman, our witness is
Caruso. The *defendant* is Migliacci."

"Excuse me," said Kaufman, smiling coolly at the judge
and then at the jury. Judge Galston performed that little
shift from one buttock to the other that experienced trial
lawyers come to recognize as the earliest symptom of judicial impatience. Kaufman continued to examine Caruso on
track for about four or five minutes. Then he said, "And
now, Mr. Migliacci, what happened next?"

A few of the jurors tittered; defense counsel started to
rise; the judge not only shifted from one haunch to the
other but cleared his throat in what lawyers would recognize as the sign of the transition from judicial impatience
to judicial displeasure. I grasped Kaufman firmly by the

sleeve. "Look, Mr. Kaufman, this witness is *Caruso*. The *defendant* is Migliacci." Both affirmations were accompanied by a vigorous aiming of the index finger—first at the witness and then at the defendant.

Kaufman nodded his acceptance; this time he apologized openly to the judge, the jury, the defendant, and the witness. He continued running down the fact sheet; the trial seemed to be back on the rails. Then I heard him ask, "And after that, Mr. *Migliacci . . .*"

The jury exploded into guffaws; I reached for Kaufman's sleeve, but I think I missed.

The judge lifted his entire posterior from his chair. "Mr. Kaufman," said he, "please approach the bench. Bring Mr. Gould with you." When we got to the bench, the judge spoke: "Mr. Kaufman, are you aware that this is a criminal case, in which the liberty of a human being is at stake? First, you are two hours late, and the government's interests are left in the hands of this inexperienced boy. Next, you come into court and try to take over a case with which you are obviously unfamiliar. You are not even sure of the defendant's name, and you don't know one witness from another. I know of your reputation as a trial lawyer, but I am not impressed. I will give you a choice: either you will sit down and let your assistant complete the examination of this witness while you read the indictment and otherwise inform yourself about the case, or I will declare a mistrial and set the case down before another judge at some future time. Take your pick."

Kaufman elected to sit down. A mistrial in the circumstances would have been an administrative disaster to the investigation. So the great man sat while *I* examined Caruso.

For me it was the end of innocence. I had picked a jury, delivered an opening, and examined a witness in the federal court. I had played in the big league, even if I was only a pinch runner. But I must give Sam Kaufman his due. When we went to lunch, we took the folder he had disdained. He studied it. And from there on in, he conducted a masterly trial. Our investigation was launched with a resounding victory. Never again did I see Kaufman walk in unprepared.

Within a few weeks of the conviction of Migliacci, Kaufman and Pindyck were trying another case—this one in Manhattan, in the federal court for the Southern District of New York. This was a case that was to provide that court with one of its enduring legends: the witness who spoke with God.

6

THE WITNESS WHO
SPOKE WITH GOD

In 1935 the simple beauty of the south façade of New York's City Hall could not be enjoyed from the downtown side. The view was still obscured by the staggeringly ugly bulk of the old post office and federal court building. This moldering structure was typical of the combined postal and court facilities erected all over the land in the second half of the nineteenth century.* Streetcars banged and clanged around it; the roar of traffic in what was then one of the busiest sections of the city made it almost impossible to hear what went on in the courtrooms. Just to the north, in what is now celebrated as Foley Square, a new, beautiful, almost soundproof palace of federal justice, to be topped by the now-familiar golden roof, was under con-

---

*Built in 1875, it was thought to have been inspired by some of the public buildings of Paris in the reign of Napoleon III. There is a photograph of the building in the Museum of the City of New York. With its four tiers of columns and silly little cupola surmounting its huge roof, it looks like a misplaced Babylonian temple.

struction—but it was at least a year away from completion. Meanwhile, in the old red-sandstone congeries to the south of City Hall, legal life went on. Judges, lawyers, and litigants struggled manfully to conduct their business. When New York endured its tiger summers, in those days before air conditioning, soundproofing, and other modern amenities, it became necessary to open the windows in order to sustain life. Then it was that the full horror of subsistence in the old federal court was brought home to its inhabitants. Worse even than the fetid air of the hot city, enriched from time to time by the gusts blowing across the Hudson from the Jersey dumps, was the endless noise. Now that summer was coming in, amid the clangor of the trolleys, the cacophony of the iron-shod dray horses, the din of automobiles, even the sharpest and most attentive ears had to strain to hear.

Among the judges who toiled in this judicial bedlam was one whose deafness had become legendary. It mattered not that William Bondy combined in his person qualities noble, dignified, and beautiful; that his learning and scholarship were of the highest rank; or even that in his treatment of the lawyers who came before him he was benign, gentle, and understanding. When the lawyers spoke of Bondy, it was his deafness that they mentioned and the agonies of misunderstanding, confusion, and wrangling that grew from it.*

---

*Many years later, when unmistakable signs of senility were added to the handicap of deafness, Bondy's inability to discharge his judicial duties forced Sylvester Ryan, then Chief Judge, to take action. Ryan visited Bondy with two other judicial cronies to suggest that the time had come for retirement. Of course, they were too delicate to allude to the symptoms of senility; they emphasized his *deafness*. "Deaf!" shrieked the outraged Bondy. "I've always been deaf, and it never seemed to bother anybody." Shortly after, the problem was solved by a higher agency than the Chief Judge.

Judge Bondy was then in his sixties. In physical appearance he was short, rubicund, and amiable; his voice, alas, had the shrill, high-pitched, almost toneless quality that comes to those who have long suffered from deafness. Though normally gentle and controlled, he sounded, when stimulated by a little courtroom excitement, like an outraged cockatoo.

The judge had experimented with the hearing aids of that pretransistor era, without success. But to facilitate communication across the sound barrier, he had developed a little trick: when by a blend of lipreading and black magic he understood what was being said to him by lawyers, witnesses, and court officials, his head kept bobbing in the vertical plane; when he wished to convey to the speaker that he was not getting across, his head began to move horizontally. The *illuminati* among the lawyers soon learned to keep their eyes fixed on the judge's brow. To signify his close attention to the mysteries being enacted before him, the judge had adopted the little device of sitting with one hand cupped to his better ear (the right one).

Almost every lawyer who appeared before Judge Bondy acknowledged his fine judicial qualities and ingrained courtesy, and made appropriate allowances for his physical disability.*

---

*There was one notable exception: a lawyer named Archibald Palmer. Archie has long since gone to his reward—which I can assure my readers must be a rich one. He was a little man, with a petulant lower lip that stuck out a full two inches, to signify his contempt for all his fellows. His voice was sounding brass, well lubricated with spittle; his beady little eyes darted about ceaselessly, as if to ensure that he was not about to be garroted by his colleagues, many of whom salivated over the thought of murdering him. He had established some reputation for expertise in the bankruptcy field, which brought him often into federal court and often before Judge Bondy. Archie was famous for his brazen gall, which was matched only by his ingenuity in unearthing a creditor-

In the summer of 1935 there came before Judge Bondy the first important case generated by our investigation into immigration and naturalization frauds. The defendant was Michael Hogan, a former member of Congress from the Borough of Queens, who had been indicted for subornation of perjury. In that time, Queens was a remote suburb filled with cemeteries, golf courses, vegetable gardens, and miles of genteel semidetached villas. The ex-congressman had a law office there, but his transgression resulted in fraudulent filings in Manhattan, so we indicted him in the Southern District.

It is a legal truism that you cannot convict for subornation of perjury unless you can prove a perjury. And proof of perjury requires proof that the alleged perjurious statements were made *under oath.* In this case, the false statements allegedly suborned by the defendant were expressed in affidavits filed in immigration proceedings by two Italian seamen who had deserted their ship in New York harbor and who had retained the defendant to make them

---

client with a claim for twenty dollars or a stockholder-client who owned two shares. Archie's courtroom jousts with Judge Bondy became a part of the folklore around the federal court.

The climax was reached one morning when Archie, having made a futile request for some outrageous relief, turned his back on the judge, strode to the rail of the courtroom, and trumpeted, "The deaf old son of a bitch doesn't even know what's going on!" Though Archie's words did not penetrate the judge's sound barrier, the appreciative guffaw of the spectators did.

"Ah, Mr. Palmer," said Bondy, "you must have said something very funny. Would you please come back and share it with me?"

"Oh, it was nothing, Judge," said Archie, "nothing at all."

"Well," said the judge, "perhaps the bailiff who was standing next to you would tell me."

He did, and Archie was forthwith held in contempt of court. Accounts differ as to the penalty imposed; whatever it was, it warmed the hearts of Archie's contemporaries.

"legal." The affidavits had been sworn to before a notary public, an Italian who maintained a "candy store" on the Upper East Side of Manhattan—in those days a predominantly Italian neighborhood.

The notary was carefully questioned by Watkins' investigators. He freely confirmed that he had administered the oath to the seamen, and then he was told he would be called to testify at Hogan's trial. He expressed no reservations. Indeed, his entire attitude was what prosecutors euphemistically call "cooperative."

At the appropriate time, agents were dispatched to the reaches of upper Harlem to escort the notary to the trial, already in progress in the old courthouse. Without the testimony of our little Italian notary, the prosecution must fall; the government's efforts and expense are set at naught; the guilty go unpunished; and the forces of order and light are routed by those of chaos and blackness. The notary's testimony was formal but vital.

On the day of his appearance, the old courthouse was at its infernal worst. It was late spring or early summer; the windows were open, the horns were honking, the trolleys were clanging. In Judge Bondy's courtroom the lawyers were drenched with perspiration and deafened by the din. Bondy presided over the scene with his accustomed fastidious judicial urbanity. His head kept bobbing, mostly in the vertical plane; his right hand remained cupped to his right ear, and except for the high decibel content, the proceedings were normal. Seconded by the redoubtable Pindyck, Sam Kaufman was presenting the government's case with his usual suavity. Neither heat nor noise ruffled that self-confident courtroom warrior. He was smoothly interrogating a witness on the stand. All eyes were on Kaufman.

Into this scene came one of the agents who had been sent to escort the notary to the courthouse. He tiptoed to the counsel table, betraying no sign of the inner panic he must have felt. The agent whispered a few words into the ear of Pindyck, who at first brushed off the intrusion. But after a few moments Pindyck reacted as if a stiletto had been plunged into his breast. He looked around the courtroom wildly and rushed out into the corridor.

In the corridor, Pindyck found the notary, surrounded by flushed, irate members of our staff. The notary's face wore the smile of one who knows a special secret; his demeanor was affable, but his words were like fingers of ice around Pindyck's heart. "I'm-a very sorry, but I'm-a trying to explain, I can't be a witness in this-a case-a."

Pindyck restrained himself and demanded a fuller explanation.

"It's-a very simple," said the notary. "Last night, God appeared to me in a vision, an' He said to me, 'Tony, I don't want you to testify in that-a case-a.' So, Mr. Pindicio, I can't help it, I can't go against God."

Here ensued a few minutes of fervid theological disputation, but nothing could shake the little notary from strict adherence to the divine mandate. In the mind of Sylvester Pindyck, the majestic edifice of his case lay in ruins. Distraught, he walked back into the courtroom to confer with Sam Kaufman, the great trial lawyer whose resources were supposed to be equal to any emergency. That lofty personage was engaged in the routine examination of an ordinary witness, engaged in describing conventional conversation with mortals. Aside from the heat, the noise, and the need to utter every question at the stentorian heights designed to reach the judge as well as the jury, Kaufman was clearly a happy prosecutor: he had a great case going, conviction was almost a certainty, and the newspapers were giving him the exposure that Joe Davies said was all he needed to be a U.S. Attorney and a federal judge. God was in

His heaven and all was well in Sam Kaufman's world.

Then Pindyck plucked at Kaufman's sleeve; between questions, he imparted to him in tense whispers the calamitous events of the corridor conference. "Boss," he pleaded, "you better take a recess—go out there and talk to this nut —do *something.* "

As usual, Kaufman would not easily admit that there was any courtroom situation to which his resources were unequal. "Calm yourself, my boy," he said. "I will get the court's permission to withdraw this witness temporarily. Bring your notary into the courtroom. We'll put him on the stand, and before he knows what's happening, I'll have him identify his notarial signature on the affidavits and concede that he administered an oath. No reason to get excited, just do it my way."

Pindyck did not share Kaufman's confidence, but he could not think of an alternative. So in obedience to the Chief's plan the witness was withdrawn. The notary was whisked into the courtroom by two of the agents and deposited in the witness chair. It is said that the notary's feet did not touch the ground between corridor and witness chair. While this mechanical shift was in process Judge Bondy sat beaming at the jury, the lawyers, the press, and the spectators. He alone of the dozens in the courtroom was undisturbed by the strident diapason of the city streets.

The witness sat in his chair, slightly breathless from his rapid transition from corridor to courtroom. The clerk turned to him and intoned the timeless words of the oath: "Do you solemnly swear that the testimony you will give in this case is the truth, the whole truth, and nothing but the truth, so help you God?" Now, the clerk was Mr. Johnson, who had been administering this oath for several decades, and in all that time he had received only one answer: "I do." But not now.

"Whatza this you askin' me?" inquired the notary.

Mr. Johnson repeated the ancient formula.

"The answer," said the notary, "is-a *no.*"

"What do you mean, *no?*" demanded Clerk Johnson.

Said the notary, "When I say *no,* I mean *no.* Last night, God came to me in a vision an' he tol' me not to testify, an' I'm-a gonna do what He says an' the answer is *no.*"

Judge Bondy heard nothing of this colloquy. He observed only that an air of wild surmise had settled on his courtroom, that something was slowing down the wheels of justice. He turned to the clerk and said, "Come, come, Mr. Johnson, what's going on here? What's wrong with this man?"

"Your Honor," shouted Johnson, "this witness says he cannot testify in this case because God has appeared to him in a vision and told him not to testify." His tone was flat, official, but ominous. His expression showed his consternation.

"Ha!" said the judge. "Somebody has been tampering with a government witness. We will have to do something about that."

The clerk raised his voice to the level required to get through to the judge. He roared, "I'm afraid Your Honor does not understand. This witness says *God* has told him not to testify. *God! God!*" The judge's face was flushed with righteous judicial rage.

"I don't care who told him," shrieked Bondy, his normal parrotlike shrill intensified by outrage. "I have had much experience with this sort of meddling with prosecution witnesses. I will mete out punishment." He muttered something about bench warrants and contempt.

The judge's minatory yelps were cut short by a chorus of spluttering objurgations by the clerk, by Kaufman, by Pindyck, by defense counsel, jurors, officious volunteers among the spectators, members of the press. Like the chorus in a Gilbert and Sullivan operetta, in harmony they shouted, *"God! God!"*—and their stridences were accompanied by a gesture—pointing the index finger in the direction of the spacious firmament, generally assumed to be inhabited by the Deity.

Gradually Judge Bondy's expression changed. He began to understand that he was dealing not with a *mafioso* corrupted by Sicilian bravos but with a Latter-Day prophet who appeared to enjoy access to powers even higher than those of the Circuit Court of Appeals. From anger, his mien changed to one of incredulity, even awe. *"God?"* he murmured. *"God?* Well, we can't issue a bench warrant for Him." The judge turned to the witness. His demeanor was appropriate to a mere district judge addressing a reborn Elijah. The Lord's special communicant sat up in the witness box exuding an air of utter self-satisfaction. He seemed quite pleased that he had chastised the infidel with both whips and scorpions.

"Sir," said the judge, "do you often converse with the Lord?"

"Yes, sir, Mr. Judge," said the notary. "We talk-a lotsa time, an' He tell me what to do, an' I do it."

"Does He ever tell you to lie?" asked the judge.

"Oh, no, Your Honor. He would not ever say to tell a lie."

"Does He not want you to tell the truth?" asked the judge.

"Oh, yes. He always wants me to tell the truth. He's-a very strict about that."

The judge thought for a moment. He turned to the white, tense faces of the lawyers. "Will counsel please come to the bench? The jury will be excused for a few minutes."

As the lawyers moved to the bench and the jury filed out,

the noise and excitement in the courtroom subsided. Even the sparrows on the windowsills abated their little contribution to the exterior din.

The rest, I regret, is anticlimax. But it is anticlimax that attests the quality of Judge Bondy, the quality that made us all allow with charity for his tragic handicap and revere him as a true professional. "Gentlemen," he said to the lawyers, "it must be obvious that we are dealing here with a man of deep religious feeling who has some kind of objection to taking the oath. I intend to dispense with the oath and question him myself. I assume there is no objection."

There was none. The jury was recalled, and in two or three minutes the judge had himself elicited from the notary that his signature appeared on the affidavits, that he had duly administered the oath to the seamen, and so on. Justice and good sense prevailed. The notary was excused. He strode proudly from the courtroom, still wearing his little secret smile, undoubtedly in deep communion with an authority higher than the United States District Court. The prior witness resumed his place on the stand, to tell again of the events of this world. From the open windows came the roar of the city. On the bench, the judge's head reverted to bobbing in the vertical plane. Federal justice was back on the track.

The congressman was convicted, Kaufman's investigation was well launched, and he moved a step closer to his goal.

7

THE FIX THAT FAILED

After the ex-congressman, Kaufman tried a number of cases in rapid-fire order. He convicted Fred Tuttle, commissioner in charge at Ellis Island, who had made the manifest volumes available to the racketeers. Tuttle had used his ill-gotten gains to purchase a Chevrolet franchise in East Rutherford, New Jersey. Next came Solomon Johnson, Tuttle's chief aide, a courtly black man who had risen high in the civil service, only to end in disgrace and imprisonment because he was corrupted by the immigration racketeers. Then came the trial of a Brooklyn lawyer, Louis Fried, whom Watkins and Muller regarded as one of the "kingpins" (their word, repeated ten times a day) of the fake-naturalization racket. There were two or three other trials, but the success of the Kaufman-Pindyck-Watkins-Muller team drove a score of malignants into guilty pleas. In ten months Kaufman had achieved his objective, as delineated by his mentor Joe Davies: he had obtained the "exposure" and the prosecutorial experience that was to make him a sure thing for appointment to the office of U.S. Attorney in the Southern District of New York whenever Lamar Hardy kept his promise to resign.

At the end of 1935 Sam Kaufman resigned and returned to his busy law firm. I assumed that Kaufman would take me back with him, but he told me that Brien McMahon, Assistant Attorney General in charge of the Criminal Division, had requested that I stay on with Kaufman's successor, Pindyck, to finish a few minor prosecutions in which I had been active. In addition, Dan McCormack, Commissioner of Immigration and Naturalization, had me working on a project dear to his heart,* and he, too, wanted me to stay. Kaufman told me I could come back to the firm whenever I finished my work for the government. We assumed it would take about six months. So I stayed. As things turned out, it would have been better for Sam Kaufman and his ambitions if I had left with him.

Soon after Kaufman went back to his law firm, in the spring of 1936, the attention of Franklin D. Roosevelt was drawn to an impending prosecution in the Southern District of New York of an obscure "private banker" and neighborhood *mafioso* named John Solitario. I am certain that Roosevelt had never heard of John Solitario and cared nothing about the rascal. But Solitario, as we shall see, was a man of considerable worldly substance and political clout. For several years before 1936 he had enjoyed the legal

---

*McCormack had a shrewd vision of the tragic fate of the German Jews. He devised a plan to anticipate quota numbers so we could rescue them from Hitler. I was working with him to fashion legislation and regulations to give effect to the plan. The project failed because of the hostility of the State Department bureaucracy, the preoccupation of the administration with matters that then seemed more important, and the open hostility of certain reactionary congressmen to any project that would have relaxed the strictures of the oppressive quota laws.

services of a gentleman who was a congressman and, more significantly, a member of a family that enjoyed an intimate relationship with the Roosevelt family.

The lawyer was John O'Connor, who was also a member of the House of Representatives for a district in Manhattan. He was also brother to Basil O'Connor, Roosevelt's former law partner and close friend—chosen by him to head the national foundation to establish the polio-research center at Warm Springs, Georgia. Basil O'Connor was a White House intimate, known to millions of Americans for his energetic leadership of the March of Dimes.

Brother John was quite different. He showed none of Basil's charm, urbanity, or civic devotion. He was a Tammany wheelhorse who had worked his way up in the System, and within a few years of the incident described below, Roosevelt "purged" him—drove him out of Congress and the Democratic Party for his intransigent isolationism and his opposition to the administration's foreign policies. But in 1936 John O'Connor enjoyed the favor of the White House.

There were other actors in the drama besides Roosevelt, the Congressman-lawyer, and the sidewalk *capo regime* John Solitario. There was Homer Cummings, Attorney General of the United States; there was Brien McMahon, Assistant Attorney General in charge of the Criminal Division. And on the New York end of the case there was Sylvester Pindyck, who had succeeded Kaufman as Special Assistant to the Attorney General in charge of the Special Unit that was investigating and prosecuting violations of the immigration and naturalization laws. There were Watkins in the Immigration and Naturalization Service (then a branch of the Department of Labor) and Charley P. Muller, his chief aide, the two ace investigators. There were assorted agents drawn from the Immigration and Naturalization Service and other government agencies, including the FBI. There was Sam Kaufman, and there was this writer.

At the time, I enjoyed the rank and splendid emoluments of a Special Attorney in the Department of Justice; from time to time, I would be designated as a Special Assistant to the Attorney General to carry out specific courtroom assignments. In practice, I was Pindyck's chief assistant. I was then a sublimely self-confident twenty-six-year-old lawyer, almost three years out of law school and free from doubt about any aspect of my work.

As we began the year 1936 Sam Kaufman, our peerless leader, had gone back to his law firm; Pindyck, our new chief, squinted through his triple lenses at file after file after file; Watkins and Muller controlled more than a score of agents digging up new cases. And since Pindyck preferred the tranquillity of the office to the hurly-burly of the courtroom, I handled most of the court appearances for the Unit.

During our work in 1935 Watkins and Muller had often referred to John Solitario as one of their principal targets. We were told that Solitario was the "kingpin," the tetrarch of an organization that had furnished spurious certificates of naturalization to thousands of Italians who had entered the United States unlawfully. Of course, papers peddled by Solitario and his confederates were as worthless as the papers peddled by the other racketeers we had convicted in 1935. They were issued by the federal courts, but they resulted from the use of a technique of fraud that made the match cases and the fake-manifest cases primitive by comparison.

As the jailhouse doors clanged behind the malefactors we had convicted in 1935, we were all elated. But our exultation was tempered by the knowledge that John Solitario still sat like a malignant spider at the center of a network that went right on doing business. None of the match cases, none of the fake-manifest cases, led us to his web. For a good reason. We were to learn the hard way that Solitario regarded these methods as absurdly crude. He knew a better way. As the newspapers of the day carried the tidings of the convictions we had obtained, John Solitario must have had many a merry laugh.

The Professor Moriarty of Second Avenue had perfected a method of naturalizing unlawful entrants that defied all our investigative efforts. It was proof against any method of detection except the squeal, and in the jolly Sicilian fraternity he dominated, squealing was neither widespread nor salubrious. Solitario's name recurred with amazing frequency in our investigations, but he enjoyed a charmed career; whenever we thought we had him, witnesses recanted, disappeared, refused to identify him. Some even preferred prison sentences to pointing a finger at the *padrone.*

Solitario had been indicted in the Southern District in 1931 for violating the immigration laws; but the witnesses had faded away, and the records of the court for February 10, 1933, contained the doleful entry "Entered and filed Nolle Prosequi." In other words, the case had collapsed, and Solitario had been free to resume his nefarious pursuits. The failure of the government's efforts must have convinced Solitario that *his* method was infallible, and he went right on peddling his "citizen papers." During these years John Solitario became a commanding figure in his New York neighborhood. We knew him well. For years our frustrated agents observed, photographed, followed, studied him—but no case could be perfected against him.

His stronghold was at Twenty-ninth Street and Second Avenue in Manhattan, under the old elevated line. The neighborhood was almost entirely Italian; little English was heard in the streets, and the storefronts proclaimed *pasticcerie* and *ristoranti* and *macellerie*. The plate-glass windows of Solitario's fortress announced in Italian and English that it was a bank, a safe-deposit company, a travel agency, an insurance office, a notarial office, and generally the Old Lady of Second Avenue. This type of establishment was a bridge for the confused and semiliterate immigrants to the commercial and financial mysteries of the Anglo-Saxon world that surrounded their ghettos. On the whole, such establishments afforded an honest and useful service to their patrons. Solitario had added one dangerous department. On *his* plate-glass storefront there also appeared the word *immigrazione*. And to his doors came the terror-stricken ship-jumpers, the sailors and stewards, the peasants, who had slipped in *sans* visa from Canada and Mexico. And many of them, at a cost of two to five thousand dollars per certificate, emerged from Solitario's office with the precious papers that they thought conferred immunity from arrest and deportation.

In the back of the office sat John Solitario—the nail on his right pinky grown to a length of three inches, signifying to the world that he was not required to do menial or physical work—raking in the ducats, seemingly immune to prosecution. In appearance, he was most impressive. The photographs of Solitario that Watkins and his merry men displayed to countless Italian aliens showed a sturdy, well-mustached, beautifully tailored Sicilian magnate. But his photograph never evinced a sign of recognition from the aliens. We thought of him as a criminal of infinite craft, sipping his *espresso*, smoking his curly little *toscani*, and laughing his head off at the clumsy agents of the Republic. He had become the *bête noire* of Watkins and Muller; every immigration officer, every border patrolman, knew that back in New York these two bloodhounds of the law salivated at the scent of Solitario.

One day in the spring of 1936, Frank Watkins appeared at the door of the office I shared with Pindyck in the Old Morgan Annex to the main post office. (The wreckers had driven us from our original quarters in the old courthouse and post-office building south of City Hall; rodents, roaches and the WPA had frightened us out of the battered, ancient Hamburg-American Line warehouse at Washington and Christopher Streets, where the Special Unit had for a while been housed. The workmen were applying their last touches to the new gold-domed temple of federal justice in Foley Square. And while we waited for our new quarters there the Ninth Avenue Elevated roared and clattered past our temporary office in the Morgan Annex.) Watkins brought news that drove all thought of discomfort from our minds. His face wore an expression of awe and ill-controlled ecstasy. It was the look that must have gleamed on the visage of Javert as Jean Valjean fell exhausted at his feet. He had received a telephone call from the local district director of the Immigration Service in Detroit. Three young men of obviously Italianate appearance had just been apprehended on the ferry, crossing the border from Windsor, Ontario, to Detroit, after an evening of pleasure. They had confidently displayed United States certificates of naturalization that for some reason looked fishy to the border sleuths. Interrogation revealed that the border cops were right; the certificates were as phony as a three-dollar bill! They had been purchased from John Solitario in New York. Faced with arrest and deportation, the three young Italians were cooperative: they even had relatives and friends who could supply corroboration of their evidence against Solitario. Indeed, one of the uncles actually had a canceled check for two or three thousand dollars payable to and endorsed by Solitario himself. The Professor Moriarty of the Italian East Side had slipped! Here was the case of which Watkins and Muller had dreamed. If the witnesses held firm (and the Immigration people assured us they were "on ice" in a secure place) and we acted with dispatch, this limb of Satan would be put away for years.

There was one minor problem: the certificates of naturalization were almost five years old; prosecution was indicated under our darling old Section 414 of Title 8, which had a five-year limitation provision. We had about one month to perfect the case and obtain an indictment. If we failed, Solitario would go on picking his teeth with that three-inch pinky nail and laughing up his well-tailored sleeve at the law and the lawmen. Pindyck, Watkins, and Muller agreed that I should drop everything else and concentrate on Solitario. The gods had smiled upon us—and upon me! *I* was to lead the assault on the archvillain; no fatter prize had yet been offered; the Finger of Fortune beckoned, and I eagerly followed.

Within an hour or two I was on my way to Detroit. Within a day or two I had interrogated the witnesses and arranged for their security. But within a few hours of beginning my interrogation of the aliens, a dim light began to glow in my mind. A few telephone calls established that these were *not* match cases; that the passenger manifests of the vessels on which the aliens claimed lawful entry were untouched and inviolate. Yet the certificates of arrival on their papers were actual government certificates, on special bond paper as distinctive as a treasury note.

I issued an SOS for Watkins and his vast technical expertise. Frank Watkins joined me in Detroit next morning. As we sat trying to figure out how Solitario had obtained the certificates of arrival, there came a call from the FBI laboratory in Washington. They had made microscopic and chemical tests of the specimen certificates we had sent them, and there was no doubt: the certificates of arrival were genuine government issue. We had no time to figure out *how* Solitario had contrived to have these bona fide certificates affixed to the naturalization applications of aliens whose names appeared in no manifest volumes. We knew then that he could have accomplished this feat only with the help of important officials in both the immigration and naturalization branches of the government. Certificates of arrival were kept under top security in the ports of entry. Only the highest officers had access to them. They must have been collaborating with Solitario. We knew also that convicting Solitario and forcing him to reveal the identity of his confederates was the only way we could get to these higher-ups. All the more reason for going full speed ahead.

Watkins and I came back to New York, ready to take the case before a grand jury. There was one purely technical prerequisite. Under the law, we could not present any case to a grand jury unless either Pindyck or I, was specifically designated *by letter* from the Attorney General to act in the particular matter we wished to present. In the past, this had been no problem. We would write or telephone Brien McMahon, Assistant Attorney General in charge of the Criminal Division and our immediate superior, and he would promptly facilitate the issuance of the necessary letter of authority. Invariably, we had the letter within a day or two. In Solitario's case, Pindyck had written to Washington for a letter of authority on the same day that Watkins got the call from Detroit. In accordance with normal routine, we had arranged with the U.S. Attorney in the Southern District to yield to us some grand-jury time. That gentleman had complied as a matter of course. We had arranged to bring our precious witnesses to New York under conditions of both secrecy and security; we wanted to take no risks that would enable Solitario or his henchmen to get to them.

All was ready, *except* the requisite letter of authority

from the Attorney General. We waited for it, and waited, and waited. The days passed and we heard nothing from Washington. The critical moment, when the witnesses would be in New York, was only a few days off; the allotted grand-jury time was ours, and the statute of limitations had not yet run. Haste was imperative. Delay could be fatal to the cause of justice.

In great anxiety, and at Pindyck's order, I telephoned to Brien McMahon at the Department of Justice. Surely, we reasoned, our letter had been lost in the bureaucratic shuffle. But the voice of Brien McMahon on the telephone was not that of the affable Celt who had for so many months been our guide, our friendly Assistant Attorney General. Now he was cool, he was reserved. No, he was *not* willing to discuss the matter. No, the letter was *not* in the mail. No, he could *not* tell me when it would be. No, he would *not* discuss it on the phone. He invited me to meet him in his Washington office next morning. Pindyck commanded me to go, and not to come back without the letter of authority.

Of course, I was there bright and early next morning, palpitating with the impatience of the young. All I needed was the letter of authority, and we would bring that miserable rascal Solitario to swift retribution. And then we would crown our task with the exposure and conviction of the high immigration and naturalization officers who had conspired with him. When I entered McMahon's office, I was greeted with even more than his usual cordiality. McMahon had become an intimate of Sam Kaufman; and as I was one of Kaufman's protégés, he treated me as one of the family. (Indeed, he later was regarded as a dear friend and close associate by my partners and me, and when he died, in 1952, we mourned him as a brother.)

The measure of Brien McMahon is suggested in this characterization by William S. White:

> The late Senator Brien McMahon of Connecticut was as hard and as acute a practical partisan, as the Senate is likely to see. . . .
> It was McMahon of Connecticut, a man who had elbowed his way to the top and a man who would have been quite at home in the most realistic political ward meeting in the United States, who now displayed the truly sensitive and perceptive mind, the mind of a basic disinterestedness. He saw at once where total military control of atomic energy, a Thing more powerful than ever before conceived might lead. In the Senate he stormed and fought, at first with little assistance, for the principle of civilian control that led at last to the establishment of the Atomic Energy Commission.*

This was the kind of man with whom I had to deal: smart, cunning, partisan, but honest and high-principled. Yet on that morning, green as I was, I knew I was being conned.

He began by telling me that the post of Chief Assistant to the U.S. Attorney in Alaska was available; it was mine for the asking, and in a year or two I might be U.S. Attorney there.

"Brien," I said, "who wants to go to Alaska? I'm here to talk about Solitario in New York."

"Don't like Alaska?" he said. "Too cold? You're right. How about Puerto Rico? That's a great place. Palm trees! Beautiful girls! Tropical climate. You'd love it. They need a Chief Assistant there. That will be open in a couple of months. Meanwhile, you've earned a vacation."

"Brien," I said, "I want to talk about Solitario."

---

*In *Citadel* (New York: Harper & Brothers, 1956), p. 119.

"No!" he shouted. "Let's *not* talk about Solitario! There isn't going to *be* any Solitario case! There isn't going to be any letter! Forget it!"

I knew Brien McMahon to be a decent man. If he was doing a dirty job, I knew he hated it as much as anyone could. I was confused, bewildered. I explained that not only Pindyck and I wanted the letter; I told McMahon about Watkins and Muller, of their uncompromising tenacity, of their eager desire to break through Solitario to the corrupt higher-ups in the government. But nothing seemed to impress him. Finally, he made it plain that he loved Pindyck and me as much as ever but was carrying out the instructions of the Attorney General himself, and *there was not going to be any letter of authority*. He was a good soldier carrying out unpleasant orders. No Solitario case!

I telephoned Pindyck and gave him the happy news. He screamed. He said, "Tell McMahon we won't take that shit! There's something crooked going on. Tell him we'll resign! We'll go to the newspapers. Insist on the letter. Today! Ask to see the A.G. himself." Pindyck's eyes may not have been strong, but there was nothing wrong with his voice. It was loud and frightening, and his commands only added to my panic.

I reported my conversation with Pindyck to McMahon; I explained that Pindyck demanded that I speak to the Attorney General. At this point McMahon looked as if *he* would explode with rage. "Speak to the Attorney General!" he shrieked. "Who the hell do you think you are? The A.G. doesn't deal with little punks like you! Forget it! Wait outside!"

I drifted around McMahon's anteroom for about an hour. I exchanged meaningless pleasantries with the secretaries. I wandered around to chat with Walter Gallagher and John Sirica and Tom Dodd, McMahon's chief aides.

Their attitude heightened my apprehension. They were friendly—but reserved. Plainly, they *knew* something. Plainly, I was a carrier of some unpleasant disease—something like leprosy. As I waited, my apprehension grew. I think I called Pindyck from a phone booth in the corridor. I think he repeated what he had said before: "Don't leave without the letter! See the A.G. himself! Tell him we'll resign! Threaten to spill the beans to the press." This was all right for Pindyck. He was the scion of a prosperous family—they owned Callanan's, the huge and bustling emporium on Vesey Street. His father had left him a few apartment houses in Brooklyn. If he was fired, it would be no economic calamity to him. I think my own net worth at the time was in the neighborhood of $1.85, plus a return ticket to New York. And if the A.G. fired me, would Kaufman take me back in his office? I would be a pariah. Such were the sugarplum visions dancing through my head as I waited.

At length, one of the houris that guarded McMahon's portals sought me out. Even in her eyes I thought I saw the special compassion reserved for the condemned. She beckoned, and I followed her to an upper floor, to the Office of the Attorney General of the United States, the Honorable Homer E. Cummings, of Connecticut. No one spoke to me as I ran the gamut of secretaries; they busied themselves with their tasks, averting their eyes, as from a sheep entering the abattoir.

The huge mahogany doors swung open, and I entered a room about the size of the old Madison Square Garden. Soft carpets, dim lights, silken flags, sofas and chairs fashioned from the leathers of Cordoba; photographs of presidents, justices of the Supreme Court and other easily identifiable potentates, all affectionately autographed to the great man before me. Off in the distance, behind a huge carved desk, sat the lean, gray, bald-domed figure I recognized from pictures in the newspapers as the A.G. himself.

In the light of what I am about to tell you, let me pay appropriate tribute to Homer Cummings. I know now that he was one of the progressive, idealistic young men who had rallied to the standard of the Jeffersonian New Freedom when Wilson became president, in 1912. When Roosevelt was elected, in 1932, Cummings had become one of the elder statesmen of the Democratic Party, along with Mc-Adoo; Cordell Hull, of Tennessee; John Garner and Sam Rayburn, of Texas; and Joseph Davies, of Wisconsin. In 1920 he was the party's national chairman. He had seconded Roosevelt's nomination at the 1932 Democratic Convention. Roosevelt's first choice for Attorney General had been Tom Walsh, of Montana, and Cummings was to have been Governor-General of the Philippines. But Walsh died a short time before FDR's inauguration, and the President turned to Cummings to head up the Department of Justice. From the very beginning of the New Deal, he was a member of Roosevelt's "inner cabinet," along with such presidential intimates as Henry Morgenthau, Wallace, Hopkins, Frances Perkins, and Ickes.

Brien McMahon, who worked for Cummings back in Connecticut (it was Cummings' influence that helped McMahon to become senator from Connecticut in 1944), had often extolled to me Cummings' zeal and probity. When Cummings served as district attorney in Fairfield County, Connecticut, in 1913, he had risked his professional and political career to oppose the widespread public demand there for the conviction of a man he believed to be innocent. In the end another man confessed to the crime, and Cummings' courage was justified. The whole event became a courtroom classic. (In 1947 it was made into a stirring motion picture called *Boomerang*, with Dana An-

drews in the principal role. It depicts in the classical melo-
dramatic way how one honest, conscientious public officer,
Cummings [Andrews], stands firm to protect a man un-
justly accused of murder against local prejudice and bigotry.) This was no political spoilsman I was about to see;
this was a man who had fought his own fights for decency
and justice.

In appearance, the Attorney General was one of the
most paternal figures I have ever encountered. He was very
tall, very bald, and he stooped over in an ingratiating way
as he rose to greet me. He wore gold-rimmed *pince-nez*,
attached to his old-fashioned coat with a black ribbon.
Through the glasses gleamed the friendliest of blue eyes.
His speech and demeanor were slow and kindly. He's
friendly, I thought. He's nice; he likes me.

He greeted me with the charm that had made him one
of America's premier politicians. How many good things
he had heard of me! What a friend I had in Brien McMahon! How fortunate I was to have the favor of such a great
lawyer as Sam Kaufman! What a wonderful guy Sam was!
What a great future lay before me! "Why?" he asked. "Why
waste it all over a bum like John Solitario? Forget the whole
thing! We have other work for you, better work! Stop in-
sisting on this stupid little letter!"

Laboriously, as if I were fashioning my words out of
granite with a dull adze, I explained to this kindly old
gentleman how important the Solitario case was to all of us;
how Watkins and Muller and their people had toiled for
years to get Solitario; what kind of people Watkins and
Muller were; how at the sound of Solitario's name there
came into Watkins' blue eyes the far-off look he reserved for
the snow-capped Olympian range of his native Washington. I spoke of Muller and his patriotism; I think I even
mentioned the Battle of Santiago Bay. I told him what a

sinister criminal Solitario was. I explained that dozens of people back in New York—agents, investigators, secretaries—all knew about the case, had worked on it, and were waiting for me to return with the letter that would seal the villain's doom. Finally, I told him of my own orders from Pindyck.

Cummings nodded in patient understanding; he understood everything. He wanted to extricate me from a tragic trap. "I'll tell you what to do," he said. "You go out to my secretary and ask her to call Sam Kaufman on the phone. Talk to Sam; he'll tell you what to do and how to do it. After all, he's your mentor, he put you into the job. And don't worry about Pindyck. I'll talk to him myself; Sam will talk to him. And don't worry about Watkins and Muller; we'll handle them. Just do what I say: talk to Sam and then come back to me. You'll see, everything will be all right."

Holy smoke, I thought, whatever this is, Kaufman's in on it, too! During the ten months when Kaufman headed up our unit, he had heard much about Solitario, as we all had, from Watkins and Muller. But we had not told Kaufman that at long last we had a real case on Solitario. I knew Kaufman's ambitions; I knew I was now in the presence of the one man who could fulfill them or thwart them. I left this beaming, confident figure, feeling like Major André on his way to the scaffold.

A call was made to New York; at length, Kaufman came on the line, and the incandescent instrument was placed in my hand. I stammered into the phone. "Mr. Kaufman," I said, "I'm calling from the office of the Attorney General. He asked me to telephone you. He wants you to advise me about a problem that has come up."

Kaufman made some dubious noises, asking what *I* was doing in the sacred precincts of the A.G.'s office. When he understood that it was true, that I really had penetrated the *arcanum*, that I had really talked face to face with Homer Cummings, and that I was calling him at Cummings' behest, he invited me to tell the tale. I told him how we were sure we had finally netted Solitario; how we needed the letter of authority; how his buddy McMahon had suggested that I go to Guam or the Sandwich Islands. I sang to him of McMahon's wrath and Pindyck's fury, of the probable revenge of Watkins and Muller, of the blandishments of Cummings, and, most of all, of my own terror. "What shall I do?" I cried in anguish. "I'm over a barrel here; I'm scared to death!"

There was a very long pause. Then Kaufman made me repeat *verbatim* what McMahon had said, what Cummings had said. What was going through his mind? All the years of patient planning for the glittering prizes he coveted, the U.S. Attorney's job in the Southern District, the federal judgeship? He must have understood that he had only to say the word and I would return to New York without the letter. He must have known, too, that he had only to advise me to stand firm and follow Pindyck's orders and his own chances of friendly patronage and advancement at the hands of Homer Cummings were gone forever. But he gave me an answer that became a fine and decent man, that befitted his concern for the young lawyers he had nurtured. Whatever differences I may have had with Sam Kaufman in the many years to come (and we did not always agree), the words he now spoke made me his slave for life.

"You poor kid," he said. "There is a fix in there somewhere, and you are going to be made the patsy. . . . You tell Mr. Cummings that you have spoken to me, and my advice is that if you don't get the letter, I will advise both you *and* Pindyck to resign immediately. I'll call Pindyck and tell him about our conversation, and I'll give him the same advice. You'll both resign and you'll tell the world why! And, son, don't worry about a job; you'll come back to the office and be a lawyer. You've been a cop long enough!"

So spake Sam Kaufman. I turned to Cummings' secretary and told her I was ready to speak with the A.G. I will carry to my last breath the recollection of the exhilaration and courage that Sam Kaufman had given me. I had a friend! I was not alone and afraid in a world filled with voracious old men who knew things I did not and who played with lightning!

Within a few minutes I was back in the A.G.'s office. "Well," asked Foxy Grandpa, "have you talked to Sam? Has he set you straight?"

Slowly and carefully I told Cummings what Kaufman had said. When I repeated the words "fix" and "patsy" the Attorney General became apoplectic. He screamed and shouted; he used ugly little words about Kaufman, about me, about Solitario. Finally, the tempest subsided; he sat quietly for a moment, then he said, "Okay, you little bastard, you'll get your goddamn letter. Go back to McMahon, and he'll give it to you. Now, get out! I never want to see you again. And as for that son of a bitch Kaufman— Get out!"

I started for the door. When I had got about halfway to freedom, to safety, Cummings shouted, "Come back! Come back!" He glared at me; he seemed to struggle for composure. He waited a few moments, looking directly into my eyes. Perhaps he thought he saw the reproach and accusation of a virginal child, though it must have been little more than terror, because that is all I remember feeling. Finally, he spoke. "You think we're a bunch of crooks down here, don't you? You think you have run into an ordinary political fix! Let me ask you, do you know who Solitario's lawyer is?"

I blurted out that I did know. Of course I knew; we had been studying Solitario's activities in microscopic detail. We even had photostats of the checks that had passed in recent days between Solitario and his congressman *consigliere*.

"Do you know who his family is? Do you know how close they are to the President?"

Again I signified that I knew all this.

Cummings then explained that two or three days after we had arrested the aliens in Detroit, McMahon had received a telephone call from one of President Roosevelt's principal aides, who told him that there was a case developing up in New York involving one Solitario, and that the President wanted it killed. (Of course, Solitario had known that the Special Unit was on the hunt for him. I must suppose that when he learned of the arrests of the aliens in Detroit, he communicated with his lawyer-congressman, who sent an emissary to the White House; the result was the call to McMahon.) McMahon had reported the call to Attorney General Cummings, but the noble Cummings had phoned the White House aide and flatly refused to interfere in the Solitario prosecution in any way. Within a few days, he had been summoned to the White House, and President Roosevelt *himself* had told him that he wanted the case dropped. Now Cummings told me that he had tried to explain to the President all the moral and legal implications of what he was asking. But Franklin D. Roosevelt was not one to argue with. To him, weighted down with the cares of the nation and the world, this was a petty annoyance, but it was personal and important.

So, Cummings wound up, when he received Pindyck's letter, from which he and McMahon learned that the statute of limitations would shortly run out on Solitario, it was clear: all they had to do was to pigeonhole our request for authority to prosecute and the President's wishes could be carried out.

"But now," he added, "now, I have to go back to the President of the United States and tell him that I can't do what he wants because of a couple of little snot-noses up in New York that no one ever heard of. I have to tell him that the two little snot-noses were put there by his friend Sam Kaufman, and that Kaufman not only refuses to interfere but is backing up these silly brats. What do you say to that, Mr. Tough Guy?"

I had nothing to say. My mind and body were filled only with a longing to go away, away from these great and powerful personages, and back to the comfort and security of my own simple tasks.

"All right, Mr. Wise Guy," said the Attorney General of the United States. "Go down to McMahon. He'll give you your goddamned letter. I'll work it out somehow with the President." He paused, as if a thought had struck him. He looked at me intently and said. "There is one thing you can do for me."

What could *I* do for *him?* Anything, anything to escape. I waited.

"Can you people arrange to have the indictment sealed, and open it after the election in November?"

Of course, we could do it, and we did.

That afternoon, McMahon handed me the letter signed by Cummings. I bore the letter back to New York, where Pindyck, Watkins, and Muller all bestowed on me a hero's greeting.

The criminal docket of the U.S. District Court for the Southern District of New York lies before me as I write. It records that John Solitario was indicted in that court on June 19, 1936; that the indictments were ordered sealed. On November 5, 1936, the day after the presidential election of that year, in accordance with our promise to Cummings, we moved to have the sealed indictments opened, and the defendant was arrested by our agents. He pleaded "not guilty" and posted bail. The case was set for trial at the beginning of January 1937. In the interval, there were several conferences with Solitario's lawyers. We made it clear that if we succeeded in convicting their client, we would hit him with the book and every supplement to it. We spoke of demanding ten years in the penitentiary.

As the trial was to start, before Judge Alfred C. Coxe and a jury, the defendant pleaded "guilty." His plea of "guilty" came when he saw that this time the witnesses had not faded away; there was a solid rank of his *paesani* prepared, at long last, to identify him as the villain who had extorted their hard-earned money for worthless papers.

The sentence of three and a half years in the penitentiary was comparatively light. After he pleaded "guilty," Solitario revealed the methods by which he had baffled Watkins and his investigators for years. He also inculpated the officers of the Immigration and Naturalization Service who had made his career so successful.

It was so simple, when we knew the answers. A large number of blank certificates of arrival were stolen from Ellis Island. When one of Solitario's clients filed an application to become a citizen, the clerk in the New York naturalization office who had the task of sending the application to Ellis Island was alerted. That faithless officer would be supplied with one of the blank certificates. He would pull the application from the file and take it to his home, where he not only affixed the phony certificate of arrival but also stamped the requisite dates on the papers. (The counterfeit stamps were also supplied by Solitario. The official receipt stamps had been "borrowed" from government offices so they could be copied by Solitario.) Thus, the application never actually went to the port of entry, but it was treated and marked *as if* it had. This we learned from the repentant Solitario, as well as the names of his confederates. Before long these rogues followed their leader to the federal penitentiary. The clerk who handled the certificates in the naturalization office used the extra money he received for some luxuries, including tuition at law school in Brooklyn. I had the exquisite satisfaction of supervising his arrest in a classroom in the law school.

What of Sam Kaufman and his ambition to be U.S. Attorney? I learned about the epilogue from Brien McMahon. When Kaufman's name was laid before Roosevelt, sometime in 1937, for appointment as U.S. Attorney in the Southern District, the President went off like a rocket. There was to be no appointment for Kaufman. He had heard from Cummings that it was *Kaufman* who had made him renege on a commitment to one of his best friends. To hell with Sam Kaufman! He was to get nothing. And, indeed, while Roosevelt lived, no one dared mention Sam's name to him again.

When Truman became president, in 1945, he learned the whole story from McMahon, who was then senator from Connecticut and Truman's right hand in keeping atomic energy out of military control. Truman approved Kaufman as Seth Richardson's deputy general counsel in the Pearl Harbor investigation, and in 1948 he made it a point to invite him to the White House, where he conferred upon him an appointment as a district judge in the Southern District of New York.* Sam Kaufman's courage, his integ-

---

*In the plethora of accounts of the trials of Alger Hiss, Sam is footnoted because, as the judge in the first trial, it was he who committed two

rity, and his concern for the welfare of "his boys" may have caused him some disappointment, but in the end he looks like a hero. Certainly he does to me.

---

notable acts: (1) he excluded the testimony of the psychiatrist through whom the defense offered to prove that Hiss's principal accuser was a psychopath; and (2) when Felix Frankfurter testified as a character witness for Hiss, Sam rose from the bench to shake the great jurist's hand, an act that was immediately construed by Richard Nixon and other members of the House Committee on Un-American Activities as proof that he was in the pay of Moscow.

PART III

Foley Square

Foley Square has been the scene of as much drama as any place in our world. Here, little men have become kings, and great men have fallen into ruin. Fortunes have been passed by judicial *Diktat* from one hand to another; the squalid scandals of rich and poor, high and low, have been sorted out. If there are ghosts, they must foregather in Foley Square. Like Westminster and the Old Bailey and the Place de Grève, their forlorn spirits haunt the locale. Let us look at some of them.

Geographically, Foley Square is the open space to the north of City Hall. It begins at Worth Street on the north, runs south on Lafayette to Chambers Street, its southern boundary. On the east, it runs north from the Municipal Building along Centre Street back to Worth Street. The northern bastion of Foley Square is a concrete cube that houses the city's health department; just across Worth Street is a demipark ironically named after the author of "The Age of Reason," Tom Paine. To a landscape architect it is not much of a square. It does not have the dignity of London's Berkeley or Grosvenor; nor does it have the sweep of New York's own Union or Madison. But to the lawyers of New York it outranks London's Trafalgar, New York's Times Square, and Paris' Place de la Concorde—not in the stateliness or grandeur of its buildings, or in any esthetic sense, but in its significance in their lives. For those of us who go there to court, it is our Colosseum, our Plaza del Toros. It is New York's legal center, the home of its principal courts, and the focus of our professional lives. Only the graybeards among us recall that Foley Square was named after a saloonkeeper who had nothing to do with the law but whose name is uttered daily by New York's lawyers.

Thomas F. Foley, the eponym of Foley Square, was a son of Irish immigrants, born in the Williamsburg section of Brooklyn, a broth of a boy who became a blacksmith. When he moved to New York, in 1872, at the age of twenty-four, he laid aside his sledge for a bung-starter and opened a saloon at the corner of Oliver and Water streets. This was the heart of the old Fourth Ward, as Irish as the banks of the Liffey, and "Big Tom" Foley soon became the local Tammany leader. He worked his way up in the Tammany ranks to become sheriff of New York County. He was the architect of the career of Alfred E. Smith and the archfoe of William Randolph Hearst.

Al Smith was his personal protégé, and he was generally credited with winning for Smith the nomination for governor of New York in 1922. In this, he blocked the aspirations of the ineffable Hearst, who saw the governorship of the Empire State as a step toward the presidency. This may have been Big Tom's most valuable contribution to this country.

When Foley died, in 1925, the event was recorded on the front page of *The New York Times*, and the obituary page recorded tributes from many important politicians. Even Republicans expressed their grief. According to the *Times*, when it was known that Big Tom was *in extremis*, Al Smith "made a hurried trip to the bedside of the departed leader." So golden were the last words of the dying man that "the Governor, in response to earnest pleas permitted part of the conversation which had been taken down in shorthand to be published." Alas, Big Tom's last words do not survive. Foley left two legacies: his brother, James, became a memorable Surrogate of New York County, and the grief-stricken Board of Aldermen of New York adopted an ordinance "that the square immediately north of the Municipal Building and facing the new court house [the Supreme

Court Building] shall be designated as Foley Square."

The dominant features of Foley Square are the Municipal Building; the Hall of Records (which houses the surrogates court); the Federal Court, with its famous gold-tipped tower, the Supreme Court Building; and the huge, monolithic Federal Office Building to the west. Foley Square also has some outworks and lunettes. To the south is the old Tweed Court House, standing chastely between the Hall of Records and the graceful City Hall. South of the Federal Court is the Church of Saint Andrew, patron saint of lawyers, and scene of a colorful annual Mass in which lawyers and judges of all sects join. To the north lie the Criminal Courts Building (successor to the Tombs, now a parking lot), the Civil Court, the Family Court. All of these make up the vast complex we loosely call Foley Square, after the old saloonkeeper.

There is more to Foley Square than its courthouses and auxiliary buildings. It is the home of landmarks, legends, memories, and ghosts. One of the landmarks, now almost forgotten, was Gasner's.

8

THE GOLDEN AGE OF GASNER'S

Souls of lawyers, dead and gone,
What Elysium have ye known,
Happy field or mossy cavern,
Choicer than GASNER's congenial Tavern?
Was ever food and talk more sweet
Than in that barristers' retreat?

The shade of John Keats will forgive such liberties with
his immortal apostrophe to the Mermaid Tavern. I
have read somewhere that when Keats and his fellow-
apprentices were studying surgery at St. Barnabas, in London, they frequented the Tudor Tavern in Bread Street,
where they enjoyed special amenities: solid fare, moderate
credit, a message board, and unwatered ale. Keats would
have appreciated Gasner's.

Gasner's stood on Duane Street, between Broadway and
Lafayette Street, a few steps from Foley Square. The build-

ing still stands, an abandoned derelict. Eyeless windows, broken frames, a roof collapsing on itself—only a battered sign remains, whose empty electric sockets, still spelling out the name "Gasner's," proclaim that this decrepit ruin is what remains of one of New York's legal shrines.* Like a broken tooth, it stands there amid the rubble of demolished buildings to either side, dwarfed by the gleaming bulk of the Federal Plaza complex, with which the General Accounting Office has desecrated the landscape of lower Manhattan.

The lawyers and the judges who hurry past the wreckage on their way to and from the nearby courts avert their gaze from this violated fane; they have not forgotten that for forty years, from 1933 to 1973, Gasner's was a home away from home for successive generations of bench and bar. The uptown *literati* had the Algonquin; thespians gathered in Sardi's; Jack Bleeck's sheltered the journalists from the *Tribune* and the *Times.* And in the Village the poets found credit and inspiration at Lee Chumley's. The lawyers of that Golden Age had Gasner's!

The founder of the restaurant, Max Gasner, had run a successful restaurant at the other end of Manhattan, in Washington Heights, at Broadway and 160th Street. All through the 1920s it throve as a center of social life, but with the coming of the Depression, in 1929, the good burghers of the Heights preferred to dine at home. So Gasner's closed its doors. From some downtown spy Max Gasner learned that even in the midst of the Great Depression, lawyers and judges were somehow still eating well. This economic truth was not without social implications.

---

*In late 1978 the famous sign was removed, to be replaced by one that reads "The Landmark." The quarters that once housed Gasner's are now occupied by a respectable hash house where the cuisine hardly justifies the sign.

So, with the advent of Roosevelt and recovery, in 1933, Max Gasner and his family opened the famous *auberge* at 76 Duane Street.

Max supplied it with a comfortable, no-nonsense atmosphere, a sturdy and equally no-nonsense menu, swift, efficient service, and moderate prices, all carefully attuned to the requirements of the lawyers and judges he hoped to attract. His waiters were recruited from that special breed of New York cupbearers whose philosophy of service was simple: anybody reckless enough to eat where they worked was not entitled to courtesy! Most of them had been carefully trained in arrogance and repartee in such refined resorts as Lindy's, Ratner's, and Max's Busy Bee (a different Max). Max Gasner drilled them into treating the lawyers and judges and politicians who flocked to the new spa with somewhat less contempt than they had shown to Big John, Harry the Horse, and the other Runyonesque characters to whom they had become accustomed. Under his careful tutelage, the waiters learned to abjure the fishy eye and the curled lip when they questioned the customer's culinary choices—as they usually did.

Somehow, it all worked, and before long Gasner's had become *the* favorite eating place of the Foley Square regulars. There were competitors: the celestial delights of Chinatown were equally close to the courthouses, neo-Neopolitan spaghetti-joints abounded in the neighborhood, complete with azure seascapes of the waters around Capri. There was the effete Longchamps, in City Hall Park, Art Deco in its fittings and phony French in its *carte du jour*. There was Schrafft's on Broadway, but that was really for the secretaries. There were also a handful of German restaurants, like Miller's and Suerken's, onetime beer saloons where the free lunch had escalated into *tables d'hôte*.

But none of these became an *institution*. For one thing,

the patronage in the other places was ecletic; they served all *kinds* of people: civilians, the laity, executives from the nearby textile center, even tourists. Gasner's was for *lawyers*. The stray waifs from the secular world who wandered into our cloister were served politely but without affection. Of course, while they were on duty as jurors or witnesses they were welcome as temporary *apparatchiks;* otherwise, they were intruders.

In the 1930s the upward mobility of a young lawyer could almost be measured by his progression from Nedick's to Chinatown, then to the pasta parlors, Longchamps, and, finally, Gasner's. When he reached the point where he was greeted by name at the portal, waved to a booth by Jack Gasner, and handed his telephone messages from Miriam's own plump little hand, his vanity and his hourly rates began to soar. And when the waiters betrayed their familiarity with his personal gastronomic predilections ("The usual, Counselor?") he knew he had arrived at the pinnacle of the profession.

From the beginning, Gasner's was a family affair. After 1945, the gatekeeper was Miriam, who came into the clan when she married the proprietor's son, Jack. Short, rotund, cheery Miriam, who knew every important customer by name and rank, was not above excluding from the sacred precincts the bad credit risks, however exalted their station. Her mother-in-law, Minnie, presided over the cash register, and the tiny, gimlet-eyed lady would examine a lawyer's personal check with the cold dispassion of a Monacan croupier. But from the earliest days, even when Max (who died in 1963) was still alive and active, the soul of this jolly *Brauhaus* was Jack Gasner, son and heir of the founder and the principal custodian of the *lares et penates.* For forty years, Jack fed the lawyers, the judges, and the politicians, shared their confidences, saved their tables and their tempers, and was a friend to all. He seated his temperamental patrons with skill; friends could lunch near each other, but enemies had to be kept apart, lest their recriminations interfere with the prevailing normal hullabaloo.

There was another reason for exercising care in the seating arrangements. A great deal of information was floating around in Gasner's: political, professional, and personal. If one wanted to know which way the wind was blowing, Gasner's was the place to find out. So the gentle art of eavesdropping was widely practiced. The real adepts could carry on a normal conversation and listen with a third ear to the talk at the adjoining tables. If you wanted real privacy, Jack had to help, and he did. When you consider that sometimes counsel for plaintiffs *and* for defendants, judges *and* witnesses, and even jurors hearing their cases all repaired to Gasner's at the luncheon recess, it becomes clear that the assignment of tables called for a cool head and a high level of sophistication.

Gasner's clientele during the forty years the establishment flourished was a tapestry of the New York bar during a time that must have been its Golden Age. Certainly those were the halcyon days for the true advocates, the true litigators. The complexion of the trial bar has changed greatly in the last ten or fifteen years. Today there is so much "specialization" in litigation that the colorful legal gunslingers have almost died out. Today we have "specialists" in corporate-takeover litigation, in the litigative skirmishes of the class-action suit and the proxy contest. Every facet of modern litigation has its own *beau sabreur* who knows mostly the single thrust or the single parry. But, once, New York knew the glittering jack-of-all-courts: the Steuers, the Strykers and the Smyths, the Kresels and the Gainsburgs. These were all famous trial lawyers who would be retained specially for a single case. They would

take on *any* sort of contest—financial, criminal, matrimonial—and bring to each combat that rare combination of
skills that was our heritage from the British barristers,
from Erskine and Carson, from Marshall Hall and Rufus
Isaacs and F. E. Smith. One of the most scintillating of this
very special breed was Frank Raichle, who did not even
live in New York. But such were (and are) his courtroom
talents that from time to time, desperate litigants would
import him from Buffalo. Raichle was the first outlander to
earn for himself the affection and respect of all that hard-
boiled crew who gathered at Gasner's. Their regard was
not easily purchased; the price was a blend of dispassionate
professionalism, courtroom skill, and, above all, a sense of
humor. Their most virulent scorn was reserved for the
pompous and pretentious. Gasner's was no place for gas-
conade!

It was men like these, the solid, hard-hitting professionals, who lit up our sky, provided most of our excitement,
and furnished Gasner's with much of its color. We had
such men in profusion during the age when Gasner's was
in bloom. There was even a sprinkling of redoubtable
women among them—Peggy Mangan, Birdie Amsterdam,
Constance Baker Motley, Florence Perlow Shientag—but
it was a predominantly male society.* Every court day's
luncheon recess saw these lawyers in action, preparing
their witnesses over the noonday meal, rehearsing open-
ings and summations, studying transcripts for cross-examination, and engaging in the timeless ritual dance of settlement negotiations. This brilliant scene deserves the pen of

---

*Birdie Amsterdam was one of the first female New York State Supreme
Court judges. A strikingly handsome woman, her appearance in court
raised some eyebrows. Once, an irreconcilable male chauvinist among
the spectators turned to his neighbor and asked, "What happened? The
judge sent his wife?"

a Dickens, the crayon of a Daumier or a Hogarth. It would
be nice for the historians of the era if it could be presented
as a huge painting in the antique style—with a schematic
outline in the lower-left corner, all the participants identified by number.

That tableau would show not only the great mouth-
pieces but also every New York mayor from Fiorello La-
Guardia to Eddie Koch, every New York governor from
Herbert Lehman to Hugh Carey. And the judges!

There was Francis Martin, presiding curmudgeon of the
Appellate Division, First Department. Watching Frank
Martin perform in court on one of his better days was like
watching Charles Laughton portray Lord Jeffreys. I once
saw Martin, incensed because he had been handed a brief
that was typed, not printed, fling the offending document
at an appellant's lawyer. "Who authorized this garbage?"
he shrieked. "You did, Your Honor," responded the lawyer, pointing to Martin's signature.

Martin had some imitators in courtroom punctilio from
the State Supreme Court: Wasservogel, Carroll Walter, Jim
Wallace (the ogre of general sessions). Wasservogel, a fine
judge, but sadistic in his treatment of lawyers, could gener-
ate great passion in refusing an adjournment. He did not
just turn you down: he made you feel that the mere request
was an attack on the institution of the law. Carroll Walter
came from the South and was said to be descended from the
Cavaliers. But there was nothing courtly in his courtroom
manners. He was often in pain, and he visited his wrath on
lawyers, witnesses, court attendants, and spectators with
impartial brutality. When Jim Wallace was finished imposing a sentence, the unhappy defendant had no reservations
about his own guilt. Jim flayed the evildoers with language
that was a blend of Gaelic eloquence and Old Testament
righteousness. When they were not lunching at Gasner's,

these judges feasted on lawyers in the courtroom. In these days when judicial conduct is monitored from on high, such sadistic mullahs can no longer practice their fiendish arts. But in that age there were always a few who thought that the infliction of courtroom cruelty on lawyers and litigants was one of the perquisites of judicial office.

Occasionally we would get visitors from across the Brooklyn Bridge. One of them was Sam Liebowitz, one of the greatest criminal lawyers of any time. He capped his matchless record of acquittals in capital cases with a career on the State Supreme Court in Brooklyn. In the annals of the law, Liebowitz's heroic defense of the Scottsboro defendants is our Thermopylae, our thin Red Line of Balaklava. When Liebowitz became a judge, after a lifetime of defending murderers and other assorted rascals, he soon became known as a judicial tyrant. Sometimes he had difficulty distinguishing between lawyers and defendants; he treated both with impartial severity. His sentences were savage, and he viewed the defendants who came before him as Armour must have regarded a pig. It is told that after Liebowitz had been on the bench about ten years, he was asked by a newly elected confrere to show him the ropes. "Sit here on the bench," said Liebowitz, "and I'll show you how we operate." He turned his shining bald head toward the bailiff. "Bring me a thief," he thundered.

The federal court was not as productive of these apoplectic tyrants as was the New York State Supreme Court. But, about once in a generation, the Southern District produced its own species of the lawyer-eating tiger. Archie Dawson, who came along in the early 1950s, was one of the most acerbic. Archie had been a Republican wheelhorse who specialized in utility law. In 1946 we were antagonists in a proxy battle for control of the Citizens Utilities Company. My side won, and Archie lost to me his job as general counsel. He was not very gracious about the loss, and perhaps I was less than magnanimous in victory. Within a few years I had to appear before him in court. He must have struggled inwardly to avoid any sign of retributive bias. He did not always succeed. He could be downright mean in the courtroom. Even Dawson met his match in Gasner's hard-shelled waiters, who could oppose to his courtroom choler their own studied contempt for the entire human race. But Dawson did frighten the lawyers, even the best of them!

Frank Raichle had the personality, charm, and strength to stand up to any judicial tyrant. But, like the rest of us, he was intimidated by Dawson. He tells a story that richly illustrates how we *all* trembled before the terrible-tempered Judge Dawson.

During the first of Roy Cohn's serial trials,* Raichle was dressing to go to court for another day of exposure to Dawson's Hunnish fury. The phone rang; it was Mrs. Bertha Cohn, mother of the defendant and widow of the illustrious Albert Cohn, who had been a judge in the Appellate Division (which only suggests that she should have known better). "Mr. Raichle," she said, "Roy is in his bath. He asked me to call you. Would you please tell Judge Dawson

---

*Raichle's successful defense of Cohn, the former counsel to Joseph McCarthy, in 1964 earned him the admiration of New York's trial bar. But Cohn had a feud with Robert Kennedy and the U.S. attorney in New York, Robert Morgenthau, and in 1969 he was again brought to trial on criminal charges in the Southern District. This time, he hired for his defense another fine trial lawyer, Joseph E. Brill. Brill was totally bald, with a heavy black beard. He looked like a pirate. The ardors of Cohn's second cliff-hanger in the federal court were too much for Brill. He collapsed with a heart attack. Cohn spurned the trial judge's offer of a mistrial. He had too much invested in counsel fees to start over. So, in a dramatic moment, Cohn took over his own defense. He was acquitted.

See Roy Cohn's *A Fool for a Client* (New York: Hawthorn Books, 1971).

that Roy has an important motion to argue in Supreme Court, and that he will be about an hour late for the trial?"

"Madam," said the gallant Raichle, "I have been a lawyer for many years. And in those years I have performed many heroic acts in behalf of my clients. But to tell Judge Dawson that your son, who is the defendant on trial before him in a criminal case, is too busy with other matters to get to court on time, and that the judge and the jury and the witnesses and the lawyers will have to wait for him—*that*, madam, is an act of suicidal folly that your son will have to perform for himself!"

It is recorded that someone else argued Cohn's motion in State Supreme Court, and the defendant was in his place at the time appointed.

Only a few of the judges were irascible tyrants. Gasner's regulars included many truly amiable jurists who combined great scholarship with grace and urbanity. There was the wise and witty Billy Hecht, often seen lunching with his young law secretary Charlie Metzner. Hecht never raised his voice in the courtroom; he was unfailingly courteous, even to the worst fumblers. His sense of humor was a delight. In the retrial before him of a celebrated condemnation case,* I was cross-examining an "expert" witness who was required to revise his views in the light of an earlier opinion in that matter by the Court of Appeals. After I had two or three times pointed out that his pronouncements did not conform with the Court of Appeals opinion, there occurred the following colloquy:

Gould: "Mr. Witness, it appears that you do not agree with the Court of Appeals, is that right?"

Witness: "I certainly do not!"

---

*Matter of City of New York (Fifth Avenue Coach Lines) 22 N.Y. 2d 613 (1968).

Judge Hecht: "That disagreement, sir, is a luxury not afforded to the judges of the Supreme Court."

In the middle 1940s I appeared before Hecht in a suit over a contract for the sale of guano. My adversary was a dainty fellow who paraded his delicate manners. In a conference at the bench, he said to Hecht, "Your Honor, we will have to explain to the jury what guano is. I suggest we agree to call it 'avian excrement.' "

"I suggest," said Hecht, "you call it 'bird shit.' "

Charlie Metzner graduated from being Hecht's secretary and became a federal judge who presided over many important trials in the Southern District. Then there was Henry Clay Greenberg, chief connoisseur of Gasner's smoked whitefish and one of the most beloved pragmatists on the State Supreme Court. Aaron J. Levy, another Gasner habitue, who was known to the lawyers as "the Mechanic" for his special skills in repairing breakdowns in the adversary process, could be seen often in Gasner's lunching with the lawyers for *both* sides in the case on trial before him, performing those magic arts that sent *all* parties out of the courthouse smiling. Levy was a Tammany lawyer from the East Side, less admired for his integrity than for his magnificent broken-field running toward the particular goal line he had selected. When Aaron sustained every objection you made and granted all your motions, you knew you were dead: The Mechanic was making a record for the appellate courts, to justify your interment. When he died, it is said, his entire estate was contained in a safe-deposit box in Arizona.

We will leave out of this Hogarthian tableau the occasional bibulous jurist who gave Jack Gasner his sorest tribulations—the ones who had to be mollified and spirited back to chambers to sleep off the fumes.

We had our regulars from the federal court: Knox,

Bondy, Sylvester Ryan, Sugarman, Weinfeld, Friendly, Edelstein, Wyatt, Cooper, Pollack, and others. They elevated the tone of the place. Jack Gasner once told me, "The federal judges are great. They don't spend much money but they give the place *class.*" By and large, the judges may have provided the quality and the dignified background, but it was the trial lawyers who furnished the color.

Looking back over the years, I can see Little Joe Hartfield (small in stature, mighty in clout). Hartfield was known to all as "the Colonel"—a rank conferred on him by a friendly governor of Kentucky. His accomplishments in the law defied all the rules. He was a tiny man, about four feet six inches, who came to New York from a German-Jewish background in Louisville and by some miracle of personality and skill rose to the top in White & Case, one of Wall Street's elite firms. I also see Big Joe Proskauer, massive in voice and vigor, brusque, impatient, but one of our giants in legal ability and moral force. There is John Cahill, of whom you will hear more later. He was often seen lunching with the chosen successors to his fame and power. He could not know then that these brilliant youths were tragically fated never to succeed him. There is the Jovian John W. Davis, rehashing with Ted Kiendl the constitutional argument he has just made in the U.S. Court of Appeals for the Second Circuit. Only two tables away is the exalted but ill-fated Manton, Chief Judge of that court, who has just listened to the learned constitutional argument and is now splitting a flounder with one of his fellow Olympians on that distinguished court, Chase or Swan. None of us dreamed before January 1939 that the mighty Manton would suffer judicial disgrace, that he would exchange the comforts of Gasner's for the prison dining hall at Lewisburg. Nor did we dream that the same John Cahill would be the chief engineer of his destruction.

During the great "state trials" of the 1950s—Alger Hiss, the Rosenbergs, Judy Coplon—Gasner's was part of the *mise-en-scène* for the drama. During the first trial of Alger Hiss, in 1950, you could see the celebrated defendant sharing a table with his lawyers, Lloyd Stryker and Ed McLean. Stryker was a leading trial lawyer, and his gifts as a historian and scholar were exhibited in delightful biographies of the great British barristers and judges. McLean became an indefatigable federal judge. He was once asked how he would prefer to end his career. "Certainly not in retirement," said McLean. "I'd prefer to die on the courthouse steps." He got his wish in 1971. Nearby sat the trial judge, in the first Hiss case, Sam Kaufman, my own hero, who received so much unjustified criticism for his conduct of the trial that some said it broke his heart and his health.

In an immured alcove sat Alger Hiss' prosecutors, headed by the gigantic Thomas Murphy, who later served as police commissioner of New York and went on to become one of our most honored federal judges. Murphy's stature was huge, his mustache inimitable, and his sense of humor formidable. One anecdote about Murphy requires preservation in the annals of the Southern District. It is told that an impressive black man with a Muslim name once appeared before him for arraignment. "Do you have counsel, sir?" asked Judge Murphy.

"Allah is my counsel," replied the defendant, pointing heavenward.

"Indeed," said Judge Murphy, "but who is appearing for you *locally?*"

During the trial of Judy Coplon for espionage, in 1950, Gasner's was the command post for the defense. Every day during the trial, one could have seen Judy's comely dark head bowed in contemplation beside the rough-hewn features of her unlikely lawyer, Archibald Palmer. Archie had long since established himself as the principal practitioner of confusion and rudeness at the local bar. He combined the beauty of the warthog with the amiability of a hungry barracuda. From between his tumescent lips there issued streams of unconnected words and particles (profusely lubricated with saliva), he screamed defiance at judges and poured abuse on his adversaries, all of it cunningly designed to drive both judges and adversaries to the edge of sanity. It is on the record that in a New York courtroom Archie once applied to the late Chester Bordeau, one of Joe Hartfield's partners in the proper and dignified firm of White & Case, an epithet now often used on the New York stage to describe indulgence in oral sex but in those days so frightful to the ear that when a court stenographer heard the word used in a criminal trial, he bowdlerized it to "practitioner of fellatio." Of course, it drew upon Archie a sharp rebuke from the bench. But such remonstrances meant nothing to him. Archie once engaged in conduct so obstreperous that Judge Knox, of the Southern District, said to him, "Mr. Palmer, you will appear before me next Tuesday at ten o'clock to show cause why I should not hold you in contempt."

"Sorry, Judge," said Palmer, "next Tuesday I have to appear before Judge Collins in Supreme Court to show cause why *he* should not hold me in contempt. Can we make it another day?"

Despite Archie's wiles—or perhaps because of them— Judy was convicted by the jury of turning over "defense information" to one Valentine Gubitchev, who came from Russia without love but somehow won Judy's heart. In the end Archie (assisted by some other lawyers less salivary but more scholarly) achieved Judy's deliverance via the judges of the Second Circuit Court of Appeals, Learned Hand and his fellow immortals, Thomas W. Swan and Jerome Frank.

Those savants concluded that so many of Judy's constitutional rights had been ravaged by her prosecutors that the
conviction had to be set aside.* Judy was seen no more at
Gasner's. Archie came back often—to the discomfort of
those who sat near him, for his table manners were no more
fastidious than his courtroom conduct.†

During that time the regulars at Gasner's could have
seen Judy's codefendant, Valentine Gubitchev, stripped of
his claimed diplomatic immunity by the rude hand of
Judge Sylvester Ryan, lunching with his counsel, Abraham
L. Pomerantz, who had unaccountably stepped out of his
accustomed role as the White Knight of the plaintiff-stock-
holder's suit to defend the Red Pawn.

And during those delectable days when Joe McCarthy
was saving the Republic from subversion by an army den-
tist at Fort Monmouth, New Jersey, he held a number of
hearings at the Federal Courthouse, in Foley Square. He
drank his lunch daily at Gasner's, flanked by his assistant
inquisitors, the Castor and Pollux of their time, Mr. Roy
Cohn and Mr. David Schine.

During their famous libel case, Westbrook Pegler (in the
temporary abstemiousness imposed by his counsel, Tom
Bolan) twirled the stem of his single martini and glowered
across the room where Quentin Reynolds sampled
Gasner's borscht with *his* lawyer, Louis Nizer (who later

---

*The story is told, *con brio*, in the Federal Reports, 191 F. 2nd 749 (1951).
†There is no doubt that however irritating Archie may have been at
times, he colored our scene and enriched our lives, and he had many
admirers. When he died, in 1969, Judge Edmond L. Palmieri of the
Southern District interrupted a trial to comment on Archie's good qualities. His eulogy included the following: "He was a fighter. He fought
judges and district attorneys indiscriminately. *I had the questionable distinction of having placed him under contempt more than once, and I never fined
him. He always persuaded me I was wrong in the end.* And my affection and
respect for him increased over the years."

turned the transcript of the trial into the enduring and profitable prose of his *Life in Court*).

Here, too, came often the great Max D. Steuer, lunching with clients. In that time Steuer was the most respected and most famous of New York's trial lawyers. Steuer was a small, sallow man with a pronounced New York accent. His command of English prose was superb. He always spoke in a low voice. A young lawyer who asked Steuer why he spoke so softly was told, "If you speak softly, they all lean forward to listen. After all, what you want is their attention." Steuer's reputation was studded with legends of his courtroom skills. He was the most sought after advocate of his time, equally proficient in civil and criminal cases. His fees were enormous, but his clients got their money's worth. There were also legends of Steuer's frugality; one speculates who picked up the check at Gasner's, or whether Steuer charged to the client his time for the lunch. Steuer's appearance at Gasner's was an event: the judges and lawyers flocked to *his* table, to pay court to the acknowledged lord of the jungle. So compelling was Max Steuer's presence, both in and out of court, so vast was his prestige in that age, that stories, mostly apocryphal, abounded about his supernatural litigative skills, his alleged parsimony, and his crusty impatience with the foibles of his own clients. It was said that Steuer's presence in a New York courtroom was so decisive that the Great Man did not like to go out of the city to try cases. In the hinterland the weight and importance of his prestige and personality might not be recognized. There is a yarn about him that he was once importuned by a well-heeled client (in one version it is the famous Chauncey Depew) to try a very short case in some provincial court in the Hudson Valley—shall we say, Poughkeepsie? Steuer demurred; he urged the client to obtain *local* counsel. But the client insisted on the services of the champion, and they entrained for the provinces. When Steuer and the client left the railway station and approached the bucolic, ivy-covered courthouse, they observed that chiseled across the façade was one of those lofty Latin aphorisms with which courthouse architects of the nineteenth century loved to confuse the local citizenry—shall we say, FIAT JUSTITIA, PEREAT MUNDUS? The client asked Steuer what the legend meant. Steuer did not respond. Of course, he knew what it meant: "Let justice be done, if the whole world perish." But he was absorbed in his case, and did not translate for his client. They entered the courthouse; the case was tried before a local bumpkin who had never heard of Max Steuer and who treated him as if he were named Joe Zilch.

The case was lost. The great advocate was trying to stifle his resentment over being dragged all the way to Poughkeepsie to be humbled by some rustic clowns. As he and his client emerged from the courthouse, the client glanced up at the Latin words over the Corinthian columns. "Mr. Steuer," he said, "I would still like to know what those words mean."

Steuer looked at him with scorn. "I'll tell you what they mean," he hissed. "They mean *'Always Hire Local Counsel.'* That's what they mean!"

Jack Gasner recalls that when Tom Dewey became Manhattan's exemplar of the racket-busting Mr. DA, in 1934, he and his staff lunched and dined daily in the security of a special, third-floor room, partitioned off from the bakery. How many of our future stars came from that staff: at least two chief judges of the Court of Appeals, Fuld and Breitel; Murray Gurfein, who even now illuminates the Federal Court of Appeals; Frank Hogan, every lawyer's model of what a district attorney should be. Dewey's staff became a seed bed from which the New York bar and the bench were nourished for generations. You could see most of them at Gasner's, plotting with the Little Giant the downfall of a Jimmy Hines or a Lucky Luciano.

In 1964 Bobby Kennedy came to Gasner's to beat the tom-tom for the Johnson-Humphrey-Kennedy team. So also came the Tory opposition, led by Barry Goldwater, who seems to have had more luck with Gasner's cuisine than with New York's voters.

Mine is not the first hand to limn the glories that were Gasner's. In 1965 Otto Preminger, the bald Viennese motion-picture producer, sued Columbia Pictures and its television subsidiary, Screen Gems, to enjoin them from despoiling his current masterpiece, *Anatomy of a Murder*, on the television screen. Preminger's carefully cultivated accents from the Wienerwald shrilled in the press and in the courts that his brainchild should not be chopped up for commercials and cut to fit the prime-time mold. The case came on for trial before one of Gasner's most reliable patrons, the late Arthur G. Klein, and *The New Yorker* magazine assigned the deft and witty Lillian Ross to do a piece on the trial.* Her description took the form of a make-believe movie scenario, in which the action switches back and forth from Judge Klein's courtroom to Gasner's. The script picks up Judge Klein "as he makes his way to and into Gasner's"; next come the lawyers for Columbia, headed by Myles Lane (a Gasner regular who eventually made his way to the Appellate Division, First Department), and then Preminger and his entourage. Lillian Ross must have had the ear of an FBI microphone. She has Preminger standing at the doorway addressing a "young woman" (who must have been Miriam): " 'They told me when I'd come here you would play for me the

---

*See issue of February 19, 1966.

theme song from *Exodus*. So, I do not hear it!' "

Miriam Gasner was not one to be overawed by Holly-wood producers. She answers, " 'Today our machine is broken.' "*

"PREMINGER: All right, darling, I come here anyway, for your blintzes." He *does* order the blintzes, "with extra cherry preserves." " 'This restaurant,' " he intones to the assembled lawyers and judges, " 'has the best cheese blintzes in the world!' " If the judges and lawyers looked up from their sauerbraten, it would have been with annoyance at the intruder. They did not need Preminger's gastro-nomic judgments on Gasner's.

This was Gasner's in the great days. The great resort died in July 1973. The City of New York had acquired by condemnation the entire block on which it stood to be part of a planned civic center that sounded great in speeches. But like so many such projects, it never happened. One by one, the buildings around Gasner's succumbed to the wrecker's iron ball and to the jackhammers. Finally, the city refused a long-term lease, and in that black summer of 1973, the lawyers and judges who habitually made their way to 76 Duane Street at lunchtime learned that their favorite haunt was forever closed. To those of us who had become habitués, its closing was the end of an era, fondly remembered but beyond recall. Gasner's was as close as the New York lawyers ever came to an Inn of Court.

---

*What machine? Muzak? Or a jukebox? They would have been as appro-priate to Gasner's as Bach to a bowling alley!

9

ALIEN CORN IN
THE SOUTHERN DISTRICT

With all respect to the many fine courts in New York and other parts of the United States, there has always been a special aura about the U.S. District Court for the Southern District of New York. The geographical jurisdiction of the Southern District includes Manhattan and the Bronx in New York City, and nine of New York's "upstate" counties, so that from the beginning of the Republic, its court has been at the hub of commercial activity and the concommitant legal ferment. (Local legal historians sometimes call it the "mother court," claiming that it is the nation's oldest federal district court. While the parochial practitioners in Connecticut make this same claim for their district court, we in New York persistently cling to the belief that *our* court was first. This contest I leave for the legal historians.)

The Southern District tribunal has been called the top U.S. commercial court. Judge Charles Wyzanski, writing in the *Harvard Law Review* in 1948 about the Southern

District when its judges included the two Hands and Charles Merrill Hough, said it was then the outstanding federal trial court in the country, and that "cases were diverted to the district not by necessity, but by the choice of lawyers who were free to go to any of the several tribunals and selected the Southern District as their preference because of the quality of its bench."

In 1936 the court was probably at the peak of its judicial quality. The roster of judges included such legal titans as Knox, Coxe, Caffey, Bondy, Patterson, and Woolsey. These were all judges in the Southern District who became famous for their skills. As a lawyer who grew up in that age rolls these names off his tongue, they invoke the image of Nelson's line-of-battle ships. Power! Dignity! Confidence! These were judges in the highest tradition. The New York lawyers of that era remember too well the pandemonium in New York's Supreme Court, where gigantic calendars, overstrained judges, and fractious lawyers wrought a bedlam to all but the most case-hardened veterans. Not so in the Southern District. Here, judicial light was dispensed with cool serenity and, above all, with dignity. Often a single one of these judges, without a battery of law assistants, presided over a daily calendar of two hundred motions. The law functioned with majesty in the Southern District. Particularly, it functioned with a reverence for a standard of English that bore comparison with the idiom practiced in the halls of Westminster. Here in the Southern District, the young lawyer heard, often for the first time, a noble English tongue that stretched back to Coke and Bacon and Erskine, to Marshall and Taney and Holmes. The tumult and the excitement of those days, when the American economy and the legal systems were boiling with change, seldom affected the decorum, the dignity, or the diction of the Southern District bench.

In 1936 there was projected into these realms of judicial gold a figure so atypical, so different in those traditional attributes of demeanor and speech long honored in the Southern District, that he soon became a legend. Let it be said at the outset that if Sam Mandelbaum's diction came from Second Avenue, not Whitehall, if his scholarship came not from Cambridge but from the hard and bitter world of the Lower East Side, his compassion and humanity soon captured the hearts of the lawyers. Within a short time, their sneers melted into grudging understanding, and those who came to scoff remained to admire. Even the young prosecutors of the Southern District, imbued with the adamantine self-righteousness that has become *their* tradition, grudgingly acknowledged that Mandelbaum's kindness and understanding leavened the life of the courthouse.

What makes the Mandelbaum story worth telling is that it furnishes the best illustration of a phenomenon that has appeared several times in the Southern District. More than once in the last fifty years, the vagaries of a basically political process of judicial selection have given us district judges who were not initially qualified. Of course, this imperfect selection process is not peculiar to the Southern District. All over America, judges have been selected by senators and appointed by presidents with an eye on the candidate's political qualities rather than his legal accomplishments. In New York we have been fortunate; even when a political dud is visited on us, the spirit of the Southern District enters into the man—and behold a *judge*, conducting himself in the loftiest tradition of that district. Some of us have mused that like Quasimodo, the spirit of the Southern District lives just below the Golden Tower, to stand unseen and unfelt at the side of the judge who needs his inspiration and help. At the time of his appointment, Mandel-

baum was "unqualified" by any standards.* And yet . . .
Samuel Mandelbaum was born in Poland in 1884. He
came to New York as a young man, a part of the tide of
immigration at the end of the nineteenth century. He grew
up in the Fourth Assembly District, the satrapy of John F.
Ahearn, a powerful Tammany politician. As his district
changed from being overwhelmingly Irish to solidly Jewish, Ahearn began to foster the growth of young Jewish
politicians. Henry Schimmel and Aaron J. (for Jefferson)
Levy were his chief recruiting sergeants, and they persuaded Mandelbaum to take the Tiger's Shilling.†

Mandelbaum worked his way through law school and
became a lawyer to the huddled masses. Seldom did his
meager practice take him beyond the municipal or the magistrates' courts; certainly the federal court was as remote to
him as the towers of Ophir. His clients were the people of
the Lower East Side, in those days a community carried
over, person by person, from Warsaw and Minsk, from
Odessa and Krakow. Their justiciable controversies hardly

---

*At least two judges in the Southern District, roughly contemporary
with Mandelbaum, confided in this writer that their prior experience
afforded no basis for performing their multiple and exacting duties. One
of them, from an upstate county, said he was "terrified" by the prospect
of presiding over an admiralty trial when he could barely discern the
difference between a garbage scow and a pleasure yacht. Another judge
blanched at the need to become an overnight adept in the securities field.
Let it be recorded that both jurists acquitted themselves with honor and
dignity in the fields of admiralty, securities, bankruptcy and corporate
reorganization, patents, criminal law, etc. Both are recalled by the lawyers and judges of their time with affection and respect.
†There is a delightful description of the shrewd practices by which
Ahearn retained control of his district, despite the overwhelming influx
from Eastern Europe, by the recruitment and development of young
politicians (including Sam Mandelbaum), in Irving Howe's monumental
World of Our Fathers (New York: Harcourt Brace Jovanovich, 1976), pp.
372–373.

fell into the jurisdictional orbit of the federal court. Mandelbaum's speech was the speech of those people, and it differed from the language of the Southern District as the speech of Fagin differed from that of Disraeli. His were not the accents of Harvard and Yale and Columbia; his diction was what Leo Rosten calls "Yinglish," or "Ameridish." His consonants were overstressed; his diphthongs were protracted; there was more than a hint of *v* in his *w*'s. In his cadences there was a pronounced liturgical lilt.

In due course, Mandelbaum's services to the people of the East Side were rewarded by Tammany, and in 1923 he was elected to the Assembly of the State of New York. It is not recorded that he entertained his colleagues in Albany with parliamentary dithyrambs; but, in character, he toiled for such measures as slum clearance and low-cost housing. His principal legislative achievement was a bill, bearing his name, that authorized the creation of municipal housing authorities for slum clearance. Though Mandelbaum remained a steadfast Tammany Democrat— ever loyal to the forces that molded his political career— his devotion, his humility, and his self-effacing kindness endeared him even to the upstate Brahmins on the Republican side of the Assembly. When his nomination to the Southern District was opposed, many of them rallied to his support.

From childhood Mandelbaum suffered from a form of progressive paralysis, which impaired the use of his lower limbs; he walked with extreme difficulty, and his movements were almost as painful to the beholder as they were to him. During his years in the legislature and on the bench, it was plain that his disease caused him great anguish, which showed through the little smile he habitually wore. But few words of complaint were heard from him. He once told a colleague in the legislature, "I have a terrible affliction, which the Lord has smothered with His blessings."

When Franklin D. Roosevelt became governor of New York, in 1928, Mandelbaum was selected as a member of his "Turkey Cabinet," so called because it met every Monday at the Executive Mansion, where the Governor and Mrs. Roosevelt served turkey for lunch. The members included such men as Samuel I. Rosenman, Lieutenant Governor Herbert Lehman, Senator John Dunnigan, Langdon Post, Joseph P. Higgins, Irwin Steingut, Senator Tom Burchill, and Saul S. Streit.* Of this group of self-assured adepts, Sam Mandelbaum, for all his diffidence, his limp, and his accent, became a charter member who enjoyed the Governor's confidence and trust. It has been said that Roosevelt was drawn to Mandelbaum because of their common affliction, their common pain. I think not. I think that the Governor—and certainly Eleanor Roosevelt—saw in Mandelbaum the eternal Little Man, the Schweik, the Sancho Panza, the Passepartout, of their time. There soon developed a warm friendship between Mandelbaum and the Roosevelts, particularly Eleanor. She honored his unflinching loyalty to the orthodoxy of his fathers by providing him with kosher dishes; she accompanied him in pilgrimages to

---

*Rosenman was then counsel to the Governor. He resigned from a New York State Supreme Court judgeship to become one of Roosevelt's closest advisers, an office he also discharged for Truman. Herbert Lehman, a member of the famous banking family, brother of Irving Lehman (Chief Judge of the Court of Appeals), succeeded Roosevelt as governor of New York and became U.S. senator from New York. Dunnigan was minority leader of the State Senate; Burchill was a prominent state senator. Joseph Higgins, then a member of the Assembly, was a worldly Tammany nabob who later held important federal offices under Roosevelt and Truman. Post, Streit, and Mandelbaum were important members of the Assembly. Irwin Steingut, speaker of the Assembly, was one of the leading Democratic politicians in the state; he was the father of Stanley Steingut, who became speaker of the New York State Assembly.

the slums, where he became her guide to the problems of the poor and underprivileged; he became one of the mentors to this pair of Knickerbocker patricians in their quest for an understanding of the problems of poverty and social deprivation. It was easy for Sam Mandelbaum; he had lived with these problems from birth.

When Franklin and Eleanor Roosevelt went to Washington, in 1933, they carried with them not only Mandelbaum's tutelary contribution in the field of social and economic injustice but also a warm friendship for this kindly ambassador from the slums. In the early days of the New Deal, Mandelbaum was a frequent visitor to the White House. Saul Streit recalls with affection Mandelbaum's recitals of his visits to the seats of power: how he was met at Union Station by a big black Packard with the Presidential Seal on its sides; how he was entertained with ambassadors, princes, and potentates. This child of poverty described with awe the magnificence with which his hosts were surrounded. He carried home copies of the menus and the guest lists, which he exhibited with naive pride to his legislative colleagues. For Mandelbaum had been elected to the State Senate in the Roosevelt landslide of 1932, and he soon became a personage of some importance in Albany and in New York's Democratic organization.

In 1936 there were only eight judges in the Southern District of New York. Three new judgeships were created by Congress in that year, and Roosevelt filled them promptly; he named Vincent L. Leibell, John W. Clancy, and Samuel Mandelbaum. The appointment of Leibell, an experienced lawyer, aroused little comment or opposition. Clancy, on the other hand, stirred up a storm. Clancy was known as a close henchman of Ed Flynn, the political czar of the Bronx, and it was said that his only claim to the job was that he had been best man at Flynn's wedding. Whatever the source of his nomination, John Clancy served with ability and distinction in the Southern District for many years, becoming Chief Judge after John Knox.

Mandelbaum's appointment evoked unprecedented opposition from the press and the organized bar. On the day following his appointment, *The New York Times*, the metropolitan thunderer, carried an editorial trenchantly denouncing the appointment as "judicial spoils." The word was abroad that Mandelbaum was the choice of *Eleanor* Roosevelt (as indeed he may have been), that Mandelbaum had never tried a case (as indeed he probably never had), and that Mandelbaum had never been in the federal court (except perhaps out of curiosity). Within a few days of the appointment, the pontifical Alfred A. Cook, chairman of the American Bar Association's Judiciary Committee, trumpeted his denunciation of the candidate as purely a politician, deficient in the specialized knowledge and experience required of a judge in the Southern District. To Cook, the perfect exemplar of a generation of German-Jewish lawyers produced by Our Crowd, Mandelbaum was an unlettered churl from the wrong side of the river Oder. As such, Mandelbaum was a perfect target for the selective anti-Semitism practiced by this group.

Other voices were against Mandelbaum's appointment. Charles Evans Hughes, Jr., president of the New York County Lawyers Association, stigmatized Mandelbaum as "unqualified by learning and experience for the performance of the duties of this great office." His written protest against the appointment was cosigned by a group of distinguished New York lawyers. The Association of the Bar of the City of New York joined in the opposition, its views expressed by the illustrious Grenville Clark. A "Special Committee on Law Reform" of the New York City Chamber of Commerce, stimulated perhaps by dark rumors of the sinister hand of Eleanor Roosevelt in Mandelbaum's nomination, castigated the President for the appointment.

On June 19, 1936, three days after the appointment, a Senate subcommittee began its hearing on the nomination.

There were no extensive investigations into the qualifications of FDR's candidates for the federal bench; neither the White House nor the Attorney General solicited the appraisals of the American Bar Association, the local bar groups, or of professional colleagues. Sweeping FBI investigations into the purity of the candidate's political philosophy, or his promptness in payment of his wife's charge accounts, lay in the future. *Vox regis vox Dei!* And Roosevelt was as close to *rex* as we had ever come.* Of course, friends and enemies were free to express their (unsolicited) opinions of the candidate. The Senate subcommittee was deluged with a tide of letters and telegrams supporting Mandelbaum. All of them extolled the nobility of his character, his devotion to public service. They could say nothing of his skills and experience as a lawyer, because there was nothing to say. Almost every Democratic member of the New York State Legislature penned his support for Sam. Herbert Lehman and Sam Rosenman, fellow-alumni of the Turkey Cabinet, added their voices. Max Steuer stood up to be counted for Sam, but he, too, spoke of character, not litigative skills. By June 21, Mandelbaum was confirmed, despite more editorial mutterings from *The New York Times* and the outspoken hostility of New York's senior senator, Royal Copeland. On July 10, 1936, Mandelbaum was sworn in, and he entered on the discharge of his duties.

The grapevine had been that the nomination was going

---

*Shortly after the Mandelbaum appointment, Roosevelt filled a vacancy in the Southern District with the nomination of Edward Conger. Conger had a rural practice in Dutchess County. When he was asked how he came to be a federal judge, Conger replied, "My only qualification is that I lived about a mile away from Hyde Park!"

to Saul Streit, who had already displayed those talents that later were to make him a distinguished judge in the state court. Streit has told this writer he "was being measured for the robe" when Jim Dooling, the reigning Tammany boss, telephoned to say that "the White House" wanted Mandelbaum, and all he could offer Streit was an invitation to the next Sheriff's Panel dinner. One story is that Mandelbaum had confided to Mrs. Roosevelt that it was his ambition to end his career as a judge, so that he could help the "little people"—by which he meant that he aspired to be a magistrate, or perhaps a judge of the old Court of Special Sessions, which dealt with lesser criminal cases. But the president of the United States could not appoint magistrates in the City of New York, only federal judges.

There is a reliable account of how Mandelbaum learned he was to be a federal judge.* A newspaper reporter in Albany told Sam in the spring of 1936 that his Washington office had a "leak" that FDR was going to give Sam one of the three new judgeships. Would Mandelbaum comment on this?

"Ridiculous!" said Mandelbaum. "I have never even been in the federal court!"

A few days later he was invited to lunch at the White House. Before lunch, he found himself sitting across the desk from the President.

"Sam, how would you like to be a federal judge?" asked FDR.

"Who, me?" said Mandelbaum. "That is ridiculous. I've never even been in the federal court."

---

*This account comes from the late George Zolotar, who became an intimate of Mandelbaum's as you will see. According to Zolotar, this was Mandelbaum's own description of how he learned that he was to be appointed to the federal bench.

Roosevelt threw his head back and roared the famous leonine laugh.

"Don't move, Sam," he said, "and don't say a word." The President reached forward and pressed all the buttons on his desk. In came the White House entourage: Missy Le-Hand, Steve Early, Marvin McIntyre, Eleanor, half a dozen Secret Service men.

Roosevelt: "Now, Sam, I'm going to repeat what I said to you and I want you to repeat what you said. Sam, how would you like to be a federal judge?"

Mandelbaum: "Who, me? It's ridiculous!"

The imperial court burst into laughter.

"Well, Sam," said the President, "ridiculous or not, you are hereby appointed to be a judge of the United States District Court for the Southern District of New York."

Mandelbaum's advent in the federal courthouse, in the summer of 1936, was a shocker. He came into room 318, the central criminal part, a judicial traffic-control center in which were heard assorted and varied pleadings, motions, sentences. It was a terrain populated by criminal defendants, their lawyers and relatives, bondsmen, and the assistant U.S. attorneys of the Criminal Division. Those assistants, then as now, were a *corps d'élite*—young, zealous, educated to the point of snobbery, and perhaps the most critical group before whom a jurist must perform. Within minutes Mandelbaum had them whispering to one another in disbelief. Within days he was the principal topic of lunch-table gossip around the Southern District. He was plainly innocent of the intricacies of federal practice, a deficiency partially repaired by the diligent scholarship of his law secretary, Louis Perlmutter. But Perlmutter's assiduous ministrations could do nothing about Sam's accent or his spontaneous use of Yiddish words that meant nothing to most of his listeners. His meekness, his constant apologetic manner, were in great contrast to the crisp, self-assured decisiveness of the usual federal judges. Mandel-baum's transparent, openly expressed insecurity had the lawyers and court attachés talking to themselves.

During one of his early appearances in room 318, there came before him a series of ten or twelve defendants who, by prearrangement with the prosecution, had all pleaded guilty to having committed certain offenses in naturalization proceedings. They had all, as witnesses, testified falsely as to the length of their acquaintance with the petitioners, swearing to a personal acquaintance of five years when in truth and in fact they had known the petitioners for only two or three. These heinous deeds had resulted in the filing of criminal charges to which they had pleaded guilty. Now they were on for sentencing before the new jurist.

In those days, the government routinely made recommendations on every sentence. In this instance the recommendation that emanated from the Immigration and Naturalization Service was "10 days and $250.00 fine." The first four or five cases went without incident. The judge asked the prosecutor, "What is your recommendation?" The prosecutor replied, "Ten days and two-hundred-fifty-dollar fine." And though Mandelbaum balked at the ten days' incarceration as being cruel and inhuman punishment for the trifling offense involved, he was still too new and too insecure to risk the displeasure of the prosecutor or the anger of the government, so he went along reluctantly and imposed the recommended sentence. His only reaction was a faint grimace of distaste.

Then, in the middle of the group, there appeared before him an obvious denizen of his own Lower East Side, represented by a lawyer whose accent and inflection were identical to his own. The lawyer wore the short-cropped beard that was the badge of Second Avenue's Yiddish intelligentsia, and he gave to his vowels and consonants the same values the judge did. Plainly, here were a couple of *landsleit* who sparked Mandelbaum's special concern. The lawyer made the usual impassioned plea that the ten days be suspended.

Judge Mandelbaum was plainly affected. Meekly, tentatively, he suggested to the assistant prosecutor that he reduce the recommended sentence so as to eliminate the ten days. The assistant resisted. He explained that this case was in no way different from the four or five previous cases, in which the recommended sentence had already been imposed.

Mandelbaum bade him approach the bench. "Young man," asked the judge, "are you a *yuld?*"*

"What's a *yuld?*" asked the confused assistant.

"A *yuld,* said the judge, "is a dope, a stupid. Don't you understand that this lawyer is a close friend? When I was a young lawyer on the East Side he was like a father to me. You want me to treat him like I treat everybody else?"

"Of course," said the stalwart assistant. "What difference does that make?"

"You *are* a *yuld,* " said the judge. "Please reduce the recommendation."

"No chance," said the assistant, making noises about the recommendation's having come down from the heights in Washington with the authority of Holy Script and no room for change.

"You *are* a *yuld,* " said the judge. "Step down."

The assistant prosecutor resumed his normal place. The judge turned to the court reporter. "Put this down in the

---

*Leo Rosten's invaluable *Joys of Yiddish* defines a *yuld,* or *yold,* as a "boob," a "simpleton," a "fool." He writes that the word derives from the Hebrew *yeled,* a "child" or "boy."

book," said Judge Mandelbaum. " 'The district attorney having very graciously consented to reduce the recommendation—' "

"Wait a minute," the outraged assistant shouted. "I never consented to anything."

"You shut up," said Mandelbaum with uncharacteristic asperity. "I'm not talking to you; I'm talking to the court reporter. I repeat, 'The district attorney having graciously consented to reduce the recommendation, I impose a sentence of ten days and two-hundred-fifty-dollar fine—the ten days *suspended.*' Next case!"

"The next case," said the exasperated assistant, "is just like the last one. No different."

"Do you have a recommendation?" asked Mandelbaum.

"Same recommendation. Ten days and two-hundred-fifty-dollar fine," the assistant snapped.

"Okay," said the judge. "Ten days and two-hundred-fifty-dollar fine. Next case."

One other story made the rounds. In an early criminal case before Mandelbaum, a youthful prosecutor was engaged in summing up to the jury. His summation betrayed his classical education, his Ivy League training in rhetoric, and his extensive vocabulary. After a number of Latin phrases and polysyllabic words, there came an interruption from the bench. "Counselor," said Mandelbaum in his humblest tones, "if *I* don't understand them big words you're using, how do you expect twelve *schnooks** in a jury box to understand them? You better start over and talk

---

*Schnook, or shnook, is strictly Ameridish. It was an East Side term for a poor slob, one unable to take care of himself. The philologists among my readers are respectfully referred to Wentworth & Flexner, *Dictionary of American Slang* (New York: Crowell, 1966), and *An American Thesaurus of Slang* (New York: Crowell, 1943). For a witty exposition of the word's subtle nuances, see the old reliable, Leo Rosten's *Joys of Yiddish.*

plain English!" There were one or two snorts from those jurors who knew what *schnook* meant, but the summation was resumed in monosyllabic Anglo-Saxon.

It is said that the defendant was convicted, and that on the appeal, the colloquy between Mandelbaum and the young prosecutor came to the attention of the Jovian panel of the court of appeals that sat in review. The story is that one of the panel—Swan or Chase or one of the Hands—interrupted the argument to ask the assistant who had prosecuted, "Counselor, can you enlighten us as to the meaning of the word *schnook?*"

"Your Honor," responded the nimble youth, "I believe it to be a pejorative derived from the Yiddish. Beyond that I have no information."

Louis Perlmutter served as Mandelbaum's law clerk, amanuensis, guide, philosopher, and link with the English language during most of the judge's time on the bench. Perlmutter recalls that Mandelbaum never overcame his lack of confidence, his inner sense that he did not really belong in the Southern District. He manifested this uneasiness by assuming an apologetic tone for every ruling. He almost bled for the lawyers against whom he ruled. He would telephone lawyers to explain why he had ruled against them and assure them that there had been no fault of advocacy on their part.

Most poignant of all was Mandelbaum's anguish over the imposition of sentence on criminals convicted before him. Here, too, the overflowing compassion of the man would manifest itself. Mandelbaum's sentencing practices were at best unconventional and aberrant; at worst they were hair-raising. Almost always, in imposing sentences, he betrayed his secret guilt that his job as a judge should include the requirement that he occasionally visit punishment on fellow-creatures.

Former judge Raphael P. Koenig relates a vignette of Mandelbaum that illustrates his reluctance to send men to the penitentiary. Judge Koenig was the son of Samuel Koenig, the East Side lawyer who became one of the exalted panjandrums of Republican politics in New York in the first quarter of this century. Though Mandelbaum, as a Tammany wheelhorse in the legislature, was a nominal foe of Sam Koenig, it was widely understood that there was a general accommodation between the reigning Democratic chieftains of Manhattan and their Republican antagonists. To Mandelbaum, Raphael Koenig was just another fine young man from the Neighborhood. "The Neighborhood" was a standard euphemism for the Lower East Side: denizens of that area, and the fortunate escapees therefrom, spoke of it as alumni of a certain law school in eastern Massachusetts are accustomed to speak of their alma mater as *The* Law School." As a certified product of the Neighborhood, Raphael Koenig was entitled to the special red-carpet treatment that Mandelbaum reserved for his *landsleit*. This usually meant that the judge addressed the privileged lawyer by his first name—or even by some intimate childhood nickname that made its bearer squirm in embarrassment. (There was once a lawyer, a contemporary of Mandelbaum's, who escaped from the Neighborhood at an early age. He went from Hester Street to Harvard and thence under a false flag to an important Wall Street law firm. One day, he appeared before Mandelbaum armored with his fastidiously Anglicized name, his vested gray-flannel suit, and his Hasty Pudding accent. Mandelbaum instantly penetrated the disguise. "Hello, Yitzker!" said the judge. "I haven't seen you since we stole apples together from the pushcarts!" There is no record of the lawyer's reaction, or of the impact of the greeting on his career.)

Raphael Koenig had no such troubles. He wore no disguises and he was accustomed to the informality with which the irrepressible Sam ran his court. But neither sincerity nor experience could protect him from Sam's unorthodox sentencing practices. In the late 1930s, Koenig found himself before Judge Mandelbaum, representing a notorious securities swindler, Walter Gutterson, who was tried with some other confidence men, all charged with bilking the widows and orphans of New York (including some from the sacred Neighborhood) in violation of the Securities Act of 1933. While the jury was working its way toward the inevitable verdict of "guilty," Mandelbaum called Koenig into the robing room. "Raphie," said the judge, "you and I know from the Neighborhood that Gutterson is a thief and a rascal. Him I will sentence immediately. The others can wait. Now, Raphie, if you are Sam Mandelbaum, knowing what a terrible crook Gutterson is, what would you give him?"

Koenig wriggled in discomfort. "Judge, I am his lawyer; how can you ask me what his sentence should be?"

"Raphie," said the judge, "you better think it over, because I am going to ask you the same question when the jury comes back!"

The jury returned with the expected verdict of "guilty." Mandelbaum wasted no time. "Stand up, Gutterson," he said. "Stand up and listen. Okay, Mr. Prosecutor, what does the government recommend for this man?"

The youthful prosecutor, flushed with victory and virtue, recited all the details of Gutterson's sordid career, and finished with a ringing recommendation that Gutterson be removed from society for a period of seven years.

"All right, Mr. Raphie Koenig," said the judge, "you have heard the recommendation of the government. Now, if you were Sam Mandelbaum, what would you do with this bum?"

Koenig made some appropriate professional noises about his duty to the client.

"Never mind all that," said the judge. "Raphie, I ask you again, if you were Sam Mandelbaum, what would you give him?"

Koenig thought hard. He knew that Gutterson had a gruesome record of convictions, that previous exposure to the rehabilitive processes of Lewisburg had been futile; most of all, he knew that the government's recommendation of seven years made it certain that Mandelbaum would have to impose a substantial penitentiary sentence.

He swallowed hard. "Your Honor," he said, "knowing the defendant's background and history, I think if I were the sentencing judge I would impose a sentence of *three* years."

The judge fixed his severest glance on the unregenerate rogue who stood before him. "Gutterson," he intoned, "you are a thief and a scoundrel. You are a disgrace to your family! The government recommends that I put you away for seven years. *Your own lawyer recommends three years in the penitentiary. But I am going to show you that Sam Mandelbaum has a bigger heart even than your own lawyer. The sentence is two years in the penitentiary.* Bail is canceled. The motion for a stay is denied." Hurriedly the judge left the bench, choking back the tears of anguish that flowed always when the law required him to sentence another human being to penal servitude—especially when the miscreant came from his own milieu.

The ungrateful Gutterson stood stunned both by the sentence and by its immediacy. He felt the hand of the marshal on his shoulder. He turned to Koenig. "You dumb bastard," he shouted, "why didn't you recommend a year and a day? He might have given me a suspended sentence!"

Mandelbaum's artless judicial adventures were not lim-

ited to sentencing. Jim Foley was the law clerk to Judge
Vincent Leibell, whose chambers were on the same floor as
Mandelbaum's. Tom Reddy was Judge Edward Conger's
law clerk, also with chambers on the same floor. Foley,
Reddy, and Lou Perlmutter enjoyed regular sessions in
which they collected Mandelbaumisms. Here is one.

During the late 1930s, a notorious libel case came before
Mandelbaum and a jury. The plaintiff represented herself
as a titled European lady of impeccable reputation. She
professed to be a baroness whose name and virtue had been
besmirched by allegations of the defendant (also a sprig of
Europe's lesser nobility, a countess). In the eyes of both
ladies was the twinkle of Budapest; in their voices was the
lilt of Lehár. The facts in the case might have been composed by any of a dozen librettists of the Dual Monarchy.
Both ladies were vying for the favor and affection of a
wealthy New York businessman. The gravamen of the action was that the "countess" had imputed a lack of virtue
to the "baroness." The countess, in an unusual breach of
professional courtesy, had publicly averred that the baroness had engaged in a concupiscent relationship with some
other lady's husband. In that age such allegations were
taken much more seriously than they are today. The tab-
loid newspapers of that time gave a great deal of space and
attention to the trial before Mandelbaum. It was Mandelbaum's first exposure to the sensual luxuries of the *haute
monde*, and he reveled in the details of the baroness's lubric-
ity.

The defense, of course, was "truth." In its efforts to
establish that elusive quality, the defendant called to the
stand a former maid in the household of the baroness:

Q. Were you employed in the household of the Baroness in the month of August, 1937?

A. Yes.

Q. Did you have occasion to see the Baroness and Mr. P———— together?

A. Yes.

Q. At what time and under what circumstances?

A. I saw them on the morning of August sixth. I opened the door to the Baroness's bedroom and I saw her in bed with Mr. P————. . . .

Examining Counsel: [*with a triumphant leer first at the jury, then at the defendant*] Your witness.

Mandelbaum: Wait, wait! Go on, go on. What were they doing?

Mandelbaum had no illusions about his professional shortcomings. But he did not like to be reminded that he was hardly the peer of Holmes and Cardozo. Any show of superior erudition by a lawyer appearing before him nettled him. One day a lawyer arguing a motion in Mandelbaum's court made a pontifical exposition of a legal point with profuse citation of authority. He referred to a case that was unknown to Mandelbaum. Sam admitted he had never heard of the case.

"Your Honor," said the lawyer, "I am astonished that you are unfamiliar with *Smith* v. *Jones.* It is one of the leading authorities in the field."

"Counselor," asked the judge, "did you ever hear of a case called *White* v. *Brown?*"

"No, Your Honor," said the lawyer. "I am not familiar with that case."

"You better look at that one before you start talking about *Smith* v. *Jones.* The motion is taken under advisement. Next case," said the judge.

Soon after, Mandelbaum went into the robing room,

where the faithful Perlmutter awaited him. "Judge," asked
the diligent law secretary, who had heard the colloquy in
the courtroom. "What's all that about *White* v. *Brown?* I
never heard of it."

"Of course you didn't," said Mandelbaum. "Neither did
I. He gives *me* a case—I give *him* a case. Forget it!"

One of the things that disturbed Mandelbaum about his
job as a judge was that he was frequently required to decide
cases in favor of the rich and the powerful against the poor
and oppressed. He had an almost instinctive revulsion
against power and authority. The folk heroes of his early
life were not just politicians but also the socialist labor
leaders who in that era were waging daily warfare for the
rights of labor and especially for union recognition. To
Mandelbaum, there were no greater figures than men like
Hillquit, Barondess, and Gompers, who were struggling
for the little people against the banking and industrial establishment.

John Lewin, then a Special Assistant to the Attorney
General of the United States in the Antitrust Division,
once obtained a criminal indictment under the antitrust
laws against a group of union officials. The indictment was
presented to Judge Mandelbaum. He summoned Lewin to
his chambers. Lewin found the judge on the edge of tears,
trembling with indignation and rage. He stormed at
Lewin, "Why do we prosecute *them?* Why union leaders?
We should be protecting them from the big shots, the
bosses! *They* are the people we should prosecute!"

Mandelbaum's most severe professional travails were in
the field of corporate reorganization.* He soon learned that

---

*This is a branch of bankruptcy work in which corporations, usually
publicly owned, are not liquidated but are reconstituted to continue in
business. In Mandelbaum's time, these were called "77-b" cases, after the
provision of bankruptcy law then applicable. More recently, they are

safety lay in placing great reliance on the skilled shock troops of the Securities and Exchange Commission, who were only too eager to be his mentors. His chief aide in this department was George Zolotar, an able lawyer then in charge of the corporate-reorganization work in the New York regional office of the SEC. Mandelbaum's rule was, When in doubt, let Zolotar take charge.

Mandelbaum was the judge in charge of the reorganization of P-R Holding Corporation. The case clearly presented some particularly thorny points that required a philosophical choice between principle and pragmatism.* Confronted with a frightening strain on his cogitative faculties, Mandelbaum abdicated in favor of Zolotar, who appeared for the SEC. Zolotar obliged by furnishing Mandelbaum with an excellent draft opinion, which was accepted without question. Of course, the opinion was affirmed in the Court of Appeals for the Second Circuit, with an opinion written by Judge Jerome Frank, surely one of the wisest heads and most facile pens ever to inhabit that great court. Shortly after Frank's opinion appeared, Mandelbaum encountered the philosopher-jurist in the judges' lunchroom. Frank was fulsome in his praise of Mandelbaum's opinion; it constituted, he said, a thoroughgoing *practical* solution to a troublesome problem. "Sam," he said, "I want to compliment you on that fine opinion. You did the right thing! You cut the Gordian knot!"

Mandelbaum, whose only contribution to the opinion was the signature at the bottom, had not the first inkling of what Frank was talking about. But he could hardly wait

---

called "Chapter X" or "Chapter XI" cases. The SEC is usually an active participant in Chapter X cases.
*The case appears in the Federal Reporter at 14 F. 2d 895. Students of the style of Judge Jerome Frank should read his footnote 2, p. 898.

to get back to his chambers to call Zolotar, to tell him that his work had drawn such praise from one of the princes of the bench. He called Zolotar. "George," he said, "you have no idea how delighted Jerry Frank was with the opinion we wrote in *P-R Holding*. He says it is a great piece of work. He says we cut Gordon's knot. Who in hell is Gordon?"

One of the best-known landmark decisions in the federal judicial system is *Erie Railroad Co.* v. *Tompkins*. Every lawyer and law student knows it as the Supreme Court's rejection in 1938 of the classical doctrine of *Swift* v. *Tyson*, in which the Supreme Court had held, in 1842, that upon questions of general law, in the absence of a state or local statute, the federal courts were free to exercise their independent judgment as to what the state law is. The 1938 decision overturned a century of precedent and required federal judges to apply state law as interpreted by the state courts. Few cases have been the subject of as much exegesis as *Erie* v. *Tompkins*.* But it is not widely known that it was the first civil trial over which Judge Mandelbaum presided, and for the rest of his life he spoke about *Erie* v. *Tompkins* as a general would speak of his first victory on the battlefield. The late John Cahill once told this writer that in arguing before Mandelbaum, he once questioned whether the judge correctly understood a principle of law in question. Mandelbaum smiled at him indulgently and asked, "Mr. Cahill, did you ever hear of a case *Erie* v. *Tompkins?*"

"Of course, Your Honor," said Cahill.

"Do you know, Mr. Cahill, *who* was the trial judge in that case?"

---

*My lay readers will have to pardon a little show of pedantry. The usages of legal writing dictate a flow of citations. The Supreme Court's opinion is reported at 304 U.S. 64, reversing the Court of Appeals opinion reported at 90 F. 2d 603. *Swift* v. *Tyson*, the venerable victim of the *Erie* decision, appears at 41 U.S. (16 Petrie), 1 (1842).

"I'm not sure, Your Honor," said Cahill.

"I was," said Mandelbaum, "and Learned Hand and Judge Swan agreed with me, even though the Supreme Court later on got a little confused and reversed us. So don't tell me I don't understand the law!"

Though Mandelbaum preened himself for the rest of his life over his part in this monumental case, a careful reading of the opinions suggests that he had little to be proud of, or to be ashamed of. *Erie* v. *Tompkins* was a conventional accident case, of the type that abounds in the state courts. It was brought in the federal court only because the plaintiff was a citizen of Pennsylvania and the defendant railroad was a New York corporation. This "diversity" conferred jurisdiction on the federal court. Tompkins was injured one dark night when, returning from a convivial evening, he was walking along the Erie's right-of-way. He claimed he was lawfully on the Erie's property because he was walking on "a commonly used beaten footpath" that ran for a short distance alongside the tracks. The law of Pennsylvania was clear: as declared by the highest court of that state, persons who use paths along the right-of-way are deemed trespassers and cannot recover in court for injury received by negligence, unless the negligence is wanton or willful.

There was a four-day trial before Mandelbaum and a jury. He had been on the bench only two months; Louis Perlmutter confirms that this was certainly his first civil trial. Both sides were represented by skilled counsel, the Erie Railroad by Theodore Kiendl, a partner of John W. Davis and one of the most respected trial lawyers of the time. Mandelbaum refused to instruct the jury in accordance with the Pennsylvania decisions, and he ruled instead that the question of the responsibility of a railroad for personal injury was one of general law, as to which the federal courts exercise independent judgment. In short, he followed the rule laid down in 1842 in *Swift* v. *Tyson.* There was a verdict for $30,000 to Mr. Tompkins, and Mandelbaum promptly denied the railroad's motion to set the verdict aside.

On appeal, the Second Circuit Court of Appeals affirmed the verdict unanimously, in an opinion by Judge Swan (Learned Hand and Manton concurring) in which he never cited *Swift* v. *Tyson.* The right of the federal courts to find the substantive general law for themselves was clearly taken for granted.

The U.S. Supreme Court agreed to review the case, and Mr. Justice Brandeis fulfilled an old hatred against the doctrine that there could be a federal common law different from the common law of the state in which the federal court sat. He persuaded a majority of his brethren, and they vaporized *Swift* v. *Tyson.**

After this reversal, in 1938, the new doctrine of *Erie* v. *Tompkins* became the subject of countless law-review articles, and there was much speculation among the lawyers of the Southern District as to whether Judge Mandelbaum had any true understanding of the substantive storm in which he had played such an important part. Any of us who assumed that at the trial, and in his denial of the motion to set aside the jury's verdict, Mandelbaum consciously rejected the notion that he should follow the Pennsylvania rule, and just as consciously clove to the hoary doctrine of *Swift* v. *Tyson,* can now be assured that the

---

*The Supreme Court's opinion in *Erie* v. *Tompkins* infuriated many federal judges. Learned Hand said that the decision emasculated the federal judiciary. He wrote that since the *Erie* decision, "We merely play the well-known aria from the opera *Le Fin de Brandeis* entitled *Erie R.R.* v. *Tompkins.*" See Marvin Schick, *Learned Hand's Court* (Baltimore, Md.: Johns Hopkins U. Press, 1970), p. 130.

judge had never heard of *Swift* v. *Tyson*. The proof appears in Mandelbaum's own handwriting.

When Sidney Sugarman became a judge of the Southern District, in 1949, he inherited Mandelbaum's library. Edward J. Ryan, now a respected bankruptcy judge in the Southern District, was then Judge Sugarman's law clerk. Some years ago, Ryan chanced upon the volume of 304 U.S. in which, on page 70, Mandelbaum had written in the margin "Because the Swift Tyson case *although before this case I never knew of its existence to be truthful* and for the confusion this decision brought about, it might have been better to leave it alone and stand by good old Swifty."

The italics are mine. The thought, the syntax, and the punctuation are pure Mandelbaum.

Sam Mandelbaum died in 1946, after only ten years on the bench. His illness had become almost completely disabling, and he grimaced with pain as he took his place in court. Among his chief mourners were his judicial colleagues, who had recovered from the initial shock of his atypical personality. Along with the lawyers who appeared before him, they had come to honor his humanity and kindness. At his death, there were no tributes to his scholarship, but many references to his heart.

10

THE CASE OF
THE FATAL PHOTOGRAPH,
OR,
DON'T KICK THE TIGER

In the late 1930s the federal court in New York was the scene of a major fraud trial that had so many bizarre elements as to make it worthwhile to recount. Ironically, in this instance, the machinery of prosecution was in the actual process of cranking out a voluntary dismissal of the indictment when the defendants, by an act of arrogant folly, revived the case, and effected their own downfall.

A decade earlier, before the Great Crash, Americans seemed to be obsessed with the attraction of easy money. In this era there flourished a widespread confidence scheme —a complex and sophisticated variation of the fabled "sting." Technically, in the *patois* of the crooks, it was called the "payoff game." A group of confidence men toured this country and Canada, luring the gullible into believing that they could win large sums on inside information on horseracing and stock-market speculation. The glib, smooth-talking con men deceived their incredibly susceptible victims into thinking that to collect their "winnings" they had to travel to Reno, Nevada. Once there, they had to produce proof of their financial ability to have paid, had they lost, the amount they were permitted to receive as profits. The pigeons flocked to Reno to collect their winnings, carrying with them evidence of their financial responsibility in the form of government bonds, marketable securities, and other tangible indicia of worldly wealth.

In Reno, the credulous suckers were informed by the con men that cash and *only* cash would serve to convince the chiefs of their financial responsibility. To obtain the cash, the victims were sent to sell their securities or to hypothecate their other assets through a particular bank, the Riverside Bank of Reno. The bank translated the assets into cash, and these trusting folk carried it to the con men, who then introduced them (and the cash) to the kingpin, the pretended payoff man. To him the swindlers displayed the cash obtained from the bank, together with the cash "winnings." The payoff man then expressed his satisfaction with the "proof," and in the presence of the victims there was paid over to con men the cash resulting from the sale, plus the spurious winnings. At this point, the infallibility of the scheme having been demonstrated, the victims were persuaded to risk everything—their own money and the "profits"—on one last phony bet or market speculation. Of course, it failed, and the fleeced lambs were persuaded to leave Reno, either with a promise of restitution or some other cock-and-bull concoction.*

---

*Those of my readers who doubt that there were such gullible fools, and who think my description of this hoax is drawn from the romantic yarns of O. Henry or from a W. C. Fields film, should compare it with the recital of the facts in the opinion of Judge Harrie Chase (Learned Hand concurring) in *U.S.* v. *Graham*, 102 F. 2d, 436 (1939). In the language of grand opera, *"Incredibile ma vero!"*

Central to this scheme were two prominent citizens of Reno, William J. Graham and James C. McKay. There is some indication that they owned or controlled the Riverside Bank. Certainly, they provided the con men with the needed front money (for the "profit" and expenses) and "safe" facilities for the payoff. Whatever may have been the contribution of these two pillars of Reno society, they presided over the division of the loot among the participating swindlers, retaining fifteen percent for their services.

Now, Graham and McKay were important fellows in Nevada's rugged frontier society. It has been said that in addition to their proprietary interest in the Riverside Bank, they owned a nightclub and a newspaper. What other commercial interests they had in the lustier pastimes of Reno can only be imagined. From the available evidence, they seem to have been drawn from the "bad-guy" types of Hollywood's Westerns, the saloonkeeper–banker–land speculator who cheats the honest prospector out of his mining claims or the honest cattleman out of his rangeland.

In due time the anguished screams of the victims reached the ears of the postal authorities. Graham and McKay and some of their henchmen were indicted in 1934 in the Southern District of New York for using the mails in furtherance of a scheme to defraud, and for conspiracy. A number of their codefendants pleaded guilty or were convicted of the offenses growing out of the swindles involved in the case. But Graham and McKay enjoyed charmed lives. Two trials, in 1934 and 1935, ended in jury disagreements. There was considerable speculation among the courthouse *cognoscenti* as to *why* the juries disagreed. Invidious suggestions were made that the juries had been the subjects of some tampering, but intensive investigation failed to provide a basis for a jury-tampering charge.

The prosecutors and postal inspectors had just about

concluded that further prosecution was futile, that the case should be dropped and the taxpayers rescued from the burden of further proceedings. From February 1936 to February 1937 there were no entries made in the docket. During that period the usual communications were passing between New York and Washington, recommending dismissal. The case was practically dead. And the word was abroad in Reno that the two prominent citizens of that community were at the end of their troubles. But official confirmation was slow in coming. Apparently, the cloud over them was impeding their careers, and Graham and McKay began looking for a "sign" that their struggle with government was over. They searched the Western skies for the dove. Soon these worthy citizens thought they discerned the happy omen in the person of a visiting dignitary from Washington.

At that time, the Assistant Attorney General in charge of the Criminal Division was Brien McMahon, of Connecticut. McMahon, the epitome of the rising young politician, was plainly destined for high office. He knew that he was a man of destiny; his eyes were already raised toward the Senate and even to the other end of Pennsylvania Avenue. Of course, he was always fastidious about his reputation; no whisper of scandal was permitted to mar the perfection of his public image. He was vigorous, he was zealous, and in the pursuit of high political office he was painfully sensitive about his good name.

I can confidently assure my readers that McMahon was completely oblivious of the proceedings in New York against Graham and McKay. True, his office in Washington was examining a recommendation that the New York indictments be dismissed. But this was a routine matter that had never reached the level of McMahon's attention.

During 1937 McMahon set out on an inspection trip to

the Far West, to observe at first hand the functioning of the U.S. Attorney's offices, and probably to mend a few political fences. He was accompanied by two of his aides, one of them an obscure young lawyer named John Sirica. In due course he arrived in Reno, where he was received with enthusiastic hospitality by the local U.S. Attorney. During the first evening, he was taken by his host to a pleasant night spot, where he was regaled with a Lucullan feast. During the repast, there appeared at the table two hearty, friendly Western types who were introduced to McMahon as Mr. Graham and Mr. McKay, the proprietors of the watering place. Their names meant nothing to McMahon. As McKay shook the great man's hand, Graham draped an arm in friendly greeting over his shoulder. A roving photographer snapped a picture of the convivial group, and left. The wine flowed and the music played. The inner McMahon was happy; his ears were stuffed with eulogy. He knew nothing of the skulduggery being practiced on him.

When McMahon awoke on the morning after the night-club meeting, his euphoria was shattered. On the front page of the Reno newspaper was a photograph of the Assistant Attorney General in fraternal embrace with the defendants. The skeptical citizenry of Reno clearly understood that the long conflict between these two local celebrities and the United States government had come to an end? If there was any doubt, the caption under the picture and the accompanying newspaper story put it to rest. The dove had come out of the East, the hatchet had been buried, and Graham and McKay were plainly at peace with the government. What better proof than the prandial photo of the little band of brothers? Did Torquemada dine with tomorrow's bonfire? Did Jack Ketch sup with his victims?

McMahon realized he had been diddled by these two

master diddlers. He had visions of being called before a congressional committee; plainly the immaculacy of his good name was threatened. The aroma was that of the "fixeroo." The Celtic feudist in McMahon's heritage screamed for reprisal; he vaulted into action. He called his chief aides in Washington. "Who in hell are Graham and McKay?" he demanded. Shortly, by telephone, he was given the substance of their dossier. He cut short his Western tour. By the next morning he was back in Washington, breathing fire and plotting revenge. The first step was to inform the U.S. Attorney in New York that any thought of dropping the case was abandoned; there must be a third trial for the two miscreants. Next, he called his close friend in New York, Samuel Kaufman. He told Kaufman of his ordeal in Reno. "Sam," he said, "who is the meanest, toughest, most ornery prosecutor in the Southern District?" Kaufman never hesitated. There was an ambitious, energetic zealot in the U.S. Attorney's office who in Sam Kaufman's view would have convicted St. Cecilia for singing a false note. "There is a kid here," said Kaufman, "who eats defendants for breakfast. He gets convictions; they may not stick, but he gets convictions. If you get him a strong judge to keep him straight, he's your man. His name is William Power Maloney." Within minutes, *U.S.* v. *Graham and McKay* had been committed to the tender ministrations of William Power Maloney.

Maloney's reputation for ferocity had been well earned. Short, pugnacious, eloquent, industrious, with the voice of a bull and boundless brass, he was the darling of the Foley Square claque—the unemployed trial-watchers who followed criminal trials and had a great appetite for blood. Those of us who inhabited the federal court in those years regarded Maloney with the highest respect. He was the incarnation of the tough prosecutor.

At the time of which we speak, Maloney was in the early stages of a career that was in the next year or two to be marked by excessive vigor in the courtroom. In *United States* v. *Dubrin,** Augustus Hand said that Maloney "made some statements not justified by the record, and at times did not show proper self-restraint." But the court felt that his "ebullitions" resulted in no prejudice to the defendant because of the curative measures effected by the trial judge, John Knox.

In *U.S.* v. *Buckner,*† in which Maloney's alleged prosecutional excesses were again a substantial point on appeal, Judge Clark wrote:

> All defendants . . . complain of the spectacular and prejudicial manner in which he managed the trial as a whole, and also attack particular instances of misbehavior. . . . Even from the printed record we can see the vigor with which the prosecutor pressed the case, vigor which at times went beyond the canons of decorum and dignity which an officer of the United States should observe. The prosecutor was not averse to indulging his talent for spectacle: chorus girls and movie stars were paraded to the stand to prove only minor portions of the Government's case. Theatrical demonstrations, however diverting to the spectators and jury, have no place in a United States court room. Nor was the intemperance of several attacks made upon defendants and their counsel in keeping with the Supreme Court's reminder that the prosecutor is to regard himself as "the servant of the law." We cannot approve such conduct.

But again, the vigilance of the trial judge preserved the integrity of the trial.

---

*93 F. 2d 499, 505 (1939).
†108 F. 2d 921 (1940).

In *U.S.* v. *Viereck,* Maloney's enthusiasm drew a sharp rebuke from Chief Justice Stone. He wrote:

> As the case must be remanded to the district court for further proceedings, we direct attention to conduct of the prosecuting attorney which we think prejudiced petitioner's right to a fair trial. . . . In his closing remarks to the jury he indulged in an appeal wholly irrelevant to any facts or issues in the case, the purpose and effect of which could only have been to arouse passion and prejudice. . . .
>
> At a time when passion and prejudice are heightened by emotions stirred by our participation in a great war, we do not doubt that these remarks addressed to the jury were highly prejudicial, and that they were offensive to the dignity and good order with which all proceedings in court should be conducted. We think that the trial judge should have stopped counsel's discourse without waiting for an objection.*

These quotations give some idea of the fervor with which Maloney stalked his prey.

Plainly, Kaufman's nomination of Maloney to be the instrument of McMahon's vengeance was a shrewd one. But remember his *caveat:* "If you want to make it stick, you must have a strong judge." Graham and McKay had become the puppets of fate: *"Fata viam invenient,"* says Vergil. McMahon found his "strong judge" in the person of Willis B. Van Devanter, who had just retired from the U.S. Supreme Court. Just how McMahon managed to get Van Devanter assigned is not quite clear. One of his aides has told this writer that McMahon made a pilgrimage to the Supreme Court and induced the Chief Justice to designate Van Devanter under the provisions of a statute

---

*318 U.S. 236 (1943), pp.247–48.

that made retired Supreme Court justices available for duty in the district courts.

Van Devanter was born in 1859. At thirty he became Chief Justice of the Wyoming Supreme Court. Theodore Roosevelt named him to the Eighth Circuit Court of Appeals in 1903, and Taft appointed him to the Supreme Court in 1910. On the Court he became a constitutional fundamentalist. With Butler, McReynolds and Sutherland, he was a member of the reactionary bloc that goaded Franklin Roosevelt into the abortive court-packing experiment in 1937. His production on the court slowed to one or two opinions a year, but he clung to his post, despite failing health and personal tragedy, because he believed himself to be part of the dam that contained the anarchic flood of New Deal reforms. He resigned from the Court just in time to join Maloney as the second member of McMahon's *posse comitatus*. Cold, humorless, a fanatical reactionary, he was the "strong judge" that McMahon needed.

The third Graham-McKay trial began on January 24, 1938. We are told that the jury-selection process was one of fastidious precision, and the jury was immured from any such influences as may have affected the first two trials. Crucial to the case against Graham and McKay was the testimony of one Moore, a professional swindler whose evidence was needed to connect them with the grand hoax. Though there was some independent evidence to link Graham and McKay with the scheme, in the two previous trials the strongest nexus had been Moore's testimony.

Now, in the climactic trial, Moore's memory began to falter, and Maloney's efforts to "refresh" his memory by references to the two previous trials were unavailing. Moore resisted the process of refreshment. Maloney advised Judge Van Devanter, "The witness's refusal takes the prosecution by surprise." With Van Devanter's support, Maloney took Moore through every question and answer from the two previous trials, all in the presence of the jury. Objections were overruled. The witness then sought refuge in the allegation that his testimony about Graham and McKay in the two previous trials had been false—that "the government had previously resorted to subornation of perjury in its prior attempts to convict Graham and McKay and was still persisting in that attempt." This was strong stuff, and Van Devanter allowed the prosecutor to cross-examine Moore extensively, in the presence of the jury, as to every circumstance of this alleged subornation. The screaming objections of defense counsel were silenced with cold scorn.

As the testimony developed, it became clear that before being called to the stand, Moore had told Maloney that he had testified falsely before and would not repeat his false testimony in this trial; thus Maloney's claims of surprise were disingenuous. But the trial judge professed that although the impeachment of one's own witness normally involves only credibility and should not be treated as affirmative proof of fact for any purpose, this was a very different stew. With the issue of subornation of perjury raised, he said the evidence elicited was something more than impeachment. Maloney was permitted to show that Moore, *his own witness,* had been convicted half a dozen times of robbery, swindling, even pimping.

When Maloney and Van Devanter were finished with Moore, the jury was convinced that Moore had testified truthfully in the first two trials, that the defendants had a hand in his recantation, and that the story about subornation was pure fiction. Worst—or best—of all, in the process, the witness's recanted testimony in the prior trials had been repeated at length. The effect on the defendants was catastrophic, and their fate was sealed. Van Devanter delivered a strong "government" charge to the jury—which means he practically instructed the jury to convict. Let us say that this was a no-nonsense trial, which under the direction of Van Devanter's pioneer mind came close to that of *The Ox-Bow Incident.*

The verdict was "guilty," on February 12, 1938. On February 17 the two defendants were sentenced to nine years and $11,000 each in fines. (The five-day delay, according to the docket entries, resulted from an "indisposition" on the part of Judge Van Devanter. I would not want my readers to think that he needed a probation report or any such ornamental trumpery.)

The conviction was affirmed on March 6, 1939,* and Graham and McKay passed into the federal correctional system and thence out of history. Had McMahon stayed in Washington, or even delayed his western trip a few weeks, their little empire in the Rockies would have remained undisturbed.

---

*U.S. v. *Graham*, 102 F. 2d 436 (1939); certiorari denied, 307 U.S. 643. There is a poignant note at the end of the opinion in the Court of Appeals: "This decision has been made without the concurrence of Judge Manton, who sat at the argument, but resigned before the opinion was written." Graham and McKay must have encountered the equally ill-fated Manton in Lewisburg. As you will learn, he arrived there soon after.

11

THE LAWYER WHO
FELL FROM THE EAVES

In 1940 Jack Gruber, still only in his early forties, was on the threshold of a new and glittering career at the bar. Already he had two significant professional accomplishments behind him. He had served as a Deputy Assistant Attorney General in the Department of Law of the State of New York, where he had made a considerable reputation in detecting and prosecuting wrongdoers in the securities business. This was during the freebooting days when there was no SEC, "boiler shops" flourished, and widows and orphans needed the protection of the state against unscrupulous stock swindlers who diddled the unwary into exchanging their heritage for worthless stocks. In the pursuit of these scamps, Gruber was a zealous hound of the law.

With the advent of the federal securities laws as part of the New Deal, in 1933 and 1934, vigorous young men were needed to carry out on the national scene what Gruber had been doing so effectively for New York's Attorney Gen-

eral. Gruber was among the first recruited by the newborn
Securities and Exchange Commission to enforce its salu-
tary policies. Now he added a second row to his campaign
ribbons. He was bright, quick, and effective, and he was
entrusted with the investigation and prosecution of some
of the first important enforcement cases at the new agency,
where he worked under the tutelage of such men as Joseph
P. Kennedy, Ferdinand Pecora, William O. Douglas, and
James Landis. His talents and accomplishments brought
him considerable public and professional recognition. By
1940 he was ready to leave government service for private
practice in securities law. There were so few lawyers at
that time with his special skills and experience that his
successful future seemed assured. When Gruber resigned
from the SEC, William O. Douglas, then chairman of the
agency and soon to be a Justice of the U.S. Supreme Court,
deplored Gruber's departure, extolled his high qualities,
and moaned, "I hate to see you leave our service."

Gruber opened a small, luxuriously appointed office on
Wall Street, and the clients came quickly. Among them
were two brothers from Chicago felicitously named Smart.
The brothers Smart were widely known in financial and
publishing circles as the principal entrepreneurs of two
magazines, *Esquire* and *Coronet*. In the middle of the Depression, these dynamic men had forced their way into an
industry dominated by such giants as *Time* and *Life*, *Look*
and *The Saturday Evening Post*. By 1940 their magazines had
acceptance and success.

But whereas their rise in the publishing world drew to
them subscribers and advertisers in profusion, it also attracted the attention of the SEC's enforcement staff. It was
suspected by SEC officials that in their ascent to success
and wealth in the publishing world, the brothers Smart had
failed to touch some bases. It was thought that they had

effected illegal sales of their company's securities. Specifically, there was suspicion that they had engaged in public sales of stock without compliance with the registration requirements of Section 5 of the Securities Act of 1933, which required that any person making a public offering of securities must first register with the SEC and furnish a detailed registration statement to purchasers.

An investigation was ordered. In overall command was Chester Lane, then General Counsel of the SEC. Lane was a perfect example of the legal zealots of the New Deal. He devoted himself to the contemporary passion for smiting the Philistines of the old order, hip, thigh, and pocketbook. His sense of ethics was derived from John Calvin.* Lane supervised the activities of both the New York and Chicago regional offices of the SEC in the commission's investigation of the Smarts. In the New York office, the supervising officer was Peter Byrne; in Chicago, Earl Edden was in charge. All three men spoke regularly on the phone about the case. Byrne and Edden were known for selfless and efficient dedication to their task; they both had worked with Gruber in the agency and were said to have a distaste for Gruber's arrogance, obstinacy, and flamboyance. They were also suspicious of his methods.

In the New York regional office, the telephone traffic was handled by the chief operator, Elizabeth Miller, a cheerful, vivacious lady who was a great favorite of the young lawyers in the office. She had spent her whole business life in the service of the government—first at the State Department and then at the SEC, where she had been friendly with Gruber. They were nothing more than office friends who exchanged smiles, greetings, and pleasantries;

---

*Lane was a close friend and associate of Alger Hiss. After he left the SEC, he played a leading part in Hiss' trials and appeals.

but the dynamic, virile Gruber had touched a soft spot in the romantic heart of Elizabeth Miller. She had voiced her admiration of the handsome, witty, and scintillating young lawyer so often that her fellow-workers teased her about him.

As the investigation into the *Esquire-Coronet* matter became intensive and somewhat dangerous to the brothers Smart, they resolved to retain the services of an expert. Who was better qualified in this field than the erstwhile hound of the securities law, Jack Gruber? He became their chief counsel, and before long he was engaged in acrimonious contention with Messrs. Lane, Byrne, and Edden. Gruber defended his clients with the same élan that had characterized his work as a prosecutor. He stoutly maintained that the Smarts, his clients, were being persecuted by the SEC people. The basic controversy between Gruber and the SEC officers seemed to have been whether their conduct justified criminal prosecution. Gruber, of course, was urging a resolution of the case by nonpenal techniques; Byrne or Edden (or both) appeared to be inclined toward recommending the more severe penalties.

The matter became extremely serious for the Smarts when the government began presenting a case against them to a grand jury in Chicago. But Gruber kept presenting evidence and arguments designed to convince the SEC staff that they should follow the high road of a civil case, not a criminal one, and he was understandably curious to learn how they were reacting to the arguments he was making. At several meetings in the New York offices, Gruber not only assailed Lane, Byrne, and Edden for scarifying his blameless clients; he also let drop some remarks that suggested he knew as much about the SEC's case as did the agency's own lawyers. He seemed to know what witnesses the SEC was going to call in the presumably secret grand-jury proceeding in Chicago and what they were going to testify to.

"By gosh," said Mr. Lane to Mr. Byrne one day, after one such meeting with Gruber. "This guy talks as if he had been listening in our telephone conversations."

When it happened again, Mr. Byrne said to Mr. Lane, "Remember what you said the other day about Gruber listening in on our phone calls? It occurs to me that he was always pretty palsy-walsy with our telephone operator. Maybe he *is* listening in."

Lane was a gentlemanly and courteous lawyer, reared in the most fastidious Ivy League traditions. Electronic eavesdropping was not widely practiced in his circles. His patrician instincts were revolted by the thought that a member of the bar should resort to such undignified snooping. But he had no great respect for Gruber, whose plebeian pragmatism had been offensive to him when the two men had worked together in the SEC, and he had an odd questing trait in him. Lane pondered Byrne's half-jocular remark and he went to the FBI. He told them of his suspicions, and those resourceful gentle-men took steps to ascertain whether Gruber, with Miss Miller's aid, was indeed enjoying the conversations among the SEC investigators. They installed in the wall behind Miss Miller's switchboard a wide-lens slow-motion camera capable of recording the mechanical steps necessary to effect the telephone connections be-tween the duly authorized parties in New York, Chi-cago, and Washington and the office of Gruber. A few test conversations were set up.

Before long, the sleuths reported enough to Lane to send him flying to the office of the U.S. Attorney in the Southern District. There, Lane was informed that an unused but vital provision of the Federal Communications Act* made it a crime for an unauthorized person to "intercept" an interstate telephone conversation. The statute had never been invoked in a criminal prosecution—but why not? A grand-jury inquiry was set in motion.

Up to this point, the story has little to recommend it to a connoisseur of Foley Square ghost stories. Many lawyers have come to grief in that place. Compared to Judge Manton or Alger Hiss or Jim Landis, Gruber is a minor ghost. Up to the moment when he is summoned to the grand jury, his case is not really noteworthy. Though his conduct is certainly unwise and censurable, it hardly rises to the level of career-destroying criminality. But now, when he hears of the grand-jury investigation, Gruber puts his head down in a bull-like rush to self-destruction.

Consider Gruber's position. He was an able and resourceful lawyer. As Henry Hallam once said of Bacon, he was "possessed of adroitness and incomparable ductility." Whatever he had gained from exploiting his relationship with Miss Miller was patently trivial and ephemeral. It is doubtful that any substantial tactical or litigative advantage could have come from snooping on the conversations among the SEC functionaries. True, he was understandably curious as to which way the SEC pendulum was swinging in the case against the Smarts. But then, it is part of the lawyer's daily life to wonder what decisions are coming out of the courts or administrative agencies. It is part of our schooling to learn how to wait, to restrain our anxiety. There is more waiting in litigation than in the infantry. We all know that the decisions for which we pant as the hart

---

*Federal Communications Act of 1934; U.S. Code, Title 47, Section 605 (as the statute then stood).

for the stream are lying in draft on some judge's desk or in some bureaucrat's file drawer. But we wait. We do not burgle the judge's chambers or rifle the bureaucrat's file cabinet just to discover what will be made known in due time. There is no value in advance information; even when there is a leak, no lawyer would dare to act on it.

Gruber received a subpoena to appear and testify before the grand jury in Foley Square. Miss Miller had already been interrogated and had denied everything. Gruber's secretary had also been questioned, and she professed to know nothing of the clandestine participation in the official calls. Byrne, Edden, and Lane had also testified to the conversations with Gruber that had aroused their suspicions. But they proved nothing; his apparent familiarity with their views could have derived from his experience and sagacity. Prescience is a virtue, not a crime. The "case" needed something—and Gruber, in his blind folly, supplied it.

Gruber, it appears, had these choices:

1. He could appear before the grand jury and claim his constitutional privilege against self-incrimination. The overwhelming probabilities were that with the two ladies professing to know nothing of the calls, it would have been almost impossible to prosecute him successfully on any criminal charge. Since there was no wiretap, there was no proof that the calls had actually come to him. The *prima facie* case was very fragile.

2. He could appear before the grand jury and tell what seemed to be the truth: that he had listened in on the calls. There is no way to tell, but a penitent Gruber, admitting his guilt, might have been able to get off with some kind of disciplinary action.

3. He could appear and deny the entire story. In this

case, he would be adding the serious offense of perjury before the grand jury to his other comparatively less serious misconduct. Before electing this course, he should have foreseen that if Miss Miller finally admitted making the connections, he was lost. Her corroboration of the autoptic proof of the FBI would make the defense of his position virtually hopeless.

After Gruber received the subpoena, he consulted several wise and experienced lawyers; from them he received sage and useful advice. The substance was that he should either (1) go to Chester Lane, admit the truth, and work out sanctions short of professional extinction, or (2) refuse to testify, keep his mouth shut, admit nothing, and fight out the charges (if any) in court. Any middle course would lead to disaster.

My first sight of Gruber came when I was called into Sam Kaufman's office in the spring of 1940. Gruber was there, accompanied by two men who later became my good friends: Frank Meehan and Gordon Poole. They were not lawyers but rather stock-market technicians who had worked with Gruber at the SEC and had resigned from the agency to become private advisers to Wall Street brokerage firms in matters of compliance with SEC requirements. Both were men of great experience and sagacity. It was immediately plain that they, as Gruber's friends, were counseling him to follow the first course. Sam and I listened. We agreed with Meehan and Poole. We also advised that if Gruber did not follow their judgment, he should stand on his constitutional rights and remain silent. But Gruber was obstinate. He had devised a third course that left him naked to his enemies. He could not bring himself to tell the tale as it happened, and he scornfully rejected the course of invoking his rights against self-incrimination by refusing to testify. In his distorted view, a lawyer of his stature could not afford this latter approach.

Instead, he went to the grand jury and gave them a narrative, the gist of which was that poor Miss Miller had indeed *offered* to make him privy to the calls, but that he had disdained to use her proferred help.

When the luckless telephone operator learned that Galahad had thus incriminated her, loyalty and affection evaporated. She changed her story. She admitted that at his request, she had twice cut him in on calls between the New York and Chicago offices of the SEC by using the "conference" setup. She said that though she herself had not listened in, she had connected Gruber's office with the Chicago calls and told him to "keep quiet." For her services she had received nothing but a smile from her former hero.

Gruber got no smiles from the government. He was promptly indicted, along with Miss Miller and his own secretary. The indictment charged Gruber with conspiracy to (1) "defraud the United States of the distinterested services of its employee"; (2) "defraud the United States of money" by making long-distance calls for the benefit of Gruber, which were charged by Elizabeth Miller and paid for by the Securities and Exchange Commission; (3) "violate the wire tapping section of the Federal Communications Act." The indictment also charged Gruber with "the substantive offense of aiding and abetting Elizabeth Miller in intercepting interstate telephone communications."

When the indictment was handed down, it attracted considerable attention, not only because of Gruber's prominence but also because it was the first time in history that there had been a criminal prosecution for intercepting an interstate communication—i.e., "wiretapping"—under the Federal Communications Act.

Gruber went to trial in the Southern District in May 1941 before Judge Robert A. Inch and a jury. (Judge Inch usually sat in Brooklyn, in the Eastern District, and was assigned to the case because there was no member of the Southern District bench before whom Gruber had not appeared as a lawyer. There was a need for objectivity.)

Sam Kaufman tried the case for Gruber, and I assisted him. The government witnesses told their tale. Miss Miller tearfully told hers.

We sat in the courtroom and watched Gruber's shining world dissolve. If he had any chance at all, it evaporated when he insisted on taking the witness stand and exhibiting those qualities of wrongheaded obstinacy that had brought him to his ordeal. Kaufman did his best for Gruber, but there was no hope. Gruber's personality, exhibited on the stand, was the most compelling proof of how he had cajoled the hapless little telephone operator into folly. The jury rejected his story and found him guilty on all counts.

The case against his secretary was dismissed by the judge, and Miss Miller, who pleaded guilty, was given a suspended sentence. Gruber was sentenced to serve a year and a day in a federal penitentiary and to pay a fine of $1,000; the service of the sentence was deferred pending appeal.

Characteristically, Gruber argued his own case in the Second Circuit Court of Appeals. To no avail. On the eve of Pearl Harbor, that court affirmed his conviction. Augustus Hand (with Learned Hand and Swan concurring) wrote Gruber's professional obituary:

> The evidence adduced on the part of the government was ample to justify the charge that Gruber induced Miss Miller to connect his office telephone by means

of what is known as the conference system with calls from one Earl Edden, an employee of the SEC in Chicago, who was calling the latter's superior, Byrne, in New York.*

And in December 1941, as America went to war, Gruber went to the penitentiary at Danbury.

There is a heartrending irony in Gruber's fall. His fault was not avarice but arrogance. Success had not come easily; he had fought hard and ably for every step up the professional ladder. And he was close to the top; he was almost certainly marked for a high place in his profession. Consider then the elemental folly of his fatal slip, the meaningless choice he made to risk career and reputation for the shabby benefit of hearing Edden speak to Byrne. The price was a glittering career in ruins, pride turned to ashes. That a man should risk his career and honor for the possession of knowledge so useless, so trifling, is an ultimate exercise in arrogance. Again it is that old fiend who bedevils the lawyer: hubris.†

If the shade of Jack Gruber still stalks Foley Square, it must be accompanied by another ghost—the wraith of the man who was the uncrowned king of the federal court. Martin Manton fell from an eminence far loftier than Gruber's. His descent from grace shook the foundations of our judicial system. I was drawn to recount Manton's story

---

*U.S. v. Gruber, 123 F. 2d, 307, 308.
†There is a footnote to Gruber's fall that is of interest to lawyers of our own time. In 1941 the state of the law in New York was that a lawyer convicted of a felony was automatically disbarred in New York State. But if the conviction was for a felony under federal law that did not constitute a crime under New York law, as in Gruber's case, disbarment was *not* automatic. In the normal order of things the facts were considered by the state courts and disciplinary action followed. For some reason, the facts in Gruber's case were not pursued by the state authorities. Though he was disbarred in the federal courts, he was able to come back to New York and practice law.

when I realized that his name and his tragedy are unknown to the lawyers of today, for when his name is mentioned to some of my younger associates, their faces are blank. When I tell them that there was once a Chief Judge in the Second Circuit who went to prison for judicial corruption, they are incredulous.

12

A KING DIES:
THE FALL OF MARTIN MANTON

I have written elsewhere in this book about the standing and reputation of the Southern District and the Second Circuit. They are among the top courts in the land, and New York lawyers are justifiably proud of their quality. For decades, many lawyers and legal scholars have regarded the Court of Appeals for the Second Circuit as "the most distinguished and admired Bench in the United States."* Today it is almost forgotten that this renowned court was once the setting for the public disgrace of its presiding judge. In the long run, not even this catastrophe would spoil the majesty of the institution. Under the leadership of Martin Manton's successors, Learned Hand, Edward Lumbard, Henry J. Friendly, and Irving R. Kauf-

*Karl Llewellyn, *The Common Law Tradition* (Boston: Little, Brown & Co., 1960), p. 48. The senior judge in the Second Circuit was called "the tenth highest in the Federal judiciary . . . second only to the nine members of the Supreme Court" (*The New York Times*, November 18, 1946).

man, the Second Circuit has attained such stature that the
memory of its only rogue has been all but extinguished.

Oddly, the tragic revelations about Martin Manton came
at a time when the court was at one of its periodic zeniths
of judicial quality. When Manton fell, in 1939, his colleagues on that bench included some of the most revered
deities in our legal pantheon: Learned Hand and Augustus
Hand, the famous cousins whose names are spoken with
awe by every American lawyer; Thomas Swan, who came
to the court from the deanship of the Yale Law School,
heavy with academic honor; and Harrie Chase, a respected
legal scholar from Vermont, who, once removed from
Manton's baneful influence, showed he was far above average.

When the revelation of Manton's corruption came, it
seemed strange that it had taken so long to unmask him. So
widespread and flagrant were his indiscretions and importunities that it was said that scores of New York lawyers
knew, or should have known, of his venality.* In the 1930s

---

*Every student of judicial improbity is indebted to Joseph Borkin's
incisive book *The Corrupt Judge* (New York: Clarkson N. Potter, 1962).
In his able exposition of the facts that led to Manton's fall, Mr. Borkin
speculates: "In view of the facts later developed at the trial, the press
which covered the Federal Courthouse and the bar which practiced
there, Manton's colleagues on the bench would have been extremely
myopic not to have noticed the strange assortment of questionable characters who were frequently seen in Manton's company. More than that,
these curious figures were constant visitors to his chambers and seemed
to have free run of the place."

I think this is more rhetoric than history. If the passage is intended
to convey that such men as the Hands or Swan really knew of Manton's
obliquity, I must reject it. Manton's associates were, in the main, people
of apparent respectability; until the disclosures of his trial, they were
thought to be respectable. As for the few known scamps, they could be
in a judge's chambers on perfectly legitimate business. How could
Augustus Hand know *who* was in Manton's private chambers, or why
he was there?

there *was* much resentment of Manton among members of the New York bar—angry muttering about his arrogance, his high-handed treatment of lawyers and other judges. But he was not the only judge who acted as if he were an organ of divine emanation. Lawyers' complaints against these self-anointed avatars are usually futile. There was no attack on Manton's integrity. If the lawyers of the time were unconscious participants in a conspiracy of grudging silence, it is understandable and forgivable. Attacks draw reprisals. When you shoot at a king, don't miss. Undoubtedly, there were many portents that might have led to earlier disclosure, but Manton's aura was majestic, and though many resented his arrogance, apparently no one wanted to believe that "the Chief"* was a crook.

Of course, when the story of his crimes came out, there were a number of self-appointed oracles who claimed they knew it all the time. I doubt that there were many who knew about Manton's corruption for years. Sam Kaufman learned in 1937 that Manton was a crook, but all he could do was to remove himself from the danger of contamination.

In 1934 the firm of Kaufman Weitzner & Celler was appointed as co-counsel with Thomas Cradock Hughes to the two trustees of the Prudence Corporation in a reorganization proceeding in the federal court in Brooklyn. Prudence was an enormous company engaged in selling participation certificates in real-estate mortgages to the public. Its securities were regarded as gilt-edged and were eagerly sought by widows, orphans, fiduciaries, and charities.

---

*Like his predecessors and successors, Manton was called "Chief," or "Chief Judge." Until 1948 the correct title was "Senior Circuit Judge." This was changed to "Chief Judge" in 1948 when the "Circuit Courts of Appeal" became "Courts of Appeal."

When the company collapsed, early in the Great Depression, a piteous lament arose from the victims. Even in its extremity, the Prudence empire included office buildings, apartment houses, theaters, hotels, golf and country clubs —all worth hundreds of millions of dollars. New York State's Superintendent of Banking, George W. Egbert, promptly took over the task of managing the floundering corporate giant. In the ordinary course, that official would have controlled the company's reorganization or liquidation under the laws of New York. But some events followed whose origin is shrouded in mystery. In the light of what we now know about Manton's *modus operandi*, and given a few incontrovertible facts, I believe I know how the Prudence Company came into the federal courts and how its rich opportunities for patronage and leverage fell into Manton's hands. I believe it was planned by Manton, and when the plan worked, it gave him both valuable patronage and the means to extort money for his bankrupt personal empire.

Plainly, as long as the Prudence Company was in the hands of New York's Superintendent of Banking, it did no good for the personal cause of Martin Manton. Only if it passed into the jurisdiction of the *federal* courts, his special domain, could he get any benefits. Manton's quick eye must have assessed this. The officers and directors, the "management" who had led Prudence into collapse, could expect neither mercy nor emolument from the New York Superintendent. To them, he represented grief and retribution. Either they came to Manton, through one of his bagmen, or he sent for them. They arranged for a friendly creditor, the American Brake Shoe Company, to file a petition for reorganization under Section 77-B of the Federal Bankruptcy Law with Judge Grover Cleveland Moscowitz in the federal court in Brooklyn; the petition was approved by

Moscowitz, who appointed two trustees to supersede the Superintendent in operating the company. Of course, the Superintendent contested this assumption of federal juris- diction, but Moscowitz rejected the challenge, and on ap- peal to the Second Circuit he was sustained by that court, led by (who else?) Martin Manton.*

One of the two trustees appointed to command of the vast Prudence Empire was John McGrath, a vice-president of the Sterling National Bank, later unmasked as one of Manton's principal minions. In 1939 Manton admitted under oath that it was *he* who had suggested the appoint- ment of McGrath to Moscowitz. The other trustee was William T. Cowin, a close personal friend of Moscowitz'.†

Once appointed, McGrath installed, in a private office adjoining his own in the Prudence Company, one Bill Fal- lon, the most ubiquitous of Manton's familiars. Fallon had no official job with Prudence; he functioned as McGrath's adjutant—and Manton's ambassador.

In any corporate reorganization, the most lucrative pa- tronage is the appointment of counsel to the trustees. As I have said, Moscowitz appointed Thomas Cradock Hughes, of Brooklyn, and Kaufman Weitzner & Celler, my employ- ers, as co-counsel to the trustees. I know nothing about the selection of Hughes; it may have been in recognition of his enormous scholarship in the field of bankruptcy and reor- ganization. I doubt it. I believe he, like McGrath, was "sug- gested" to Moscowitz by Manton.

As to the origin of the appointment of Kaufman Weitzner & Celler, that was explained to me later by Sam

---

*79 F. 2d 77.
†Cowin was unscathed by the scandals that engulfed McGrath. He went on to a long and illustrious career as a lawyer and State Supreme Court judge in Brooklyn.

Kaufman. In 1929 Judge Moscowitz had been charged with improprieties in appointing his former law partners to rewarding bankruptcy positions. The matter was under study by the Judiciary Committee of the House of Representatives, of which Mannie Celler was an important member. According to Kaufman, the committee was then considering impeachment charges against a federal district judge in the Southwest; the Republican members of the committee were hot for the blood of the Westerner, a Democrat and a Baptist; the Democrats were equally hungry for the head of Moscowitz, a Republican and the first Jewish federal judge in Brooklyn, a huge Jewish community. Celler, although a Democrat, led the support for his fellow Brooklynite. The committee traded off the errant Baptist for the Brooklyn Israelite. *Neither* was impeached. Moscowitz was cleared,* and he was greatly indebted to Celler. Kaufman said that our firm's appointment by Moscowitz was in somewhat belated gratitude for Celler's support of Moscowitz in 1929.

At any rate, to return to the question of how much of Manton's venality was known to lawyers before his unmasking, this Prudence matter is the background to my meager personal knowledge of the situation.

After the Solitario case, my future in the Department of Justice was, shall we say, clouded. But Sam Kaufman had kept his promise, and as soon as Solitario was safely in the clink, early in 1937, he took me back as an associate in Kaufman Weitzner & Celler.

Shortly after my return, I assisted Kaufman in a criminal

---

*But not without sharp criticism by the committee, which deplored his judicial practices. Two Congressmen voted to impeach Moscowitz, one of them his fellow Republican from New York, Fiorello La-Guardia, who never was strong on party loyalty.

case in the Southern District. One afternoon, as the trial proceeded before Judge John Clancy and a jury, Manton's secretary, Marie Schmalz, came into the courtroom and whispered a few words into Kaufman's ear. Kaufman nodded affably. When we recessed for the day, he told me that Judge Manton wanted to see him in chambers "about some Prudence matter." I should explain here that although Weitzner and various associates in the firm had been heavily occupied with the affairs of Prudence, Kaufman took little part in its reorganization. I accompanied Kaufman to the Chief's sanctum. Manton came out to the anteroom and greeted Kaufman with a great show of affability. The two men disappeared behind doors. I sat waiting. When Kaufman reappeared in the anteroom, all traces of amiability had vanished. He was grim and tight-lipped; he said nothing, but motioned me to follow him. When we were settled in the back seat of his limousine, there was none of the usual friendly discussion of the courtroom happenings that came at the end of each day. Sam was tense and preoccupied; as we neared Wall Street, the silence embarrassed me. I made some fatuous remark about the obvious regard with which he had been received by Manton. Kaufman glared at me; the words seemed to explode out of him. "He's a thief!" he said. "He just asked me to 'lend' him fifty thousand dollars. We have two Prudence appeals that are coming before him. Both are important; we should win both of them. Of course, I turned him down. Now, God knows what will happen!"*

---

*Certainly some things happened. There were in fact *four* appeals pending in Manton's court affecting the Prudence Company. All of them were decided by panels over which Manton presided, by opinions that Manton wrote. See *In re Prudence Company*, 88 F. 2d 628, 89 F. 2d 689, 90 F. 2d 587; and *Brooklyn Trust* v. *Prudence*, 92 F. 2d 419. Just about this time, Celler resigned from the Kaufman firm and became a partner in

For a decade there had been premonitions that all was
not well with the federal bench in the Second Circuit. Even
the hallowed Southern District, staffed at the time with one
of the most respected panels of district judges ever assembled, was the scene of a scandal. District Judge Francis A.
Winslow was attacked for improprieties in bankruptcy and
receivership matters. A grand jury issued a presentment
that he was guilty of "indiscretions," and the matter went
to the House Judiciary Committee to consider impeachment charges. Winslow obliged everybody by resigning
from the bench. But this resignation, in circumstances that
were widely construed as an acknowledgment of culpabil-
ity, led to some substantial modifications in bankruptcy
and receivership practices in the Second Circuit. These
changes were to become germane to that ultimate in judicial scandals, the fall of Martin Manton.

Before it happened, there were rumblings of dissatisfac-
tion with still another judge in the Second Circuit, Edwin
S. Thomas, district judge in Connecticut. It was not known
at the time that Thomas had become Manton's creature,
and that in his judicial transgressions he was responding to
the Chief's machinations. Indeed, Thomas had the questionable distinction of being the only other member of the
bench who surrendered himself to Manton's corrosive influence. If lawyers have an occupational hazard, beside gar-
rulity, it is what the Germans call *Schadenfreude*, delight
over the discomfiture of their peers; so, when Dewey
stripped Manton of his disguises, many lawyers anticipated
that his colleagues on the bench would be more than em-

a firm headed by Milton C. Weisman. Weisman's close relationship with
Manton is described later in these pages. Kaufman's firm ceased to
represent the two trustees. Any observation by me as to cause and effect
would be pure speculation.

barrassed. But all of them were cleared of the faintest suspicion. Only Thomas was destroyed after a comic-opera effort to avoid subpoenas, including pell-mell flight to Panama, barricading himself in his New Haven chambers against federal marshals, and, finally, taking refuge in a mental hospital.

Martin Manton's fall was the most momentous judicial disgrace in the Anglo-American judicial system since Francis Bacon was impeached in 1621. Before we come to a consideration of the circumstances, let us examine the man.

Manton's career could have been fashioned by Horatio Alger. He was born in Long Island of Irish immigrant parents. His childhood was marked by poverty, industry, and piety. He worked his way through Columbia Law School at hard menial jobs; after graduation, he established an office in Brooklyn. In 1911 he became the junior partner of W. Bourke Cockran, a distinguished lawyer, one of the most potent figures in New York politics, an important member of the House of Representatives, and a leader of Tammany Hall.* Manton became Cockran's protégé; he also became an expert in admiralty law and in patent law, and was sufficiently skilled in criminal law to be selected as the lawyer for Police Lieutenant Charles Becker in his sensational trial for the murder of the gambler Herman Rosenthal.†

---

*Manton was himself a gifted and forceful speaker, in and out of court. He must have learned much from Cockran, whose gifts of rhetoric were acclaimed by no less an orator than Winston Churchill. Churchill wrote in his memoir, *Amid These Storms,* "In point, in pith, in rotundity, in antithesis and in comprehension, Bourke Cockran's conversation exceeded anything I have ever heard." Cited in James McGurrin, *Bourke Cockran* (New York: Scribner's, 1948), p. 76.

†For a description of Manton's able if unsuccessful labors in the *cause célèbre* that shocked and thrilled New York from 1912 to 1916, the reader

After the Becker case, Manton was highly regarded in legal circles. In 1916, through the influence of Cockran and the redoubtable John McCooey, Democratic czar of Brooklyn, President Wilson appointed Manton to be a district judge in the Southern District. Within two years he was elevated to the Second Circuit Court of Appeals. There, he quickly established a reputation for ability, iron-handed self-confidence, and an arrogant disdain for conventional usages. By 1922 he had been elevated, at the age of thirty-nine, to the chief judgeship of that circuit.

It was not generally known that in his spare time Manton was building a personal real-estate empire that ran into millions. His savings from the practice of law and sums borrowed from friends were used to amass equities in a number of valuable buildings in New York. In 1916 his net worth was at least $1,000,000, and it must have increased during the 1920s. There is no indication that he engaged in any corrupt or illicit activities as he fashioned this personal empire; so long as the buildings were occupied by responsible tenants who generated a copious cash flow, he apparently had no problems. But when the Depression began, in 1929, the cash flow from his tenants began to dry up. It was Manton's need for money to avoid forfeitures and foreclosures in that frightening time that pushed him into the shoddy and corrupt practices that in the end led to his ruin.

In 1922 Manton came close to appointment to the U.S. Supreme Court. Only the determined opposition of Chief Justice Taft and the Judiciary Committee of the City Bar Association prevented the appointment.* Their opposition appears to have been both political and personal. Manton

---

is referred to Andy Logan's delightful book *Against the Evidence*, 1970, pp. 252 *et seq.*
*Marvin Schick, *Learned Hand's Court*, p. 63.

was a Democrat of Irish-Catholic origin; the administration was Republican and conservative, and the members of
the city bar's Judiciary Committee were drawn mostly
from the reactionary nabobs of New York's Wall Street
elitists. Manton was not their type, and their opposition
defeated him. Manton kept trying, but he never came as
near to elevation as in 1922* when he was publicly recognized as the leading candidate.

Concern was expressed about Manton's personal financial problems as early as 1931. When the Bank of United
States collapsed the year before, it was learned that Manton
had been a heavy borrower. At that time he had succeeded in
concealing the extent of the disaster in his huge personal
real-estate enterprise, but now Manton submitted to a voluntary examination with respect to his financial status and
ability to pay his indebtedness to the Bank of United States.
He was treated gently but persistently by Carl J. Austrian, a
well-known lawyer who represented the New York State
Superintendent of Banking, who was in charge of the bank's
liquidation. Austrian's task was to determine if there was
any purpose in trying to collect Manton's debt to the de-
funct bank. To this end, he led Manton through the details
of his financial ruin. What emerged was Manton's depiction
of himself as a decent man who had combined legal and
judicial talent with a flair for business but who, like millions
of others, was flattened by the juggernaut of the Great
Depression. It was a virtuoso performance.

---

*Manton's campaign to gain a seat on the Supreme Court is described
in David J. Danielski's *A Supreme Court Justice Is Appointed*, 1964, pp. 64
et seq. According to that author, Justice Jackson said, "Manton had come
within an ace of being appointed to the Supreme Court at the time of
the appointment of Pierce Butler. I understand that it was only due to
the intervention of Chief Justice Taft that his appointment was prevented." (P. 146.)

The bench, the bar, the newspapers, the public, now knew that the Chief had been pauperized, but in that time, when so many millionaires had become impoverished overnight, he was as much an object of pity as of public concern. Still, it became evident that in his official judicial conduct, Manton was living on the edge of impropriety. His audacity was a subject of general comment, but it was not recognized as a smokescreen for corruption.

Judge Winslow's disgrace in 1929 had resulted in a major reform in bankruptcy practice. The judges of the Southern District adopted a rule under which no personal friends, no political henchmen, no hungry relatives, could be appointed to receiverships in bankruptcy. All such golden patronage went to the Irving Trust Company. Many lawyers and judges resented this rule, some for obvious motives of self-interest, some because they sincerely felt that it undeservedly impugned the integrity of both bench and bar. No one was more outspoken in his disapproval of this monopoly than Manton. He openly attacked the district judges for their action and threatened to disregard the rule.

In 1932 he carried out his threat. The huge theater empire of William Fox, one of the tycoons of the motion-picture industry, had fallen into bankruptcy in the Southern District. Plainly, the receivership of this enterprise was a post of great responsibility—and of rich rewards. In an act of unparalleled judicial arrogance, Manton cast aside the rule of the district judges, which would have given this function to the Irving Trust as a matter of courthouse routine. The Chief appointed *himself* a district judge and, in his capacity as the senior circuit court judge, entered an order directing the district judge (himself!) to take jurisdiction over the Fox bankruptcy. Then, in his capacity as district judge, he appointed two personal cronies as receivers. Soon one of them died; the other "moved down to

Virginia and asked to resign." In their place, in 1934, this judicial Pooh-Bah appointed Milton C. Weisman and Kenneth Steinreich. Five years later, we learned that Weisman's law firm acted as Manton's lawyers in "settling" claims against him, and handled large amounts of cash for him. And we learned that Steinreich had a number of personal transactions with Manton; he obtained loans for Manton and guaranteed some of his debts.

Manton was tireless in milking the Fox receivership. When Fox needed an ancillary (i.e., local) receiver for Fox's New England properties, he arranged for the susceptible Judge Thomas in Connecticut to appoint a man who (as later appeared) paid for the appointment by making a contract to buy one of Manton's insolvent properties at a fancy price.

After the appointment of the Fox receivers, there was an unseemly, undignified, and unprecedented tussle between the district judges and the Chief. Many lawyers are accustomed to view the federal judiciary as an orderly pyramidical hierarchy, in which judges of the circuits are superior in rank to judges of the districts. But certainly in 1932, and perhaps even now, in some instances the district judges regarded themselves as virtually supreme in their own rule-making, including in bankruptcy. Their response to Manton's imperious assumption of power in the Fox case was to revise their rule to restrict applications for bankruptcy receivers to the district judge assigned to bankruptcy matters, "and to no other judge." Manton reacted to this like Charles I to the dictates of his Parliament. He publicly announced his purpose to disregard the new rule, as he had the old. He sneered at the suggestion that a large impersonal banking corporation could effectively administer the affairs of an important publicly owned bankrupt company. In a statement that in retrospect would evoke many horselaughs, he emphasized the need for "personal integrity, honesty, and understanding" in the fulfillment of a receiver's tasks.

But Manton did not confine himself to words. Within months of the promulgation of the new rule, he repeated on an even larger scale the audacity of his action in the Fox case. He arranged that an application for appointment of receivers of the Interborough Rapid Transit Company should be made directly to *him* and not to the district judge presiding over the Bankruptcy Part. In open defiance of the published rule of the district court, he again appointed himself a district judge, and again directed himself to assume jurisdiction over the affairs of Interborough.*

Interborough was no run-of-the-mill bankruptcy. The company owned and operated most of the rapid-transit system in New York City. The continued operation of the subways and elevated lines was vital to millions of people; its cash flow, even at the five-cent fare ("world's longest ride for a nickel"), was stupendous. Manton named as receivers Thomas E. Murray, Jr., and Victor J. Dowling. On the score of personal accomplishments, both men were well qualified. Murray was one of the early exemplars of the successful Irish American who moved from shanty through lace-curtain to the boxwood hedges of Southampton. He was a highly successful engineer and businessman, worthy of the confidence of any judge or court. Dowling's career in the law was parallel to Murray's in industry. He had risen from obscurity to be a State Supreme Court judge, then a judge of the Appellate Division, First Depart-

---

*Manton's interest in the affairs of Interborough dated back to 1928, when he presided over a special statutory court (with Judge Knox and Judge Bondy) to rule on the propriety of a seven-cent subway fare. He wrote an opinion granting the increased fare, but he was reversed in the State Supreme Court and the fare remained at five cents.

ment, and had retired from the bench as Presiding Justice of that respected court. On his form sheet he, too, was a splendid candidate for the receivership of the Interborough. He was also "of counsel" to the law firm of Chadbourne Stanchfield & Levy. And that large and powerful Wall Street establishment was promptly named as attorneys for Interborough in receivership—surely one of the most lucrative pieces of legal patronage in the gift of any court in those years. One of the principal partners in the firm was Louis S. Levy, who, as later events were to prove, was among Manton's principal companions on the descent to Avernus.

In 1932 there was as yet no reason to suspect that the relationship between Manton and Levy was unwholesome or irregular. They had been classmates at the Columbia Law School, where Levy outshone his classmates in personal panache and academic glitter. He was brilliant, well-to-do, personable. The gods had indeed smiled on him. He had even penetrated the *cordon sanitaire* with which the anti-Semites of Wall Street excluded people with names like Levy from their private hunting ground. The relationship formed at Columbia between Manton and Levy was long and close.

To return to Interborough Rapid Transit. . . . Creditors and stockholders of that company attacked the appointment of both receivers and their counsel with ferocity. The appointment of the Chadbourne firm was too audacious even for Manton and Levy to defend, and the firm graciously withdrew. Manton thereupon appointed a Brahmin of Wall Street Brahmins to replace it: Nathan L. Miller, former governor of New York and a senior partner in a substantial Wall Street law firm, became counsel to the receivers. But the attack on Manton's two receivers was not so easily repelled.

An Interborough stockholder challenged the validity of the designation of the receivers in the district court on the ground that Manton had no authority under the bankruptcy rules to make such an appointment. Judge John M. Woolsey, a sturdy pillar of the district bench and one of the authors of the rule, vacated the appointment of Murray and Dowling. The receivers appealed to the Second Circuit, where a panel consisting of Learned Hand, Swan, and Chase unanimously reversed Woolsey, confirmed the validity of Manton's appointments, and reinstated Dowling and Murray. The imbroglio now moved to the U.S. Supreme Court.

The appeal in that court is celebrated not only because of its intrinsic importance but also because of the prominence of the lawyers who appeared before the highest court. The bond holders of Interborough, who assailed Manton's appointment of receivers, were represented by John W. Davis, then at the apex of his reputation as America's leading constitutional lawyer, and by his partner Edwin S. Sunderland. The secured creditors of Interborough were represented by Charles Evans Hughes, Jr., the son of the Chief Justice, which forced his famous father to withdraw from participation in the appeal. Miller, second only to Davis in fame as a constitutional advocate, defended the validity of Manton's appointments.

The Supreme Court affirmed the order of Learned Hand's panel, approving the appointment of the receivers on the narrowest of technical grounds. But its opinion suggested substantial reservations about the wisdom and propriety of Manton's conduct. It threw out some pungent hints that though the receivership could stand, Manton should withdraw from the case. Every lawyer but Manton was impressed by the Court's suggestion. That doughty rascal laughed it off! He laughed off an application to the district judge (himself) to remove him as the judge presiding over the receivership; he laughed off an application for a writ of prohibition filed with the Supreme Court. *L'audace, toujours l'audace!* But when an order issued from the highest court restraining his further actions in the case, the hilarity ended. Manton apparently felt that he had reached the limits of judicial contumely and "voluntarily" withdrew. Chief Justice Hughes appointed Circuit Judge Julian W. Mack to replace Manton in the Interborough case. If we think of Manton as the Bonaparte of the federal judiciary in New York, this episode was the end of his Egyptian adventure. It merits description because Manton's conduct in the case foreshadows his Hundred Days, his Waterloo, and his St. Helena.

Years later, when the full measure of Manton's corruption had become known, we learned that his appointment of Murray, who received hundreds of thousands of dollars as receiver of the Interborough, was more than an act of cronyism. It was thoroughly corrupt. In 1939 it was disclosed that just about the time Manton conferred upon him the plum of the Interborough receivership, Murray had made substantial payments of money to one of Manton's shadow real-estate companies.

To many lawyers the deepest mystery that enshrouds Manton's conduct in the Interborough case is the blindness of his colleagues on the Second Circuit. Were Learned Hand, Augustus Hand, Swan, so indifferent to the appearances of impropriety, the total lack of judicial dignity that glared out at them like a neon sign? Perhaps these fine men, among the wisest and the best our system has ever produced, were so bemused by the technical "rightness" of Manton's self-arrogation of power (as found by the highest court) that they failed to perceive the folly, the indignity, the inevitable disorder, of his position (as also pointed out by the Supreme Court).*

By 1932—to summarize—anybody who read the New York newspapers knew that Manton was immersed in personal business to a point inconsistent with acknowledged standards of judicial conduct. There were public reports of his heavy borrowing from banks, of the calamitous state of his personal fortunes. By 1934 it was public knowledge that he was actually insolvent. Then, in 1937, an SEC investigation of Samuel Ungerleider (a stockbroker who had become notorious in the Teapot Dome scandals of the Harding administration) disclosed that Ungerleider had made huge loans to Manton.† The SEC inquiry touched on relationships between Ungerleider and some underworld characters who were of interest to Thomas E. Dewey, then district attorney of New York County. Wiretaps and informers revealed a connection between Ungerleider and Manton. This stimulated Dewey, who was as avid for signs of corruption as was Torquemada for those of heresy. He instituted a thorough investigation of Manton.

Manton's connection with the notorious Ungerleider was disclosed in the press. *The New York Times* at one point pontificated that such commercial interests as Judge Man-

---

*There is a spurious legend that Manton's colleagues in the Second Circuit not only defended his conduct but testified in his defense. Like most folklore, it is hard to dispel. The facts, as hereinafter described, are quite different.

†Ungerleider was a liquor dealer from Columbus, Ohio, who throve in propinquity to the great and important. When Harding moved from the Senate to the White House, Ungerleider went to Washington and became a stockbroker and source of funds to the President and his cronies. His role in the murky corruption of the Harding administration is described in Francis Russell's *The Shadow of Blooming Grove: Warren G. Harding in His Times* (New York: McGraw Hill, 1968), pp. 260 and passim.

ton's were incompatible with recognized standards of judicial propriety.

Even before Dewey acted, there were public leaks about Manton's troubles. The *World-Telegram* criticized his business activities while on the bench; the Attorney General of the United States revealed that there was an ongoing investigation of Manton's commercial activities. But there was no word of corruption, of venality. The concern was with judicial decorum and appearance.

When word came, it was from a source that at the time seemed almost irrelevant: from Tom Dewey, an elected *state* official. On the morning of January 29, 1939, the front page of *The New York Times* announced that Dewey had written to the chairman of the Judiciary Committee of the House of Representatives, detailing the results of a yearlong investigation into Manton's activities, judicial and extrajudicial.

In 1939 Tom Dewey was already well along the road to the Governor's Mansion in Albany and to the drama of the 1948 presidential election. There has been much speculation as to Dewey's reason for turning the Manton case over to the federal authorities. Certainly the case was a natural for a politically ambitious prosecutor. The conviction of Manton by Dewey would have surpassed his successes in the prosecutions of Lucky Luciano and Jimmy Hines. Dewey's admirers have insisted that his good sense, his special feel for good order, told him that this was a *federal* case, a case that belonged in the courthouse that Manton had defiled. But one of the few surviving participants in the federal prosecution has told me that it was only after Dewey and his enormously resourceful aides found it impossible to devise a case that could withstand jurisdictional attack in the courts of New York that he addressed his letter to the House Judiciary Committee. It matters little;

the unmasking of the Machiavellian Chief was Dewey's accomplishment, and the successful prosecution that followed his disclosures was based in large part on the dogged investigative work of Dewey and his gifted aides.

Dewey's letter to the chairman of the House Judiciary Committee pulled no punches. It declared in blunt terms that the evidence justified consideration of impeachment proceedings against the Chief. Nor was it a shotgun charge; Dewey named names and gave details. His letter was a catalogue of courthouse horrors. He charged Manton with taking bribes and selling his judicial office in a number of cases. Dewey's charges against Manton specified judicial misconduct in *Art Metal Works* v. *Abraham & Straus; Smith* v. *Hall; Schick Dry Shaver* v. *Dictograph Products;* and cases involving the Prudence Company, Kings Brewery, Warner Brothers Pictures, and American Tobacco. A number of individuals were identified as having had illicit relations with Manton: John M. McGrath, William J. Fallon,* John L. Lotsch, Harry M. Warner, and John J. Sullivan. (McGrath, Fallon, Lotsch, and Sullivan were later revealed as Manton's familiars, his bagmen, whose evil presence was smeared over most of his activities.) Also named as confederates were Harry M. Warner (head of the Warner Brothers movie kingdom), Kenneth M. Steinreich, a well-known New York businessman and a nephew of New York's Senator Robert F. Wagner. There were others.

To the lawyers and businessmen of Wall Street and Madison Avenue, the most titillating names in Dewey's roll call

---

*There is an almost unquenchable legend that the Fallon who was one of Manton's procurers was the celebrated William J. Fallon, "the Great Mouthpiece," a noted criminal lawyer of the 1920s. But though they shared the same name and certain traits of appetite and character, they are two different men. Fallon the criminal lawyer died in 1927. I am unaware of any connection between him and his namesake.

of the bodies buried in Manton's private necropolis were those relating to the American Tobacco case, a stockholders' suit in which, it was alleged, Manton had corruptly, for money paid to him in hand, bartered his vote.* American Tobacco was one of the largest companies in the United States, and its chief executive, George Washington Hill, one of the most colorful tycoons of the time. (Hill is widely regarded as the real-life prototype of the despotic, ill-mannered tycoon of the novel *The Hucksters.* Some of his actions in this case are certainly consistent with that character.) The allegations against Manton were larded with intimations of impropriety against Hill himself, against the venerable Albert M. Lasker† (head of American Tobacco's famous advertising agency, Lord & Thomas), and against Paul Hahn, a former partner of the Chadbourne firm. But to the New York bar, the most electrifying of Dewey's accusations concerning Manton's impropriety were those against Louis Levy, also of the Chadbourne firm. In the memory of New York lawyers, no such charges as were directed at Manton had ever been made against a federal judge. No investigation into the conduct of the judiciary had ever reached such heights.

Dewey's evidence was turned over to the office of the U.S. Attorney in the Southern District. John T. Cahill had just been named to that position, to succeed Lamar Hardy, but he had not yet assumed the office. (It is an amusing speculation that but for the Solitario case, Sam Kaufman would have followed Hardy. I think Kaufman would have felt that his experience with Manton in the Prudence reor-

---

*The case was *Rogers* v. *Hill,* 60 F. 2d 109, 289 U.S. 582. The facts, the proceedings, and the tragic *sequelae* are described in the pages to come.
†In the end, Lasker's conduct was not only blameless; he was an innocent victim of the duplicity of the officers of American Tobacco and their lawyers.

ganization would have disqualified him.) Cahill, whose memory is still green in the minds of many New York lawyers, was a gifted trial lawyer, and he applied his gifts to the Manton case with deftness and alacrity. He became famous as a result of the case, and his fame would grow over the next three decades.*

When Dewey's charges became public, the roof of Manton's world began to collapse on him. After a brief discussion with Attorney General Frank Murphy, Manton resigned from the court. Within days Dewey announced that his office would take no further action, leaving Manton's fate to the pursuing furies of the federal system, where, indeed, it belonged. On Murphy's orders Gregory F. Noonan, acting U.S. Attorney in Manhattan, convoked a special grand jury in the federal court in Foley Square, and the parade of witnesses began. Mr. Roosevelt ordered his Attorney General to "investigate *all* efforts to influence the Federal judiciary"; state and federal income-tax authorities began an inquiry into Manton's affairs; FBI agents armed with search warrants "raided" the offices of real-estate agents who had worked with Manton's network of companies; bank records were seized by the ton; John McGrath, Manton's familiar, resigned as trustee in the reorganization of the vast Prudence Company, and Judge Thomas took ship for Panama.

At this point it was discovered that Noonan, acting U.S.

---

*Cahill became one of the leaders of the New York bar in the period 1940–1970. When he resigned from the office of the U.S. Attorney, he became a partner in a leading Wall Street law firm in which he had previously been an associate. When he rejoined it, it was known as Wright Gordon Reindel & Cahill. So many clients sought Cahill's services that before long his name moved from last place to first place on the letterhead. And Boykin C. Wright, who had been senior partner in the firm, moved from first place to a different firm. "The Cahill firm," as it is still called, survives as one of New York's most important.

Attorney in charge of the investigation, somehow "without his consent" was listed as a stockholder in one of Manton's companies. He promptly withdrew from the case, retired as acting U.S. Attorney, and Cahill's entry on his duties as chief houndsman was expedited. Manton retained as his attorney Martin Conboy, Roosevelt's personal friend and his first selection as U.S. Attorney in the Southern District. Conboy was a lawyer of towering prestige in the New York bar. The legal community of New York lapsed into a state of shocked anticipation. Some shook their heads sadly, asking, "How could this happen?" They were matched by those who affirmed, "I've known about this crook for years."

In bridging the gulf of the years, I have had the benefit of the recall of one of the lawyers who assisted Cahill in the Manton prosecution.* He tells me that when Cahill replaced Noonan, the atmosphere in the prosecutor's office was one of suspicion and distrust. Cahill was under great pressure from the White House and the Attorney General to bring the Manton case to a rapid disposition. But at first he was reluctant to draw on the resources of the large staff already ensconced in the U.S. Attorney's office, for he had been shaken by the revelation that Noonan had a close relationship with Manton, and he was suspicious of lawyers who had served under Noonan.† After a careful scrutiny of the staff, Cahill selected his own team for the Manton case from associates in his former law firm. His chief

---

*Robert L. Werner was then a young assistant in the U.S. Attorney's office. He had been appointed by Lamar Hardy and was serving under Noonan when Cahill took over. He was general counsel to RCA until he retired from that distinguished post in 1978.
†There never was the faintest basis for questioning Noonan's integrity. In 1949 Noonan became a judge in the Southern District, where he served for many years with distinction.

assistant was Matthias F. Correa; under him were Silvio J. Mollo and Jerome Doyle. Robert Werner and another assistant U.S. attorney, Frank Gordon, were the backup men for research.

The prosecutors reacted to the pressures of the case by keeping the special grand jury going under full steam. J. Edgar Hoover told *The New York Times* that he had taken personal charge of the agents who were working with Cahill's staff to ferret out the evidence. The process was slightly delayed when Manton went to the hospital for minor surgery, but on March 1, 1939, barely more than a month after the detonation of Dewey's bombshell, Manton was indicted with one George Spector for conspiracy in fixing the decision in *Schick* v. *Dictograph*. Other indictments followed. On April 26 a superseding indictment charged Manton, William J. Fallon, John L. Lotsch, George M. Spector, and Forrest W. Davis in a single count with conspiracy to obstruct justice and to defraud the United States. (Significantly, the indictment did *not* refer to Manton's part in fixing *Rogers* v. *Hill*, the American Tobacco case. As we shall see, there was a reason for this—and there were important consequences.) Fallon, Lotsch, and Davis soon pleaded guilty and aided the prosecution.

The trial of Martin Manton in the federal court in Foley Square is one of the great legal dramas of that era. Because of Manton's relationship with the judges in his own circuit, it was manifestly necessary to have the presiding judge in this case come from foreign parts. Chief Justice Hughes designated W. Calvin Chestnut, a hardbitten judicial martinet from Baltimore. Manton also went to foreign parts for his counsel: on the eve of trial, he replaced the venerable Martin Conboy with John E. Mack, a highly respected lawyer from Poughkeepsie. But the actual trial was conducted for Manton by a team of experienced lawyers from

Philadelphia headed by Benjamin N. Golder. Of course, John Cahill took the lead for the government. His aides included Correa, Mollo, Doyle, Gordon, and Werner.

The trial began on May 22, 1939. An experienced trial lawyer reading the trial record must come away filled with admiration for the skills displayed by Cahill and his aides, for the case against Manton and Spector was constructed with architectural felicity. Essentially, the case was presented as a succession of judicial infamies. Under federal criminal law, as it then stood, bribe givers and bribe takers could not be charged in the same indictment for conspiracy to commit bribery. But Cahill needed the flexibility of the conspiracy statute* to present his tapestry of crimes. His staff ingeniously came up with conspiracy to defraud the government of Manton's honest services as a judge, a novel theory that stood up under appellate review. John L. Lotsch and Forrest Davis gave especially damaging evidence against Manton.

The first of Manton's crooked cases was *Art Metal Works* v. *Abraham & Straus & Evans Case Company.* This civil action had begun in 1932, when Art Metal charged that the famous Brooklyn department store had sold lighters manufactured by Evans that infringed patents it owned. The defense was assumed by Evans. The judge in the Eastern District Court who heard the case decided against Evans, and the defendants thereupon appealed to Manton's court. That court not only affirmed the lower court's decision but held that even another patent had been infringed.† The U.S. Supreme Court denied review.

Reilly, president of Evans, was faced with economic di-

---

*In that time, Title 18, Section 88 of the U.S. Code; now, Title 18, Section 371.
†61 F. 2d 122.

saster. Through a friend, he met Bill Fallon, an intimate of Manton's who served the judge as a procurer of litigants in need of a judicial fix. Reilly paid $10,000 in cash as a down payment to Fallon. Fallon introduced Reilly to Judge Manton and there ensued a jolly social relationship. They lunched together at the Lawyers Club, at the Belle Terre Hotel in Port Jefferson, and at Manton's home; there were parties at the St. Regis and the Waldorf Astoria. They played golf together. Manton devised a virtuoso scheme for relieving Reilly and his company from the threat of doom. As the money flowed from Reilly to Fallon to Manton's near-bankrupt companies, Manton instructed Reilly's lawyers to apply to his court for permission to amend the original answer in the case, to add a new defense, and to return the case to the district court for retrial. The application was granted, as a matter of course, by a panel over which Manton presided. The case was retried before Judge Galston in the Eastern District. Galston had no Fallon in his entourage. He called it straight and found against Evans; promptly, his decision was appealed to the Second Circuit. This time Manton presided over the review panel, and it reversed Galston (with a bitter dissent from Learned Hand). Reilly's company was saved. Lawyers and law-review editors raised eyebrows over this strange outcome, but no one smelled the rat.

But in 1939, after Dewey's letter and just before Manton's resignation from the bench, the fun went out of the relationship. As Mr. Justice Sutherland described the sobering end of the Evans caper:

A day or two before the resignation was to take effect Manton called Reilly on the long-distance telephone and told him he understood that he had Bill (meaning Fallon) on the payroll [of Evans]. Receiving an affirmative reply, Manton said: "That will be very embarrassing for me if found out, because I heard they intend to investigate. Couldn't you pull out those pages?" Reilly answered he knew nothing about bookkeeping and would not know where to begin. Manton repeated that it would be very embarrassing for him, and Reilly responded: "I don't know what to do about it."

After the lapse of a few hours, Reilly had another long-distance telephone talk with Manton, first asking him if it was all right to talk. Manton answered: "I don't think exactly." Manton then asked Reilly for his telephone number and said that he would call him back under another name. Later in the same day, the call was made. In the course of this conversation, Manton spoke of the statute of limitations and said that it would protect them in the Art Metal investigation; that anything that was three years old was outlawed. Manton again spoke of Fallon being carried on the [Evans] payroll, saying that it was a great embarrassment to him and to get rid of the records because of the Art Metal investigation. Manton admitted that telephone conversations between himself and Reilly occurred and that he initiated them, but gave a different version of what was said.

A few days later, Reilly directed the bookkeeper to procure all the records and to destroy them. The bookkeeper destroyed the records of the company up to 1935—cashbooks, ledgers, bills, vouchers and everything with the exception of some papers subsequently discovered and turned over to the Government.*

The second case that Cahill presented in his evidence against Judge Manton was *Smith* v. *Hall,* also a patent-infringement case. Here, again, Fallon was the intermediary. In 1934 the brothers Hall operated a commercial chick

---

*As reported in 107 F. 2d 834, p. 840.

hatchery in Wallingford, Connecticut. A patent-infringement suit was filed against them in the federal court in
Connecticut by one Samuel Smith, alleging that the chick
hatchery used incubators that infringed patents he owned.
The district court found against the defendants, the Halls,
and it seemed inevitable that they would have to pay substantial damages. Almon Hall later testified that his company produced four and a half million chicks then; that the
damages "might have been on the basis of five cents an egg
and might have amounted to as much as a million and a half
dollars." At this price, he was very susceptible to the blandishments of Manton and his team.

Fate brought Hall to Forrest Davis, who led him to Fallon's office at the Prudence Company, on Madison Avenue.* An appeal in his case was pending in the Second
Circuit. Through Fallon, Manton demanded $75,000 as the
price of a reversal. After some haggling more appropriate
to an oriental bazaar than to the federal court, the deal was
struck at $60,000. The depth of the villainy appears from
the trial testimony of the hapless chicken farmer: "Fallon
told me that he would be able, through his friend Judge
Manton, to secure a unanimous decision in our favor at a
cost of $75,000." Hall was understandably dubious about
Fallon's authority to speak for the Chief, but Fallon soon
laid the doubts to rest. In return for a $5,000 advance, he
delivered a promissory note for that amount payable to
Forrest Davis (their mutual friend) and signed "Martin T.

---

*Fallon was a lawyer without an office. When McGrath became a trustee
of Prudence, he provided Fallon with a rent-free room adjoining his own
. suite at the company's main office. For several years, it was a great
convenience for Manton's two familiars to be so closely situated. In the
end, it was a disaster for Fallon, who was convicted in the New York
courts, for commercial bribery; to wit, the sale of services to Prudence
to people who paid him for his access to McGrath.

Manton" (the authenticity of the signature was never questioned). Some of the caginess usually attributed to the peasantry of the Nutmeg State survived Fallon's ministrations, for Hall retained a photostat of the note, and he turned it over to Cahill for use at the trial, where it furnished compelling corroboration of Manton's complicity. Additional "loans" were made via Fallon until Hall had $25,000 invested in the fix. It worked. Manton delivered an opinion in which the Second Circuit reversed the district court.* Hall now paid Fallon an additional $35,000, and Fallon got back his notes (but not the photostat with Manton's signature!).

There is a strange irony in the final outcome of *Smith* v. *Hall*. When Smith appealed to the U.S. Supreme Court to review the case, Hall asked Judge Manton, through Fallon, to find a lawyer to handle the appeal in the highest court. Manton suggested another crony, Thomas G. Haight, of Jersey City, a retired judge of the Court of Appeals for the Third Circuit. Haight must have done a splendid job, for the Supreme Court affirmed Manton's decision. How Haight was rewarded and the character of his relationship with Manton does not appear from the testimony. But Haight testified that the appointment for his first meeting with Hall "had been made either by Judge Manton or Judge Manton's secretary."

John Lotsch was heaven's richest gift to the financially beleaguered Manton. For many years Lotsch was a successful lawyer in Brooklyn who specialized in patent litigation; he was also chairman of the board of directors of the Fort Greene Bank of Brooklyn, a small but apparently flourishing bank on the more modest bank of the East River. Imagine: a corrupt patent lawyer who also ran a bank! In 1935

---

*As reported in 107 F. 2d 834, p. 840.

he represented the unsuccessful defendants in an action for patent infringement brought by the Electric Auto-lite Company against P&D Manufacturing Company and its owners. The suit charged the misuse of patents relating to automobile ignition systems. Lotsch shared the legal work for the defendants with a patent law firm in New York of the highest repute, Kenyon & Kenyon. The case was tried before Judge Robert A. Inch (one of the most respected district judges in the Second Circuit), who found for the plaintiff. Lotsch's clients faced heavy damages. A mutual friend led Lotsch to Fallon in the snuggery provided by McGrath at the Prudence Company. Fallon guided him to Manton's chambers. This was probably a mark of respect for Lotsch's membership in the bar. None of the other pigeons was received in chambers. Lotsch described his first meeting with Manton: "There was a conversation at that time in connection with securing a loan for Judge Manton of $25,000 from the bank [with] which I was connected." When Manton said he was unable to provide collateral, Lotsch hesitated. But Manton was equal to this impediment. "Judge Manton said to me that if I could arrange a loan there would be substantial deposits [in the Fort Greene Bank] made by the Prudence Company and the Fox Company." The loan was made, and the bank's file was sweetened by a terse if wholly untruthful note from Manton:

Gentlemen:

This is to certify that my net worth is upwards of $750,000.

> Yours very truly,
> MARTIN T. MANTON.

Within days the Fort Greene Bank received a deposit of $50,000 from Milton C. Weisman, receiver of Fox Theatres Corporation (appointed by Manton), and $25,000 from the Prudence Company, Debtor in Reorganization, John McGrath Trustee ("recommended" to the appointing judge by Manton).

The appeal of Lotsch's clients was argued before an apellate panel composed of Judges Manton, Swan, and Augustus Hand on June 18, 1935. On July 8 the appellate court reversed Judge Inch's decree. In those intervening two weeks, there occurred one of the most meretricious episodes in the history of any court. It is best described in the words of Lotsch.

> After the argument of the case in the Court of Appeals Mr. Fallon called me and asked me to come over to his office. I came over to his office in the Prudence Building, and he told me that I should arrange to get an additional loan promptly or immediately for Judge Manton, and that there would be a favorable decision, and that he wanted $5,000. I asked him did he want a $5,000 loan. He said no, he didn't want it as a loan. He also told me I should draft the opinion for the Court of Appeals and he would hand it to Judge Manton.
>
> *Q.* And what did you do after Fallon told you to draft the opinion?
>
> *A.* I went down to see Mr. Theodore Kenyon . . . the attorney for the P. & D. and also one of the counsel who argued the case with me in the Court of Appeals. I went down to Mr. Kenyon's office, down on lower Broadway, and had him prepare the draft opinion, which I delivered to Mr. Fallon.
>
> *The Court:* Kenyon prepared a draft opinion for the Circuit Court of Appeals?
>
> *The Witness:* That is what Mr. Fallon asked me to do. . . .

Q. Now, thereafter did you have further conversation with Fallon in regard to the $5,000?

A. Yes, sir, I told Mr. Fallon that I would arrange to get him $5,000 and I paid him $5,000 from a period in July to about the end of September, $4,500 in cash and $500 in check.

*   *   *

Q. Tell us what you told Mr. Kenyon of the law firm of Kenyon & Kenyon when you went down to ask him to get up a draft opinion.

A. I told him I had a talk with William J. Fallon, who was a friend of Judge Manton's, and that he should draft the opinion in the case for me and I would deliver it to Mr. Fallon, and Mr. Fallon said he would take it to Judge Manton.

Q. Now, thereafter—and according to the stipulation the date is July 8th, 1935, your Honor—the C. C. A. rendered a decision in favor of your client, did it not, that is the Circuit Court of Appeals?

A. I would not say it was my client. I was of counsel for defendants. I was not attorney of record in the lower court. I was of counsel with Mr. Kenyon for the defendants.

Q. And the decision of the Circuit Court of Appeals was in favor of the defendants?

A. Was in favor of the defendants.

The Court: Did you say what became of this so-called draft opinion prepared by Mr. Kenyon?

The Witness: I delivered it to Mr. Fallon. I don't know what became of it afterwards. . . .

Q. Well, now, after the decision came down, did you have a further conversation with Colonel Gunther (President of the Ft. Greene Bank) in regard to this further loan for $15,000 to Judge Manton?

A. I did.

Q. Will you tell us that conversation?

A. I told him that I would like to arrange for the additional $15,000 for Judge Manton, which I had discussed with him a couple of months previously.

Q. And was the $15,000 loan made?

A. The $15,000 loan was made. . . .

Q. After the decision?

A. After the decision.

Q. By this time—I am referring to the time of the further loan to Manton of $15,000—had substantial deposits been received by the Fort Greene National Bank from the Federal Court Receivers of the Prudence Company and the Fox Theatres Corporation?

A. There had.

Any doubt about the accuracy of Lotsch's testimony is resolved by the testimony of Kenyon, one of the most highly respected patent lawyers of the time. Kenyon was asked by Cahill:

Q. Did you have a conversation with John L. Lotsch relative to drafting an opinion for the Court in this case?

A. I did.

Q. Will you tell us what that conversation was, when, where, and who was present?

A. The conversation took place in my office. Mr. Lotsch came in and he said, "We have won the case. The Judges have had their conference and have decided in our favor on all of the issues, and Judge Manton has requested that we prepare a draft opinion."

Q. Did you prepare a draft opinion?

A.   I felt there was no alternative but to defer to the wishes of the presiding judge. I did prepare such an opinion and handed it to Mr. Lotsch.

When Kenyon gave this testimony, Judge Chestnut, whose austere probity was a local legend in Baltimore, took over Kenyon's cross-examination. He was pitiless in stripping him of his sham piety. I cannot find that any disciplinary steps were ever taken against Kenyon.

Shortly after Lotsch's success with Manton in the Auto-lite case, the two conspired to fix an even weightier patent-infringement suit, again from the Eastern District. This was *General Motors* v. *Preferred Electric & Wire Co.* Again, Lotsch shared the representation of the defendants with the pharisaical Kenyon. Again, the district judge found for the plaintiff, and the defendants appealed to the Second Circuit. There was danger that during the pendency of the appeal, General Motors, the successful plaintiff, would take further litigative steps against Lotsch's clients. The district judge had denied a stay of action by General Motors pending the appeal; the issuance of a stay by the appellate court was imperative for the defendants. By now, Lotsch knew the way to Manton's lair; he needed no guide. He went to the judge's chambers and emerged with an *ex parte** order to show cause. The order included a temporary stay pending argument of a formal application for a stay pending appeal, which would continue the plaintiff's impotence through the period of appeal. Again, Lotsch's testimony:

---

*Issued on the application of one side in a lawsuit without notice to the other side. An order to show cause is lawyers' language for a written direction from the court to appear and be heard.

Q. And thereafter, on the date set in the order to show cause for argument, did Judge Manton alone sit on that argument?

A. The argument on that motion was in Judge Manton's chambers.

Q. And he was the only Judge who sat?

A. Yes, he being the Chief Judge, he was the only Judge who sat.

Q. And what was his decision on the return date of the order to show cause?

A. He enjoined the defendant—the plaintiff, General Motors, from prosecuting any further suits and ordered us to—ordered the Preferred case to be heard on the opening of the term of court in October, 1935.

Thus, by Manton's fiat, General Motors was unable to act on its judgment. The appeal was argued by Lotsch and Kenyon on October 7, 1935, before Judges Manton, Swan, and Learned Hand. On November 4 these judges reversed the decree of the district judge, and the case was decided in favor of Lotsch's client. Service of this kind commanded a high price, and Manton lost no time in demanding it.

Q. Following that argument, did you have a conversation with Judge Manton relative to further loans to him, after the argument and prior to the decision of the General Motors case in the Circuit Court of Appeals?

A. I did.

Q. The case was argued on October 7, 1935, and after the argument, what was the next communication, if any, you had from Judge Manton, and when did it occur?

A. Judge Manton called me on the telephone the afternoon of the argument.

Q. He called you at your Office?

A. 500 Fifth Avenue. . . . I was not in, but the next morning I called Judge Manton on the telephone and went down to see [him].

Apparently, Manton had no doubt about his ability to persuade his two famous colleagues. The conversation on the morrow of the argument was about as subtle as a solicitation in the Place Pigalle.

Q. And did you have a conversation with him there?

A. I did.

Q. Will you tell us the conversation, please.

A. Judge Manton wanted me to arrange an additional loan of $25,000 for him. I told him that I could not do that, but if he could give me someone else to make a loan with securities, I might be able to put that through for him.

*　　　*　　　*

Q. Now, still later, in the month of October, did Judge Manton personally guarantee a loan from the Fort Greene National Bank to James J. Sullivan in the amount of $25,000?

A. He did. I delivered the guarantee to Judge Manton and had him sign it.

Q. Well, now, I show you this piece of paper and ask you if you can tell us what that is?

A. This is the guarantee which was prepared by me and printed for use by the Fort Greene National Bank, and I had Judge Manton sign it and acknowledged before a notary.

Though nominally the loan of the $25,000 was made to Sullivan, in fact Manton received the proceeds. Now came the "accident," the peripeteia so dearly loved by the Greek

dramatists in depicting the downfall of the great and powerful: Sullivan dropped dead of a heart seizure. It is perhaps
understandable that one living at the vortex of Manton's
activities should be susceptible to heart failure.

But the Chief never wavered. He summoned Lotsch into
his presence and commanded him to have the note rewrit-
ten. Lotsch, of course, obeyed: "I had Judge Manton sign
a collateral note in place of Sullivan's note with the same
collateral put up and then had Sullivan's note released."
Why not? Manton had received the proceeds of the loan; he
was hopelessly insolvent, anyway. The collateral was Manton's, and it was worthless. Most important, in December,
Lotsch himself was in a desperate personal situation from
which only Manton could rescue him. And Manton did his
best—for a price.

In 1935 Lotsch had been indicted in the Southern District of New York for accepting a bribe in a case in which
he had acted as special master.* The evidence was that
Lotsch had solicited money from one of the litigants to
influence his recommended decision. Judge Knox had set
Lotsch's case for trial at the opening of court in March
1936. In February, Lotsch applied to Manton for help.

Manton acted with his characteristic vigor and with unparalleled audacity. He assigned to sit in Room 318, the
Criminal Part of the Southern District, Judge Thomas, his
longtime flunky from Connecticut who had been so helpful
to him in the Fox receivership. The judge sitting in the
Criminal Part controlled the criminal calendar. On March
1 Manton met with Thomas at the Hotel Edison and made
the arrangements necessary to pluck Lotsch from the burning. On the evening of the same day, he met with Lotsch

---

*A "special master" is a referee appointed by the court who takes proof
and reports to the judge.

at the Commodore Hotel. Lotsch described the rescue operation:

> I met Judge Manton in the evening at the hotel and
> we went to the ice cream salon which is in the corridor
> of the Grand Central Depot and we had a ginger ale,
> and he told me that he had seen Judge Thomas and
> that Judge Thomas would take care of my case, but he
> wanted $10,000 from me, and that I had to pay him
> $10,000 before the trial.
>
> *Q.* What did you do the next day?
>
> *A.* The next day I arranged—the case was on the
> calendar, so I called on the telephone to get hold of
> someone at the bank and so that I could borrow this
> $10,000.
>
> *Q.* Did you ultimately get the money?
>
> *A.* The $10,000 was delivered to me in this court-
> house on March 2, 1936. . . .
>
> *Q.* Mr. Lotsch, let me just go ahead with you. Did
> there come a time when you gave to Judge Manton
> two payments of $5,000 each in cash on or about
> March 2nd or 3rd, 1936?
>
> *A.* Yes, on March 2nd I delivered to Judge Manton
> $5,000 in his chambers, and on March 3rd I delivered
> $5,000 to Judge Manton in his chambers.
>
> *Q.* Did you ever have any conversation with Judge
> Thomas about Judge Thomas receiving any of the
> money?
>
> *A.* I had no conversation with Judge Thomas about
> my case. . . .
>
> *   *   *
>
> *Q.* This $10,000 was given to you in cash, was it not?
>
> *A.* Correct.
>
> *Q.* And after you received the $10,000 in cash, what
> did you do?

A. I went upstairs to Judge Manton's Chambers on the 24th floor of this building and gave Judge Manton $5,000 of it.

Q. Did you have a conversation with Judge Manton at the time you gave him the $5,000 in cash?

A. I did. I told him I was only able to get $5,000 and I gave him the $5,000.

Q. What did he say when you gave him the $5,000?

A. That I had to get the other $5,000, that Judge Thomas wants it.

Q. And was anything further said [about] when you had to get the other $5,000?

A. Before the trial opened.

*　　*　　*

Q. What did Judge Manton do with the $5,000 in cash when you gave it to him in his Chambers?

A. He got the $5,000 from me and put it in his safe.

Q. In his safe in his Chambers?

A. In his Chambers; yes, sir.

Q. What did you do after you left Judge Manton's Chambers?

A. I came downstairs and I gave back to my brother $7,500 in cash, and took cash checks from him, which I could use next morning.

Q. What did you do the next morning?

A. I had the cash checks cashed at the Fort Greene Bank.

Q. And received $5,000 in exchange therefor?

A. Received $7,500.

Q. In currency?

A. Yes, sir.

Q. What did you do thereafter?

A. I took the $5,000 and took it up to Judge Manton's chambers.

Q. What did you do then?

A. I handed the balance of the $10,000 that he said Judge Thomas wanted. He took that $5,000 and put it in his safe.

* * *

Q. And did the case come on before Judge Thomas?

A. The case was assigned to Judge Thomas and came on trial on March 5th.

Q. And what was the disposition on that trial?

A. The final disposition was a directed verdict of acquittal by Judge Thomas.

Q. Now, what happened in court immediately after Judge Thomas directed the jury to acquit you?

A. A special agent of the Department of Justice immediately rearrested me.

* * *

Q. What did you then do?

A. Later in the day I went up and saw Judge Manton.

Q. Did you have a conversation with Judge Manton?

A. I did, and I told him what happened and that my attorney said it was double jeopardy.

Q. What did Judge Manton say?

A. He agreed with that.

Q. Now, in the course of this conversation, did Judge Manton give you anything?

A. Yes, sir; Judge Manton gave me a copy of the Government's trial brief, which Judge Thomas had handed to him.

Manton was as good at law as at larceny. He recommended that Lotsch file a petition for habeas corpus on the ground that the new charge presented a case of double jeopardy; that is, Lotsch could not be prosecuted again for the offense on which Judge Thomas had directed his acquittal. The two conspirators anticipated correctly that the district court would dismiss the writ and the case would come before Manton on appeal. This is precisely what happened; the appeal was heard in the Second Circuit by a panel over which Manton presided. While the case was *sub judice*, Manton met with Lotsch again, made suggestions about an additional brief, and even showed him a draft of the court's proposed opinion, which Lotsch edited. Of course, Manton's court reversed the lower-court decision and Lotsch was discharged.

In 1938 Lotsch was again convicted of a violation of federal banking laws, this time in federal court in Brooklyn, for accepting fees from people who wanted loans from the Fort Greene Bank, of which he was an officer. Of course, he applied to his mentor, the Chief. But by 1938 Judge Manton was aware of Tom Dewey's investigation of his relationship with Lotsch and knew that Dewey's people were trying to serve a subpoena on the desperate man. This time Manton could not protect him but only counsel him to hide out in Connecticut until Dewey's interest waned.

Lotsch saw Manton once again before he faced him in the courtroom as one of the government's chief witnesses at Manton's own trial. Just after Manton's resignation from the court, in early 1939, he urged Lotsch "that that matter with Judge Thomas you should carry to your grave," and, if asked by the grand jury about the $10,000 paid to Thomas, he should say he paid it to former Judge Millard (his lawyer in the case). "Judge Millard is dead," Lotsch quoted Manton as saying, "and no one can testify against him."

If there can be a masterpiece in the art of judicial corruption, it was attained by Manton and his confederates in an action brought in 1936 by Schick Industries against Dictograph Products. This was another patent-infringement case, which Schick won handily after a trial before Judge Moscowitz in federal court in Brooklyn. Moscowitz enjoined Dictograph from further acts of infringement and appointed a special master to hear and report on the damages. Every sign pointed to a huge judgment against Dictograph. In the fall of 1936, the defendant posted a bond, and further proceedings were stayed pending an appeal to the Second Circuit. Translated into Mantonian terms, this means that the case moved into the sights that the jurist fixed on substantial patent litigation.

The chief executive officer of Dictograph was Archie M. Andrews, a tireless entrepreneur who was no more reluctant to fix a case than to steal a patent. While his appeal was pending, Andrews encountered one Morris Renkoff, who described himself as being in the real-estate business. In November 1936 Renkoff assured Andrews that he "knew a man who could fix things up" in the circuit court. The fixer was, of course, Bill Fallon. Renkoff's description of the arrangements could come from the pen of a Runyon or a Lardner. Accompanied by a bookmaker named Selinsky, he went to the Prudence office to see Fallon and told him of Andrews' problem. Fallon said he would have to take it up with Judge Manton and would let Renkoff know what could be done. Next day, Fallon reported on Manton's terms. It must be savored in the words of Renkoff:

> I came up to see Bill Fallon. I asked him how he was getting on. He told me he saw Judge Manton and here is the arrangement I would have to make in order to get what Archie Andrews wants. He said to me, "In the first place you have got to take a lawyer by the

name of Milton Weisman, which I and Judge Manton would work with only that lawyer, nobody else," and second he said $50,000 would be the price and he will get whatever he wants when the case reaches the Circuit Court.

Renkoff recounts this conversation to Andrews, who balks at the price. He offers $25,000. There is another meeting at the Prudence office, and Fallon advises "that $25,000 was O.K. and to make sure that Milton Weisman was in the case." The money is to be paid in advance of the circuit-court decision. Andrews does some more bargaining.

I told him (Andrews) to give me the money and I asked him whether he had made arrangements with Milton Weisman, that Milton Weisman should be in the case. He said yes, he did. He called upon Milton Weisman and he is going to be counsel. He said, "About the money, I can only give you $10,000 and $15,000 I will give you after the decision comes down."

More haggling follows, and Fallon accepts the $10,000 down payment.

I went over to Bill Fallon's office at the Prudence Company, and I threw the money on the table. "Here is the first payment of the $10,000." He said to me, "Count." At the time Selinsky was present, Frank Selinsky, and we all started to count. There were seven single thousands and three thousand dollars in tens and in twenties, and we counted the money on the table, and it was correct, 10,000.

He says, "Let me get out of here fast, because I got an appointment with Judge Manton at Schrafft's at 58th Street and Madison Avenue." He says, "He is waiting for the money." . . .

I waited for over an hour and Fallon came [back] and he said, "Everything is O.K. You can go and tell Archie Andrews that he is going to get the decision in his favor." He says, "There will be a bond of $25,000 and no man in the business."*

Renkoff reported his success to Andrews, who remained skeptical:

I told Andrews that everything is arranged, that the money was delivered to the Judge, and that he shouldn't worry, and when the decision comes down he should have the money ready to pay the balance. He asked me then, how sure I was that this is going to be accomplished. I said, "I will tell you how sure I am. I will bet you two suits of clothes made by the best tailor in New York, and I am going up to order them right now, and if I lose, I will pay it, but I am sure I will win," and there is the suit. This is the suit that I am wearing right now, and I didn't have to pay for them. I didn't pay for them.

Thus, eventually, Renkoff was able to report to Andrews:

"You got it, the bond is $25,000 and there will be no man in your business." He says, "I am very happy to hear it. Get a bottle of Egg Cognac out," he said to the girl, the secretary, to get a bottle of Egg Cognac out.

Now the balance of the $25,000 "down payment" was due. Andrews stalled, but in his Ritz-Carlton suite he finally confronted Fallon. The money was paid.

But all this money, paid through the embassy of Renkoff, had purchased only temporary relief for Andrews. He had

---

*That meant no special master to assess damages.

his stay of the decree, pending appeal, his nominal bond, and immunity from "a man in his business." But, alas, in early December 1936 Andrews lost his ambassador to the Court of St. Martin. Renkoff had been convicted in January of receiving stolen bonds. Although he paid Manton $7500 through an intermediary, the Chief was unable to deliver a reversal of the conviction, and in December, Renkoff had to surrender to serve his sentence in Lewisburg.

There was a touching epilogue. When his conviction was affirmed, Renkoff said to the hoodlum who had acted as broker:

> "Why wasn't it [the reversal] delivered? I paid the money for it." He says: "Morris, you will get your money back. Judge Manton could not help it. The other two judges wouldn't go with him. Therefore, he had to go with the other two."

Renkoff threatened Fallon that he would "expose this entire proposition," but Fallon returned the $7500 that he got from Manton. Renkoff wanted more. He demanded and received a letter from Manton to Alexander Holtzoff, the pardon attorney in the Department of Justice, urging executive clemency for Renkoff. The document signed by Manton concludes with the words "I unhesitatingly say I think he is entitled to executive clemency." This is probably the only case in history in which an appellate judge in the federal system urged executive clemency for a criminal defendant.

Renkoff went to Lewisburg, and Andrews and Dictograph had lost their link to Fallon and Judge Manton. But the miscreants proved accessible to a new embassy. George M. Spector was Andrews' insurance agent and his *homme d'affaires*. He knew Fallon and carried on where Renkoff left off. From December 1936 through 1937, a steady stream of money was advanced by Andrews through Spector to Manton, to his secretary, and to his failing companies. Of a total of $35,000, $20,000 was traced into Marie Schmalz's account. These were booked as "loans," and Manton asserted at his trial that "all but $4,000 had been repaid." But poor Marie Schmalz had to admit on cross-examination that less than $4,000 had ever been repaid.

Meanwhile, Manton was zealously discharging his end of the crooked bargain. Several weeks before Dictograph's appeal was docketed, Manton peremptorily denied an application by Schick's lawyer to vacate the stay pending appeal; he set the case down for argument on January 4, 1937, a day on which he was scheduled to preside over the court. By now, Schick's counsel were desperate to avoid Judge Manton. They must have sensed that their cause was not being considered with dispassionate objectivity. They succeeded in adjourning the argument to January 11, when Manton was *not* scheduled to sit. Manton then directed the clerk to revise the schedule so that he would preside on that date, too. The appeal was argued before a panel that included Manton, Augustus Hand, and Chase, and on April 12, 1937, with a vigorous dissent by Hand, the majority so modified the decision of the lower court as to decide in favor of Andrews' company on both patents.* Simon Cameron, Senator from Pennsylvania and a member of Lincoln's cabinet, is reported to have said that "An honest politician is one who when you buy him, he stays bought."

When Cahill and his staff were finished erecting this edifice of corruption and betrayal at the trial, Manton had little chance. He opened his defense by calling Alfred E.

---

*89 F. 2d 643.

Smith and John W. Davis as character witnesses.* Other judges and lawyers followed them to attest to Manton's excellent reputation for veracity, integrity, and honesty. The most dramatic moments of the trial were provided by the appearance of Manton's colleagues on the Second Circuit, Learned Hand, Augustus Hand, Thomas Swan, and Harrie Chase. But they did *not*, as the legend has it, voluntarily appear to affirm Manton's reputation for good character; each was called by the defense to testify that in those appeals in which they sat with Manton they *observed* nothing that led them to believe "he was acting otherwise than according to his oath of office and the dictates of his conscience"—which only proves that Manton was as accomplished an actor as he was resourceful a rogue.

In the end Manton staked everything on his ability to

---

*Until the trial of Alger Hiss, a decade later, no defendant in the Southern District had character witnesses as impressive as Manton's leadoff sluggers. Davis, the Democratic candidate for president of the United States in 1924, was the uncrowned king of the New York legal establishment. Smith, former governor of New York, was the Democratic candidate for president in 1928. So Manton had as character witnesses two of the best-known losers in the country. They lost this one, too.

The term "character witness" is misleading. A defendant in a criminal case can call witnesses to testify to his reputation for veracity, for truth-telling—*not* to his character. Most experienced lawyers have grave reservations about the effect of character witnesses on jurors. But the clients love the parade of notables; it is an ego trip that consoles them in the dark, desperate days of a criminal trial. They think that the little men and women of the juries are traumatized by a defendant's power to command the appearance of the great, the powerful, the ultrarespectable. So most important criminal cases are enlivened by a procession of bishops, bankers, and ballplayers. I once asked a juror in such a case about his reaction to the character witnesses. "Oh," said the shrewd little man, "it did the defendant more harm than good. If he could convince all those big shots that he was a decent fellow, he must have been the slickest crook in the world!" Still, most experienced lawyers do not deny their clients the solace of the parade of "character witnesses." Who knows? It may be effective.

confront Cahill and outwit him. No chance. His own admissions on direct testimony and his hopeless tergiversations on cross-examination destroyed him.

Some of Manton's "explanations" are almost pitiful in their transparency. He admitted having met Reilly in 1935, but *not* in connection with the Art Metal case. "If this name was mentioned in the record on that appeal it escaped my attention." Certainly, he never heard of Reilly from Fallon. How did he come to know Reilly? "There was a Venetian lady named Madame Jolles who my wife had become acquainted with," and Manton continued that she had brought Reilly to lunch at his Port Jefferson summer home. Only later did he learn that Reilly "was the man in that case." How about Hall? "Never met him," said Manton. Finally, he recalled a telephone conversation with the Connecticut chicken farmer in 1939, but that was only to see if he could help Manton's son with *his* chicken business.

As Cahill chopped away at Manton, his defense crumbled into ruin. The jury needed little time for deliberation. And on June 3, 1939, Martin Manton and George Spector were found guilty; on June 20, Judge Chestnut sentenced Manton to two years in the penitentiary and fined him $10,000. Spector was sentenced to one year and a $5,000 fine. Of course, they appealed.

The appeal of Manton and Spector was heard by a special panel appointed by the Chief Justice of the United States. It included Mr. Justice Sutherland and Mr. Justice Stone of the Court, and Charles E. Clark, newly appointed to the Second Circuit, who had never served under Manton. The convictions were affirmed in an opinion that disposed of an array of technical points, and it includes a paragraph that deserves a place in the literature of the American law. For a unanimous court, Mr. Justice Sutherland wrote:

We cannot doubt that the other judges who sat in the various cases acted honestly and with pure motives in joining in the decisions. No breath of suspicion has been directed against any of them and justly none could be. And for aught that now appears we may assume for present purposes that all of the cases in which Manton's action is alleged to have been corruptly secured were in fact rightly decided. But the unlawfulness of the conspiracy here in question is in no degree dependent upon the indefensibility of the decisions which were rendered in consummating it. Judicial action, whether just or unjust, right or wrong, is not for sale; and if the rule shall ever be accepted that the correctness of judicial action *taken for a price* removes the stain of corruption and exonerates the judge, the event will mark the first step toward the abandonment of that imperative requisite of even-handed justice proclaimed by Chief Justice Marshall more than a century ago, that the judge must be "perfectly and completely independent with nothing to influence or control him but God and his conscience."

On February 27, 1940, the Supreme Court rejected Manton's application to review his conviction. And on March 7, 1940, the former Chief Judge of one of America's greatest courts went to Lewisburg to begin the service of his sentence.

The conviction of Manton does not close the book on his offenses. You will remember that when Tom Dewey wrote his fateful letter to the House Judiciary Committee, the case that attracted the greatest public notice was the American Tobacco case, but no allegations about this matter were contained in the indictment under which Manton was tried. Manton was vigorously cross-examined by Cahill at his trial about his knowledge of the transaction, but Manton denied any "personal knowledge of it at the time."

(The cross-examination of this matter, outside the scope of
the indictment, was allowed by the trial judge "on the
ground of what we call similar transactions possibly re-
flecting on the defendant.")

There is little doubt that the facts in the American Tobacco fix would have furnished some of the racier moments in Manton's trial, had they been included in the
indictment. They were not, because they had occurred
beyond the statute of limitations.* So that resplendent
Wall Street lawyer Louis Levy, his striped-pants partners,
and the powerful clients who were his confederates in the
plot were saved from a criminal case. But there is no statute of limitations on professional misconduct, and immediately after Manton's conviction, Cahill instituted disciplinary (i.e., disbarment) proceedings in the Southern
District against Levy and his former partner Paul Hahn.
The matter was heard by Judge Knox, the Chief District
Court Judge. Cahill and the team that had prosecuted
Manton presented the government's case. John W. Davis,
one of Manton's character witnesses, was Levy's counsel,
"seconded" by Harold Medina, surely one of the most lu-
minous figures of the American bar in the twentieth century—a great advocate, a superb legal pedagogue, a gifted
raconteur.† Hahn's lawyer was George Z. Medalie, who
had been Dewey's boss in the U.S. attorney's office in the

---

*There were some other transgressions that were never formally pre-
sented in court: Manton's murky dealings in the Prudence Company; his
acceptance of loans from Harry M. Warner, who had litigation before
him; his corrupt relationship with Steinreich, who brought him money
from the Kings Brewery, a gangster-controlled enterprise also in litigation before Manton. There may have been others that never came to
light. They were not needed.
†Medina served as a fine federal judge in the district court and then in
the Second Circuit. He goes on, at a great age, still one of the bar's
proudest monuments.

early 1930s and was later a distinguished judge in New York State's Court of Appeals, its highest court. The trial of Levy and Hahn, one of Foley Square's classics, rivals Manton's in the richness of its revelations about the bench and bar of the period.

Levy's firm, Chadbourne Stanchfield & Levy, handled most of American Tobacco's important legal work. Indeed, Paul Hahn became so invaluable to George Washington Hill, chief executive of the company, that in 1931 he left the Chadbourne firm and became Hill's chief assistant at a princely salary. Lord & Thomas, a huge advertising agency, was engaged in promoting Hill's Lucky Strike cigarettes and other products. The head of Lord & Thomas was Albert D. Lasker, probably the outstanding personality then in American advertising. Hill, Hahn, Lasker, Chadbourne, and Levy were all intimates, dedicated to making tons of money out of American Tobacco. And in 1931 Hill, Hahn, and Levy had devised a scheme by which the top brass at American Tobacco could make vast personal profits. They had designed a stock-subscription plan that authorized the top officers of American Tobacco (including Hill and Hahn) to subscribe for the company's common stock at $25 per share, at a time when the stock was selling on the New York Stock Exchange at $112 per share. The plan even provided for the officers to borrow the cost of the stock from the company. Richard Reid Rogers, a stockholder, sued to challenge the validity of this plan as an illegal giveaway of the company's assets. One of Rogers' actions was dismissed in the federal court in New York on February 23, 1932, by Judge Robert P. Patterson on the narrow technical ground that the case should have been brought in New Jersey. His dismissal was without prejudice to renewing the action in that state. An appeal was taken by Rogers to the Second Circuit, Manton's Happy

Hunting Ground. But in a companion action in the Southern District, in March 1932, Judge Francis Caffey enjoined the company from carrying out the stock-subscription plan, pending the outcome of the first case. From this decree, American Tobacco and its top officials appealed to Manton's court. On both appeals their counsel was Chadbourne, Stanchfield & Levy, and both appeals were set for argument on May 3, 1932, before a panel selected by Manton, with himself, of course, presiding. Both appeals were now firmly fixed in the cross hairs of Manton's judicial Winchester. Between March and May 3, Manton, his henchman Sullivan, Chadbourne, and that gifted sprig of Our Crowd's gilded youth, Louis Levy, worked out the mechanics of a fix.

First, let us consider how vital were these appeals to the personal interests of Levy's most important clients, the top officials of American Tobacco. At the spread between the subscription price and the market price when Rogers brought his actions, Hill's anticipated profit was at least $1,500,000; Hahn's was at least $250,000. These were even more enormous sums in those days than they are now; they were not lightly given up.

Next, let me remind my readers of the relationship between Judge Manton and Levy. They were not merely law-school friends; Levy *owned* Manton. He had enjoyed a psychological ascendency over the judge from their days at Columbia. Judge Knox described their relationship:

> Levy is a man of superior talents. Throughout his scholastic days, his achievements and distinctions were of a character of which any man might well be proud. Manton's youthful education and training had not been so broad and comprehensive. Thus, it was perhaps that in their law school days Levy came to

give assistance to Manton, explaining the intricacies of reported decisions and discussing with him the legal problems propounded by the lecturers.*

Manton and Levy were also business partners long before the fix in *Rogers* v. *Hill*. They were jointly interested in developing the Holmes Airport site in Flushing into New York's major air terminal. Had they succeeded in this enterprise they would have made millions. But the selection of a site a few miles to the west, the present LaGuardia Field, left them with a costly dud. Levy and his illustrious partner, Thomas L. Chadbourne, were also stockholders in Manton's National Cellulose, of which James J. Sullivan was Manton's puppet president. But they were very silent partners; the stock was held in the name of Levy's secretary. What other ties existed between Manton and the members of Levy's firm I do not know, but certainly the common interest in National Cellulose should have disqualified Manton from hearing the firm's cases. If either Levy or Chadbourne had a shred of professional honor, he would have shrunk from letting Manton hear the appeals in *Rogers* v. *Hill*. Not only did the two men not shrink; they made absolutely sure they had purchased his vote.

The method of providing the necessary funds for the fix had already been tested in a perfectly legitimate way in the previous year, 1931. Some of the American Tobacco offi-

---

In Re Levy, 30 F. Supp. 317, 319 (1939). There was so much controversy —and so much manifest lying—about the "fix" in *American Tobacco* that I have used throughout my description the facts as found by Judge Knox after trial. John Knox was Chief Judge in the Southern District for many years. He brought to the court a vast legal talent, a noble character, and a devotion to the court that won for him the admiration of judges and lawyers throughout America. Knox told me in later years that he regarded Manton as "the foulest man I have encountered in a lifetime on the bench, our Judas."

cials had pledged their stock in the company as security for loans from the Guaranty Trust. In the dread autumn of 1931, the value of the stock was melting away, and the bank issued a margin call for $150,000. George W. Hill, the only American Tobacco mogul who had this kind of ready cash, was off on a fishing trip in a remote part of Canada, unreachable by phone or wire. Levy came to the rescue. He obtained the money for the stricken officers from Lasker. He even gave Lasker his personal guaranty. In due course, this advance was repaid with interest, and Lasker had good reason to rely on Levy's promises.

Now, in April 1932, with the arguments in *Rogers* v. *Hill* set before him on May 3, Manton put a heavy arm on Levy for $250,000 to save his Esplanade Hotel property, one of the jewels of his collection, from foreclosure. There are three versions of the conversation in which the "loan" was solicited: Manton's, Levy's—and the truth. Manton testified under oath that during "the first part of May 1932" he and Levy "walked a part ways downtown" and "I mentioned it to Mr. Levy on the way down town that Sullivan [the National Cellulose puppet] wanted to obtain a loan of $25,000." Levy said "send him down to me." And that, said Manton, is how Sullivan happened to get a loan on May 10 from Lord & Thomas, the advertising agency of American Tobacco—less than a week after Levy's firm had argued the appeals in *Rogers* v. *Hill* before Manton and his two colleagues. Manton insisted he had never heard of a $250,000 loan—"only $25,000."

Levy's version was short and simple: he "absolutely never discussed with Judge Manton *any* loan to Sullivan in the amount of $25,000, $250,000 or any other amount." This, too, was stated under oath.

But a piece of paper existed that projected both versions into the midden of falsehood. On April 26, in Manton's chambers, Manton's secretary, Marie Schmalz, typed a letter to Levy on a sheet of government stationery. The letter, which set out the financial problems of the Esplanade Hotel and its immediate need for $250,000, was signed "James J. Sullivan," but it was proved that the signature was written by Marie Schmalz at Manton's direction. Can there be any doubt how the idea of the $250,000 loan originated?

Louis Levy lost no time. On May 9 the appeals in *Rogers* v. *Hill* had been argued and were under consideration by Manton and his two oblivious colleagues, Augustus Hand and Swan. Time was running out. On that day there was a conference on advertising matters at the office of American Tobacco. Present were the chief executive officer, Hill, and Hahn, as well as Lasker, president of the advertising agency. Lasker testified that when the meeting ended, Hahn drew him into a room adjoining Hill's office and said:

> "I want to speak to you on a matter that Mr. Hill is embarrassed to speak to you about. . . . You remember that loan you made at the request of Louis Levy last fall? . . . An identical situation has arisen. This time it is $250,000. Will you accommodate us?"

On May 11 Jim Sullivan received a check for $250,000 from Lord & Thomas. Lord & Thomas got Sullivan's interest-bearing note for that sum and, as "collateral," 15,604 shares of National Cellulose stock—with an equity value of zero. As Judge Knox put it, Sullivan was "a conduit through which money siphoned from Lord & Thomas by Hahn and Levy flowed into Manton's depleted reservoirs. . . . Within a few weeks after the loan was consummated, and prior to the decisions on the appeals in the Rogers suits, more than $200,000 of its proceeds had found their

way into corporations in which Manton was vitally interested." It must be appreciated that $250,000 in that year was
equivalent to more than a million in the 1970s.

Hahn gave still another version of the origin of the
loan. He testified before Judge Knox that he was drawn
into the transactions in mid-April by a telephone call
from Chadbourne, who wanted "a favor." The Chadbourne firm was "interested" in National Cellulose; its
president, Jim Sullivan, a close friend and client, needed
a loan of $250,000. Chadbourne would like to make the
loan himself, "but it was not at that moment convenient
for him to make it." Could Hahn arrange for Mr.
Lasker to make the loan? Whereupon Mr. Chadbourne
sailed off to Europe, leaving further arrangements to
that resourceful fellow, Louis Levy. Mr. Chadbourne's
interest in spending the next few weeks in Europe is
understandable. Had he known what was to come, he
might have gone to Tibet.

About two weeks later, according to Hahn, Levy reminded Hahn of the telephone talk with Chadbourne. He
added his own testimonial to the upstanding character of
Sullivan, who, he told Hahn, was "a thoroughly responsible man." But before Hahn would approach Lasker, he
cleared it with his own boss, George Washington Hill. Hill
played it cozy: "Well, all you can do is to tell Albert what
Tom Chadbourne and Louis Levy have told you." Naturally, he did *not* say to tell Lasker: "Look, Albert, we have
this case, *Rogers* v. *Hill*, before Manton; Manton wants the
money; if we lose, Mr. Hill and I and all our top brass will
have to pay back millions in stock." There was to be no
connection between the loan and the case.

Paul Hahn's association with all these glib lawyers and
merchants had apparently taught him well. Here is *his*
version of the pitch to Lasker:

I told Mr. Lasker that I had been asked to speak to
him by Mr. Chadbourne and by Mr. Levy and, to the
best of my recollection, I repeated the telephone conversation which had been given to me, telling Mr.
Lasker that Mr. Chadbourne was interested in a man
named James J. Sullivan, who was president of National Cellulose Corporation; that the company was
engaged in the business of cellulose products; that Sullivan had come to Mr. Chadbourne for a loan of $250,-
000; that it was not convenient for Mr. Chadbourne at
that time to make the loan or else he would make it;
that Sullivan offered as security the majority of the
stock in the National Cellulose Company; that the
loan was wanted for a very short time; that it was to
be repaid promptly; that I had been assured by both
Mr. Chadbourne and Mr. Levy that Sullivan was a
responsible man and that this was a good loan; and
that I had been asked to ask Mr. Lasker whether he
would see Mr. Sullivan and let Sullivan put his proposition up to Mr. Lasker.

Mr. Lasker said: "Well for how long—for how long
would this loan be?" And I said . . . "I am told by Mr.
Chadbourne and Mr. Levy that it will be repaid in a
short time. . . ." And I recall saying to Mr. Lasker that
"Mr. Levy assures me that this loan will be promptly
repaid" and I remember Mr. Lasker asking me some
questions about Mr. Levy's assurance and my answering that "Mr. Lasker well, you know from your own
experience with Mr. Levy on the matter of the $150,-
000 loan that when Mr. Levy says something it can be
depended upon!" Mr. Lasker replied, "Well, I can't see
him, I am leaving. I cannot see Sullivan. . . . I am
taking a train for Chicago this afternoon, but you can
tell Mr. Levy to send him to see Ralph Sollitt [trea-
surer of Lord & Thomas]."

Levy had a more romantic version of how the loan came
about. He testified that the first *he* knew of a loan to Sullivan is when Chadbourne came to his office and said:

"Our paper company is doing very well. *It is going to be a great success, it is earning money and paying dividends,* * but the president, Sullivan, is in a personal jam and he needs $250,000, and I don't want to see him hurt. Now he is a very necessary, important and substantial citizen, and if I had the money, I would give it to him myself. He is the whole company. But he has no collateral that a bank would take because there is no market for it and there is only one person, the only people who would appreciate the value are the people in the business, and therefore I concluded that his best chance to get the money is from Lasker who would know all about it, and I have asked Paul Hahn to arrange an introduction for him with Lord & Thomas to see whether they would not loan the money."

Nothing to do with Manton! Or *Rogers* v. *Hill!* Just the normal solicitude of that kind and generous lawyer Tom Chadbourne for the decent fellow who was running "our paper company."

The loan was made, and the money flowed into the bottomless pit of Manton's empire. Nothing happened about the loan for a couple of years. Neither principal nor interest was paid to Lord & Thomas. But something very significant did happen in *Rogers* v. *Hill,* and it happened fast. On June 13, 1932, the Court of Appeals decided in favor of American Tobacco against Rogers. Manton wrote the opinion; Augustus Hand concurred, with Swan dissenting.†

The victory for American Tobacco, its officers, lawyers, and assorted friends and creditors of Judge Manton was short-lived. Early in 1933 the U.S. Supreme Court reversed and remanded the case, with instructions to follow Judge

---

*This is not only false; it is a whopper! National Cellulose was in the most desperate financial straits.
†Rogers v. Hill, 60 F. 2d 109.

Patterson's original decision.* The $250,000 loan to Man-
ton had purchased nothing but time. In the end, the case
was settled by a payment to the company of almost $1,-
000,000 in cash and the return to the company of almost
100,000 shares of American Tobacco stock.

By all the normal rules that govern affairs of this kind,
the matter should have ended in 1933, with the Supreme
Court's reversal of Manton's dearly purchased opinion. But
now there enters on the scene one of the most powerful
figures in the New York bar of the time, Max D. Steuer. I
have referred elsewhere to the prodigious stature and prestige of Max Steuer among New York's judges and lawyers.
Steuer's performance in the American Tobacco fix, as
Lasker's lawyer, has never been as highly publicized as his
famous trials, his legendary exploits in and out of the courtroom, but it was exquisite.

During 1933 and 1934, Albert Lasker kept pressing for
the repayment of his advertising firm's $250,000. He asked
Hahn, who asked Chadbourne, who asked Levy. All he
heard was, "The loan is all right and will soon be repaid."
But Lasker did not get his money, and he spoke sharply
about it to Paul Hahn. Hahn spoke to Hill, but Hill gave
him small comfort. "Keep after Tom Chadbourne and
Levy to get this thing cleaned up, and in the meanwhile,
not to worry," said the great cigarette magnate. But Hahn
did worry; he knew where the money had gone, and he
knew that the loan was a time bomb, ticking away in the
substructure of American Tobacco—and its lawyers. He
appealed to George W. Whiteside, another partner in the
Chadbourne firm, who was emerging as the new leader of
that Wall Street institution. All he got was more excuses.

By 1936 the situation got completely out of control. Sul-

---

*289 U.S. 582.

livan died, leaving an insolvent estate in the hands of his executor, Martin Manton. When Lasker heard this, he retained Steuer to get the loan paid. And as soon as Manton heard that Steuer was representing Lasker, he wrote Lasker requesting a meeting, even offering to come to Florida to see him. Lasker refused. But when Steuer visited Judge Manton, that talented mechanic came up with a characteristic solution: "I have got a great proposition for him and he is the one man that can make a great thing out of it." The proposition: Lasker should buy National Cellulose from Manton at a price that would presumably give effect to Sullivan's indebtedness of $250,000. In furtherance of this brazen audacity, Manton furnished Steuer with an auditor's report on the company. At a glance, Steuer pronounced the report as worthless. Later, he told this to Louis Levy, who suggested that Steuer retain Leidesdorf & Co. to report on the condition of Manton's company. This Steuer did, and the cost of the investigation was paid by Chadbourne Stanchfield & Levy. The Leidesdorf report showed that the *book* value of the National stock held by Lasker as collateral for the loan to Sullivan was more than $100,000 short of the face of the loan; its realizable value at a sale was close to *zero*. That was the end of the negotiations for the sale of National Cellulose.

Now Levy and his partner, George W. Whiteside, together visited Steuer. As Steuer told it, it was offensive to Levy that a lawyer of his standing should be dunned in Steuer's persistent manner. After all, he had his *dignity* to consider! Levy now affronted his host by telling him that he, Levy, would have nothing more to do with the matter, and henceforth Whiteside would be in charge. He also regaled Steuer with a fictitious version of how the loan had come to be. Whiteside's contribution was to suggest that Lord & Thomas should get back its money from "the col-

lateral and the Sullivan estate." Steuer indignantly rejected this silly proposal, reminding the two lawyers that
Lasker's loan had been made "upon the faith and credit of
Hahn, who was acting on behalf of Hill." He wanted no
part of National Cellulose, Sullivan's estate, or Sullivan's
executor. The Old Fox must have sniffed out that the proceeds of the loan had gone to a place that was best forgotten, that the Chadbourne people were too eager to stay
out of the matter. He wanted his client repaid by the people who had asked for the loan: Hill and Hahn, the
American Tobacco people; Chadbourne and Levy, the
Wall Street legal stars.

I believe that by this time Max Steuer knew of the relationship between Sullivan and Manton and wanted
nothing more than to get out of the case. But first, he
tried to discharge his duty to his clients, Lasker and
Lord & Thomas. Steuer testified that when he rejected
Whiteside's first suggestion, that gentleman said, "I told
you that we don't want Lasker or Lord & Thomas to
lose anything on this transaction; we don't think they
ought to." How generous! How thoughtful! Whiteside
went on: "On the other hand, I repeat, we don't want to
give our recognition to this transaction." How fastidiously ethical! Now Whiteside showed the quality that
had brought him to leadership in the Chadbourne firm.
He suggested a way by which the loan could be repaid
without pain: the American Tobacco Company can always use advertising; in this business, when Lord &
Thomas gets an order, no matter what its size, they get
a fee of fifteen percent of the cost of advertising. In
sending out advertising matter to magazines and newspapers, the effort is no greater, certainly not perceptibly
greater, whether it is two million, five million, eight or
ten million. And they can give to Lord & Thomas suffi-

cient additional advertising to make up for the difference between what they would realize on the sale of the
collateral plus what they may have collected from the
estate. Whiteside urged Steuer to pass this idea along to
his client, because, he told Steuer, "neither Hill, Hahn
nor the Tobacco Company would recognize any responsibility for the money advanced to Sullivan." Of course
not. To have recognized their responsibility would have
been to acknowledge that they were parties to the fix so
clumsily arranged by Whiteside's senior partners. Steuer
rejected Whiteside's proposal, but Whiteside kept slug-
ging. He had another ingenious plan. According to
Steuer's testimony, he said, "Well, now I have another
thought. Hahn is over in England. Lord & Thomas have
an English branch. They can do advertising over there
and that advertising can make up the difference between
what can be realized always from these two sources,
from the estate or from the sale of the collateral. Put
that up to them."

Steuer turned this down, too. Plainly, he was unimpressed by the virtuosity of Whiteside's mind. In his simple
way, he wanted the money repaid by the people who had
borrowed it: Hill, Hahn, Chadbourne, and Levy.

When this ingenious solution was rejected, according to
Steuer, Whiteside came up with still a third. He proposed
that since the American Tobacco's radio programs had
been amazingly successful, and since Albert Lasker had
played a large part in their success, Lasker should make a
claim on Sullivan's estate and "send a bill for the difference
between his recovery and the amount due on the note."
Then Mr. Whiteside looked Mr. Steuer full in the face and
added, "If this proposition is not satisfactory, it is the last
I will make—you can take it or leave it." If Whiteside said
that to Max Steuer, his brass and fortitude—and his ele-

mental stupidity—exceeded even his capacity for imaginative corporate chicanery.*

At this point, Steuer withdrew from the case. He must have been revolted by Whiteside's duplicity. His testimony betrays that he was offended by the man's assumption that Steuer would lend himself to these corrupt schemes. Most of all, I think, Steuer wanted no more of Whiteside's tricks or Manton's crooked deals, or the sickening hypocrisy of Chadbourne *et al.* The Old Master must have sensed that there was an infernal device underlying the transaction and that it had to detonate sometime. Max Steuer did not want to be there when it happened.

The ineffable Whiteside testified that he never made the take-it-or-leave-it statement to Steuer. As to the serial proposals for corporate larceny, they "were never authorized by the Tobacco Company" and he made them "merely as 'bait' to ascertain Lasker's real purpose in seeking to impose liability on Hahn, Hill or the Tobacco Company. My thought was that Lasker was using the loan to Sullivan as an instrumentality of pressure to improve his relationship with the Tobacco Company." I suggest that any lawyer who believes this bland hypocrisy should find a job selling ribbons. I suggest further that Mr. Lasker was a decent merchant who had been tricked into providing a huge sum for a foul fix, and had the effrontery to require that the well-heeled mechanics of the fix pay back the money. Some nerve!

---

*When I was a young lawyer, I carried Sam Kaufman's bag to court in a number of cases in which Mr. Steuer was a participant. I had much opportunity to observe the respect, even the awe, with which he was regarded by members of the bar. Nobody—no lawyers, no judges— treated Max Steuer as he reports Whiteside treated him. But then, not all of the lawyers I observed were certified members of the Wasp Ascendancy.

When all of these negotiations ended, no claim was ever made against Sullivan's estate, or against Manton. The statute of limitations ran on the loan, and it was never repaid.

Judge Knox characterized this story as "one of the most fantastic business transactions that ever came to my ears." He wrote, "Here was a group of men . . . possessing minds as acute as any that are to be found; persons of wide experience not only in business, but in law, and yet, for some reason not clearly disclosed, acting as though they were children lost in the woods and fearful of the shadows about them." In the end, Judge Knox rejected the whole story as a pack of lies, designed to conceal the actors' actual parts in taking advantage of Manton's pervasive corruption. He ordered Levy disbarred. He treated Hahn as a victim of the deceit and imposition of his former senior partners, and dismissed the petition against him.

Louis Levy was disbarred in the courts of New York. He died in 1952, exiled from the life and profession he had once adorned. Martin Manton surrendered to the marshal in March 1940 and served his sentence in Lewisburg. His plea for parole was denied. He, too, was disbarred in the courts of New York. When Manton was released from prison, he went to live in Fayetteville, New York, a suburb of Syracuse. He never came back to New York City. He died in Fayetteville in 1946, unwept, unsung, and dishonored.

Is there an epitaph for Martin Manton? When Learned Hand was testifying before a Senate subcommittee in 1951 on certain proposals to elevate the standards of morality in public life, he intimated that he knew some things about the Manton case that had never been exposed to the public. Regretfully, the aging jurist was cut off by Senator Fulbright. Here is the colloquy:

Judge Hand: There lingers in the back of my memory some things that happened very close at home, but they shall not be mentioned.

Senator Fulbright: If there is anything wrong, it has been better concealed. At least, I am not aware of anything wrong.

Judge Hand: All right, then, I will not bring it to your attention. I could a tale unfold.

Senator Douglas: There is a former judge from New York who is serving in the penitentiary.

Judge Hand: He has gone now. I would not say to a greater penitentiary.*

Manton's story is a study in nemesis, in retribution. There is a special catastrophe visited on men who reject the elemental rules of experience and conduct themselves without respect for their duties, their obligations, and their status as individuals living within a social contract. For them, the world explodes, and the debris rains down on their heads. If a society could order its priorities, none should outrank the integrity of its judiciary. When that is compromised, the debris rains down not only on the culprits but on everyone else.

---

*From *The Spirit of Liberty: Papers and Addresses of Learned Hand,* ed. Irving Dilliard (New York: Vintage Press, 1959), pp. 171–172.

13

ITZKE, MITZKE, AND HOTZKE,
OR,
HOW THE GUARANTY TRUST
COMPANY WAS AFFLICTED WITH
THE ORIENTAL STING
(AND BENJAMIN N. CARDOZO)

During the early days of the immigration investigation in 1935, Charlie Muller made some allusions to "the Werblow case." The name was vaguely familiar to me; I recalled dimly that some people named Werblow had been clients at the firm of Kaufman Weitzner & Celler. I reported Muller's reference to Sam Kaufman, then still head of our Special Unit, and he gave some indication of recognition. Then, a few days later, he called Pindyck and me into his office. He told us that the brothers Werblow were the proprietors of the Polygraphic Company of America, a client of his law firm; that they had some problem with the Immigration and Naturalization Service; that he had reached an agreement with both the Immigration and Naturalization Service and the Department of Justice that the Special Unit was to have nothing to do with the case. He wanted to avoid a "conflict situation," and any mention of the case was taboo. Watkins and Muller were informed of this arrangement, and from then on I heard nothing about the Werblow case—officially. Unofficially, during the next two years, Muller alluded to it more than a dozen times. Whenever he did, he spoke of it as Sherlock Holmes alluded to Irene Adler, the quintessential heroine of *A Scandal in Bohemia*. There came to his face that expression of wistful yearning that he reserved for moments when he was brooding about the chief rascals who were his targets. He often wore this expression; like Watkins, he was all cop. Once or twice, he said, "Ah, Werblow! *That* will be a great case!" But not until some time after I left the government, in 1937, was there a palate-tickling feast for Charlie Muller.

In 1937, when I returned to Sam Kaufman's office, I did some litigation for the Polygraphic Company and came to know both Robert and Henry Werblow. Gradually, I began to learn about their problems with the Immigration and Naturalization Service, that in some remote way they derived from the Guaranty Trust case. Most of my contact was with Robert M. Werblow, Jr., chairman of the board of this high-sounding corporation. I learned that though Bob Werblow professed to be every inch a native-born American, he was in fact an alien, not even a citizen.

Bob Werblow had spent virtually his entire life in this country; he had served in World War I as an officer in the armed forces of the United States, had built a large and successful business in New York; in manners, speech, appearance, he was the exemplar of a successful New York businessman. He was greeted by name in the most fashionable restaurants; he served on charitable and civic committees. But United States citizenship eluded his grasp. By law, he was a citizen of no country, and he was technically subject to deportation to a world he had never known.

It was inevitable that the litigative advocacy in his naturalization case should evoke references to Edward Everett Hale's fictional outcast in *The Man Without a Country*. In fact, Werblow was one of five brothers who had come to the United States between 1907 and 1921. Their place of origin was Libau, Latvia, where the family was known as Verbelovsky—a Slavic jawbreaker almost instantly Anglicized to "Werblow" in Brooklyn, where the family became established in 1907. The parents of our subjects were not distinguishable from the millions who fled from Czarist oppression and anti-Semitism at the beginning of this century. They appear to have been honest, industrious immigrants, concerned only with their daily bread, their faith and immunity from the pogroms of the Black Hundreds. It seems that the father, Rubin, found honest employment as a shoemaker, although his parvenu progeny usually said he was "in the leather business." Our story does not concern the father and mother; nor does it concern the eldest son, Morris (né Moishe), or the youngest son, James (né Yussel). These other family members appear only peripherally in the saga of the three middle brothers.

Robert Werblow had *tried* to be an American citizen. In 1922 he applied for and received an American passport. In 1923 he caused a false record of his birth to be made *nunc pro tunc* in Fort Morgan, Colorado. In 1929 he obtained another American passport on his false representation that he was a native American. But when he returned to the United States from a European trip in 1930, he was compelled to surrender this passport because it was fraudulently obtained. Then, in November 1933, he filed a petition for naturalization in the Southern District. Curiously, in that petition he gave his status as that of a native-born American citizen but stated "that for the purposes of his petition he would concede that he was an alien and a native of Holland." The judge who denied this petition did so on the basis of one of the several reasons that the government had relied on in opposing the petition: that the "applicant was not of good moral character." He observed that "the applicant's testimony was characterized by falsehoods of the most egregious character."

It was during this unsuccessful effort to become a naturalized American that Robert Werblow first encountered Charlie Muller, who became his relentless enemy. Then, in 1940, with the war in Europe, American citizenship became more precious than ever to Robert Werblow, and he urged Kaufman and me to file a new petition for naturalization on his behalf. Though we recognized and advised him that there were technical impediments to such a petition, he insisted that we give it a try. But his application was finally denied, after an extensive hearing. The district judge expressed strong reservations about Robert Werblow's professions "that he underwent reformation and is now a person of good morals."*

But, as we shall see, this proceeding was a turning point in the lives of the Werblow brothers. For in this proceeding they finally abandoned all the lies, the sham pedigrees, that had poisoned their lives. And it was in this proceeding that their guilt in the Guaranty Trust case was finally acknowledged. When Robert was asked in the hearing before Judge Knox why he chose now to seek naturalization, despite the obligatory humiliation and risk of confessing a lifetime of lies and fraud as to his origin and lineage, he replied:

> Well, I don't know any other country but this country. I love this country. I enlisted in the last World War, and if I hadn't gotten a commission, I would have been glad to go as a private to defend this country, and I am ready to do it again if I have that privilege. I realize that I have broken some of the laws, for which I am very much ashamed, I also know that I

---

*Petition of Werblow, No. 358942; 134 F. 2d 791 CCA 2d (1943).

could have gone on as I have been without American
Citizenship, but somehow I didn't feel right every
time I salute the flag!*

A little mawkish, but moving enough to be used in an
American Legion Fourth of July oration. Here was a true-
to-life Philip Nolan, debarred by his own follies from calling himself an American. But he *was* an American! No
European would fail to recognize him as an American.

Behind this paradox there is a courthouse tale of unparalleled deception. Before the tale ended, its participants included some of the legendary figures of the New York bar
in the first half of the twentieth century. Benjamin N.
Cardozo, Learned Hand, John C. Knox, Alfred Talley,
Felix C. Benvenga, Ferdinand Pecora, George Gordon Battle, George W. Alger, Samuel Markewich, and Bernard L.
Shientag—all of them were giants of the New York bench
and bar in the first half of this century, and all of them
played important parts in the Werblow saga.

The year 1922 found the entire Werblow family living
in Brooklyn. Michel (Mitzke) Verbelovsky, born in Libau
in 1894, was now Robert Maximilian Werblow, Jr., a self-
proclaimed native American, born in Fort Morgan,
Colorado; a veteran of World War I who received a lieutenant's commission at the famous Officers' Training Camp at
Plattsburgh in 1917. He professed to be of Dutch and
French lineage and of the Episcopal faith, educated at Columbia University. At least, that was the dossier he furnished to the Chase National Bank, on Wall Street, where

---

*Throughout this narrative there are references to two different tran-
scripts of testimony. Most are to the trial of Henry Werblow in New
York in 1924. The other transcript is of Robert Werblow's naturalization
hearing in 1941. Robert's fervid patriotic cry appears in the transcript
of the naturalization case.

he was employed. He becomes the "Mitzke" of our narrative.

An older brother, who had been "Isaac" in Libau ("Itzek" in his native tongue, and the "Itzke" of our story), now called himself Elliott (or Elyot) Werblow. He was the last to come to America. In Europe he had seen and suffered much, had survived World War I, the Russian Revolution, and the carnage of the civil war and the war between the Soviets and Poland. He did not arrive in the United States until 1921. His experiences had developed in him a capacity for survival in circumstances that would have broken most men. In addition to some remarkable linguistic skills, he was adept in accounting. He also had a talent for assuming the protective coloration of the environment in which he found himself, a quality that had undoubtedly served him well in the Russian army during World War I and in the Red Army thereafter. Unlike Robert-Mitzke and Henry-Hotzke, Itzke never claimed to have been born in Fort Morgan, Colorado. Poor Itzke! Not for him the splendid security of a birthplace at the foot of the American Rockies.

The most startling change was in the personal composition of Chatzkel (or Hotzke) Verbelovsky. Now calling himself Henry H. (for Harrison) Werblow, he, too, professed to be a native of the Golden West, born of sturdy Dutch stock who had joined the pioneers in founding Fort Morgan, Colorado.* He, too, professed to find solace in the

---

*Throughout their lives, Robert and Henry Werblow persistently clung to the fiction that they were born in Fort Morgan, Colorado. "Fort Morgan, Colorado" had a special indigenous *American* ring to it. Robert was asked in the 1941 naturalization hearing, "Will you please state how it was that you picked on that place, Ft. Morgan? How did that place come to your mind as a place where you should claim that you were born?" He testified that his sister knew a man "who had a brother in Fort

Anglican faith. He, too, pretended to be a product of the Ivy League (although when he applied to the Chase Bank for his first job, his ability to write English was so frail that brother Mitzke had to write the letter). At least, that is what he had told *his* employer, the Asia Banking Corporation, the Asiatic affiliate of the proud and mighty Guaranty Trust Company of New York, by whom he was employed in 1922 in Peking, China. Henry appears to have been the most enterprising and imaginative of the brothers. In World War I he had served in military intelligence with the U.S. Army's Siberian Expedition. After the war, he served at the U.S. consulate in Vladivostok. He later described himself as the Vice-Consul in that office, and though there is much doubt that he ever had such a title, there is no doubt that he served there in some capacity. We know that by 1922, Henry was comfortably established as assistant manager in the Peking branch of the Asia Banking Corporation.

Thus, both brothers had assumed identities far more impressive than the simple background from which they had sprung. No immigrants they! They were *real* Americans. Apparently, they felt like Sheridan's arriviste Irishman who said, "Our ancestors are very good kind of folks, but they are the last people I should choose to have a visiting acquaintance with." In his testimony in the 1941 natu-

---

Morgan" and he learned that the birth records in that community had been destroyed. He said, "He implanted the seed to me as Fort Morgan, Colorado, being a place where no birth records were kept."

In 1927 Robert actually journeyed to Fort Morgan and induced an aging physician to aver that he attended at Robert's birth in Fort Morgan. On the basis of this recollection, Robert obtained a birth certificate from Fort Morgan. When brother Henry learned of Robert's success in documenting the Fort Morgan myth, he, too, made the pilgrimage to Colorado, found the same physician, and got himself a birth certificate. In the face of this imposing documentation, it was hard to kill the lie.

ralization proceeding, Robert Werblow gave this poignant explanation of the lies about his and his brothers' origin, lineage, and education:

A. Well, as I previously indicated when my brother Henry and I started to go to work we had adopted a lie as our origin. . . . And in a further attempt, or in an attempt to further that lie we have continued to— as it shows—to create new backgrounds for ourselves —new pedigrees.

* * *

Q. Explain why you did this, Mr. Werblow.

A. Well, realizing the difficulty of being foreign born and looking for a job, I foolishly adopted a lie as the beginning of my life in this country for which I am very sorry. I have lied about my birth; I have lied about my citizenship and one lie led to another, until I actually became to believe it so. I regret it very much.

Q. And you knew with respect to the false statements that you have given under oath as to your origin and pedigree that you were committing perjury?

A. Yes.

Q. In connection with your application for admission to the Officers' Training Camp at Plattsburgh, you made similar false statements as to your birth?

A. I have.

Q. And you continued these false statements until 1934?

A. Yes.

Q. During the proceeding before Judge Knox?

A. Yes.

Q. What happened at that time?

A. Well, in 1934 I realized that all of my grief and troubles which I have had were all due to my own doing because I have lived the life of a lie. It was a case of telling one lie to cover up another lie. It was a case whereas if I told one lie it involved my whole life practically up to the time of my birth, and at that time I decided to clean up my life and abandon the foolish and stupid stand which I had taken in telling lies. I decided to tell a truthful story and to live a clean life and to begin life all over again.

Q. When you say that one lie led to another, it was as a result of your stubborn or stupid insistence on attempting to maintain the origin or pedigree which you started from?

A. Yes.

In 1922 these three brothers hatched a scheme that made skillful use of their special qualities, their fraternal intimacy, their common knowledge of Yiddish, their access to banking secrets, their unusual histrionic skills—and, most of all, their utter disregard for the truth. In the end, when it seemed that the miscreants had been brought to book, they were turned loose by the Court of Appeals of the State of New York, with an opinion by Benjamin N. Cardozo that is a testament to his vast juridical intellect but that deals a karate chop to the primal instincts for justice and retribution. It really needed a Cardozo to figure out why these three perpetrators of a patently felonious international heist should be set free.

As one reviews the fantastic swindle these three brothers contrived and executed, it must be borne in mind that their daring raid on the citadels of banking could not have been carried out by any random little group of freebooters, however great their daring and shrewdness. There was one indispensable ingredient that *only* these brothers enjoyed: Henry, as assistant manager of the Peking branch of Asia Banking, was privy to secret codes used by Guaranty Trust and Asia Banking for transmitting funds by cable between

New York, London, and the principal cities of China. In conjunction with the secret codes, the Guaranty Trust and its correspondent banks also employed a common secret-cipher key. This was a carefully devised and jealously guarded system used to authenticate cables that transmitted money. The codes and ciphers were known to only a handful of the most trusted officers in each branch of the bank. In Peking, Henry Werblow was one of only two employees who had access to these valuable secrets. As Francis Bacon once wrote in tragic foreknowledge of his own temptation and ruin, "Opportunity doth make a thief."

In June 1922 a series of cablegrams passed among the three brothers, Robert (Mitzke), Isaac (Itzke), and Henry (Hotzke). These telegrams provide a clear skeletal outline of the scheme. Isaac, equipped with a draft for £100 and a steamship ticket, was to go from New York to London and, under the *nom de guerre* "Max Elliott," open an account with the Guaranty Trust's London branch. Henry, in China, was to send a bona fide cable to London transmitting £300 to "Max Elliott's account" at the Guaranty Trust's London office. "Max Elliott" was to play his part by confiding to the bank officials that in addition to the small remittance already received, he was expecting very substantial sums from China in connection with a contract between his principals and the Chinese government for the construction of a bridge. Once "Max Elliott" and his Chinese connections were made known to the bank officers in London and his credit with the bank was established, fictitious cables were to be sent, purportedly from Asia Banking's Hankow branch, using the secret codes and cipher, directing the London branch to pay substantial sums to "Max Elliott." He was then to instruct the London branch to transmit the sums so received to Asia Banking's Peking office, for the account of "Chester James" (Henry, of course). On receipt, the fictitious Chester James could dispose of the funds as he chose.

Simple, neat, and seemingly foolproof. In execution the plan proved clumsy, transparent, and stupid. But the plan floundered because of the enormous investigative resources the Guaranty Trust commanded, and because the conspirators lost their nerve and ran out of lies.

Though there is no surviving evidence as to when and where the plot was conceived, it seems clear that there must have been some communication between Robert, in New York, and Henry, in China, out of which their conspiracy evolved. Isaac-Itzke-Elliott could have been little more than their pawn—eager and willing, but still a pawn. He was a greenhorn, fresh from the old country and hardly capable of contributing to the conception. In practice, he was to prove both the luckiest and the most reliable of the miscreants.

On June 15, 1922, Henry, in Peking, cabled to Robert, in New York:

> Referring to your last telegram have simplified plan to extent of eliminating all characters except Elyot. James presence here not necessary. No outsiders participate. Advise Elyot that after arrival at his destination he is to communicate with me as follows: 'Chester James, Bankasia, Peking.' never to any other port at any time, although he may have received information indicating my presence other ports. Hozke.

Robert acknowledged Henry's cable with the following on June 19:

> Received your two telegrams, writing for funds. Will wire date of sailing. In the future use Robwerblo.

And next day Henry cabled Robert again:

For immediate funds if necessary sell Anglo stock.
Later will remit Eliot at destination.*

On June 26 Isaac Werblow (Max Elliott) applied to the
Passport Control Office at the British consulate in New
York for a visa to make a visit to the United Kingdom. He
was told that it would take a few days. On the following
day, Robert and Isaac appeared at the New York office of
the Guaranty Trust, where Isaac was introduced to the
officer in charge of the bank's foreign-exchange office as
"Max Elliott," and where he purchased a draft for £100,
paying $441.63. The funds came from a check for $450.00
drawn on a joint account of Robert and Henry in the New
York Trust Company.

On June 30 Robert cabled Henry: "Elyot waiting for
visa. In any case one of us will leave not later than July
8th."

Apparently, Robert anticipated that Isaac might have
some problem with his visa or passport and that he, Robert, might have to go to London instead and play the part
of Max Elliott. Robert's credentials as an American citizen born in Fort Morgan, Colorado, though completely
spurious, were well established, and he had already received an American passport. Robert and Henry were
evidently somewhat apprehensive of Isaac's ability to

---

*The cables that passed among the brothers, translated here into conven-
tional English cablese, were in fact written in a mixture of Bentley's
Commercial Code and Yiddish. They were later translated by a team of
skilled code experts and linguists in the employ of the Guaranty Trust
Co. For the reader's convenience, only the final English version is given
here. These English translations were never questioned by the defendants in their trials and were accepted by the trial courts and the juries.

carry off his assigned role, for on July 2, Henry cabled to Robert:

> Owing to possible recognition of Elyot use your judgment. Great caution in conjunction with visa. Will sign Xazke, Mitzke, Itzke accordingly.

The assumption that Robert was ready to stand in as "Max Elliott" is fortified by the fact that on July 5 the White Star Line issued a first-class passage to *Robert Werblow* for travel to England on the S.S. Majestic, sailing on July 8. And on the same day, Robert applied for a visa to visit England. In order to accompany Isaac on his visits to the steamship office and the British consulate, Robert had to be excused from his duties at the Chase Bank. This he accomplished by relating the fiction that his father was dying in France, and that he needed the time to make arrangements to attend the obsequies. Undoubtedly, this bunkum was designed to explain his extended absence in the event he should have to stand in for Isaac in London. But on July 5 Isaac's application for a visa to England was granted by the Passport Control Office. The ticket purchased by Robert was canceled, and a new ticket was issued for the same voyage to "Isakas Verbelovas." The price of the ticket was $285.00, and again the funds were obtained by cashing a check for that amount on the joint account of Robert and Henry in the New York Trust Company. Now there was no need for Robert to go to England. Itzke had his visa, a steamship ticket, the draft for £100, and the new identity of Max Elliott to be assumed on arrival in England.

On July 6 Robert cabled Henry:

> Itzke due to sail July 8. Use double 'l' double 't' in the name Elliott. Telegram to him of every remittance. It

is very important for the purpose of referring and also convincing in the bank. Use New York Trust Company as well as Chase for your remittances. Mitzke.

And on July 8 a relieved Robert cabled to an anxious Henry:

Itzke sailed today, Mitzke home.

The plot was in full train. The S.S. Majestic was speeding Itzke to London for his rendezvous with international fraud, and the enterprising Henry sat poised in Peking, secret cipher in hand, ready to defraud the Guaranty Trust.

On July 10 Robert-Mitzke received the following from Henry-Hotzke:

Take steps to collect dividends on Prairie Oil. Believe further communication regarding large proposition must be discontinued. Cables can be traced Itzke Mitzke. Must adopt safer communication. I am writing fully. Be cautious. Xazke.

And Itzke–Isaac–Max Elliott received this cablegram in London:

Telegraphing you from Hankow as follows: On July 17, £300, July 20, £17,430, July 22, £14,200. All of the remittances on account Hankow government. You have their authority act on behalf of government. Advise bank interested accordingly. Also funds are to be used for constructing railroad bridge amounting to £120,000 and state that you may perhaps need the bank's financial help. Give above information to the bank immediately upon arrival. State further in case bank give assistance financing your clients will give

substantial securities. When you open your account
Guaranty Trust interview with executive official and
promise to do large business in the future. Demand
large interest on your deposit. Act bravely and independent. Transfer funds to me as soon as possible. Act
according to best possible judgment. Telegraph to me
Chester James, Bankasia, Peking. Destroy by fire all of
[sic] the upon their receipt. Love, Xozke.

The subscription is a touching testament to brotherly
affection, especially since Henry-Xozke later swore he had
never seen Isaac-Itzke in his life. Henry cabled Robert on
July 16:

I have Elyot telegraphed to him £300 July 22, £17,000
July 20, £14,000 on July 22d Hozke will he be in time
for receiving. I cannot wait any longer. Reply immediately. Urgent.

In turn, Robert-Mitzke put some heat on "Itzke":

Xozke informs me that he has sent over to you £300 on
July 17,000 on the 20th and 14 on the 22d. Mixke.

The time had come for Isaac–Itzke–Max Elliott to play
his part as the occidental agent for the syndicate that was
to construct large public works for one of China's provincial governments. On the morning of July 17, 1922, a well-
dressed and self-possessed young gentleman appeared in
the London office of the Guaranty Trust Company. He
introduced himself as Mr. Max Elliott, Manager of National Trading Corporation, Vladivostok, Siberia. He wore
dark glasses, he spoke "very good English, with a foreign
accent," and he gave his temporary address in London at
a fashionable West End Hotel. All in all, he made a most

favorable impression on the people at the bank. They were delighted to open an account for him, using his £100 draft from the Guaranty Trust in New York. There was some friendly chitchat about the skin and fur trade in the Far East. After this *causerie*, the personable young Mr. Elliott let drop some references to his relationship with the Wuchang provincial government, some titivating intimations that his principals in China were building a railway bridge for the provincial government . . . there would be large remittances . . . £120,000 to start . . . could be some substantial financing business for the bank.

Itzke followed the scenario that had been laid down by Henry in his long cable of July 14. Within a day or two, a cable came from Asia Banking in Hankow to credit £300 to Max Elliott, "account of Chester James."* The money for the remittance had been delivered across the counter by "a Chinese of the coolie or servant class" (Henry's cook in Peking) to Asia Banking's Hankow office, together with a typewritten letter addressed to the manager. The composition of this letter entitles Henry Werblow to a permanent niche in the Confidence Man's Hall of Fame. It reads:

> Please remit, at my risk, by cable at your best possible rate £300 (pounds sterling three hundred—only) to 'Max Elliott care of American Express Co., London, account of Chester James.' As I have not arranged for Code messages to Mr. Elliott, and wishing to save cable expenses, I would appreciate it very much if you will kindly, while making this remittance, in the same cable at my expense instruct your correspondent to advise Mr. Elliott as follows:

---

*"Chester James" was a creature of Henry's active imagination. The name appears for the first time in his cable of July 24, "the scenario."

'Wuchang provincial government
accept our offer on bridge and
agree to remit 30% this week.'

I am sending with the bearer, my servant, funds to
cover this remittance and all cable charges. Please
give him your usual confirmation statement and re-
ceipts.

CHESTER JAMES
Legal Adviser to Civil Governor

It was later proved that this letter was typed on a machine available to Henry in Asia Banking's Peking office.

So convincing was this letter that no one questioned the
authority of Chester James, not to speak of his existence.
But if the ring of authenticity deafened the ears and dead-
ened the sensibilities of the European managers of the Hankow branch, its impact on the bankers in London was even
greater. Plainly, this well-tailored, suave Siberian who
called himself Max Elliott was, for all his youth and foreign
appearance, truly a man of large affairs, a substantial
wheeler-dealer with far-flung connections. If there were
any suspicions of his bona fides in the London office of
Guaranty Trust, they were dispelled by this remittance
and the accompanying message. Assuredly, young Mr. Elliott had important connections with that prodigious Oriental tycoon "the Legal Advisor to the Provincial Governor
of Wuchang"; he was engaged in financing and constructing major public works in that far-off land, and, most important, he had broadly intimated that he would throw
some substantial banking business in the way of the Guaranty Trust, London branch, at a good interest rate.

Within two days came fresh confirmation of Mr. Elliott's
importance and affluence. A cable dated July 20 was re-

ceived, purportedly from the Hankow branch of Asia Banking, reading:

Advise pay £17,430 to Max Elliott for a/c of Provincial Government. Governor promises to pay additional this week. Balance due you 3 months. A.B.C.

And two days later came another:

Pay £14,200 to Max Elliott Provincial Government. A.B.C. Hankow.

Both cablegrams were in Guaranty Trust's private code, and both contained the correct secret-cipher key necessary to confirm authority to pay out money.

Needless to say, the July 20 cable (£17,430) had never been signed or sent by the Hankow office of Asia Banking. It was later established that like "Chester James' " first letter, the cable was typed on a machine available to Henry at the Peking office—and even bore some words in his own handwriting.

The London office of Guaranty Trust honored all three cables with dispatch and paid into the account of the enterprising young Mr. Elliott the aggregate sum of £31,930— about $160,000 in those days.

The next stage of the swindle required Itzke–Max Elliott to get the money out of London and into safe hands. This was accomplished by drawing a series of checks on Mr. Elliott's Guaranty Trust account, payable to the Hong Kong & Shanghai Bank. That institution was then instructed to cable the funds to the Peking office of Asia Banking to the credit of Chester James. When the funds were duly received in Peking, the manager happened to be absent on leave, and Henry-Hotzke, as his deputy, was in

complete charge of the Peking office. Now we understand
the urgency in the early cables. Henry had known for some
time that Klingsmith, the manager, would be away from
Peking in late July, and that at that time he would be in
complete charge at the Peking branch when the money
arrived.

Henry promptly opened an account at Asia Banking in
the name of "Hilliard & James," and the funds received
from London were credited to it. He himself opened the
account in the bank's ledger, filled out the signature cards
himself, and attended to the entire transaction. No other
employee touched a paper or heard a single word. None of
the employees of Asia Banking in Peking ever saw or heard
of Chester James or Hilliard & James.

Now to transfer the funds from China to New York.
Henry had to invent a reason for resigning so that he could
go to New York to preside over the division of the boodle.
But first the money must get to New York. This was ac-
complished by obtaining Japanese drafts on the Hilliard &
James account through Oriental banks other than the Asia
Banking Corporation and transmitting them by mail to
Robert-Mitzke in New York. Robert received the drafts on
August 28. On August 30 one of the drafts was sold to the
New York banking firm of A. B. Leach & Co., where
James,* the youngest Werblow brother, was employed as a
clerk. A check for the aggregate amount was made out to
brother James, who endorsed it to Robert, and, in accord-
ance with the original plan, the funds were deposited in the
joint account of Robert and Henry at New York Trust.

The deposit of the funds in New York had hardly been

_____

*Brother James is not to be confused with Chester James. There is no
connection. His name may have inspired Henry in inventing the mythical Chester.

recorded when the first small omen of discovery and disaster appeared. Early in September, the Hankow office of Asia Banking received letters from Guaranty Trust in London confirming that on Hankow's instructions it had made the substantial payments to Max Elliott directed by the cablegrams of July 20 and July 22.

What cablegrams? asks Hankow. We know of no such cablegrams! There is consternation; London, Hankow, Shanghai, and New York burn up the transoceanic cables with questions. Who is Max Elliott? Who is Chester James? An investigation is ordered; since the recipient of the stolen funds, the Chester James (Hilliard & James) account, has been traced to the Peking branch, the investigation focuses there. Henry, in charge at Peking, is among the first to know of the trouble.

On September 5 Henry-Hotzke, in Peking, cables to Mitzke, in New York:

> Itzke shall hide himself. They are looking for him.
> Bad.

And on September 16 he sends this portentous telegram to Robert:

> I have sent cable from N.Y. They say that you have 96000 Japanese money. You have made a great mistake. It is known that you have given a check to Itzke to by £100. Now you must say that you know nothing about it. You must say that Itzke requested your check gave you cash. You shall say that I sent you Japanese money to keep for a Chinese friend. His name is Chen Pan Fu. You should hide all your money. It is not very good. You and I are being shadowed. You will be arrested. You should prepare accordingly. Hoske

Now, it was part of the plan that once the money was safely in New York, Henry was to resign from his job in Peking and return to share in the enjoyment of the spoils. Accordingly, in early August, he had advised the general manager of Asia Banking in Shanghai that he had been slighted by his superior in Peking, and he wrote, "I wish you to take my resignation, to take effect the latter part of August."

But the hand of fate now intervened. Dr. Holder, president of Asia Banking, happened to be in China when he learned of Henry's resignation. Holder regarded Henry as a valuable employee, one plainly destined to higher responsibility in the bank. What bank wants to lose the services of an employee so loyal, so devoted, and so clearly deserving of advancement? Holder went to Peking, spoke with Henry, gave him a substantial increase in salary, promised him that he would be promoted to manager, and induced him to remain in Peking. Of course, Henry was persuaded to stay.

Maybe his decision to stay in Peking was affected by a cablegram from Itzke, in London, who wrote, "Hotzke must stay for at least five months longer to allay suspicion, to make it all safe and secure." At any rate, this loyal hoplite stayed on guard at the pass.

This was during the interval when one of Asia Banking's top men in China, Tisdall, was quickly sent from headquarters in Shanghai to Peking to assist the investigation by the local people. Klingsmith, the manager, was on leave. Henry Werblow was the number-one man on the scene when Tisdall arrived. Tisdall consulted with Henry, who gave him an impressive show of zeal and efficiency. He was in all respects the loyal servant of the bank. The two men agreed on one point: they must find Chester James. And Henry became both detective and dragoman to Tisdall (who did not know Peking and was unfamiliar with the dialect of North China) in pursuing the trails in Peking's murky alleys.

While Tisdall and Henry were searching files and running out "leads" in Peking, London was following the spoor of the evanescent Max Elliott. That fine young man was now established in a suite at the Hotel Adlon, in Berlin. There he awaited news from Robert-Mitzke, and for his share of the loot.

Ah, what a splendid movie it would have made. One can imagine the late Peter Lorre, lispy accent and all, in the role of Itzke, hiding his anxieties behind a mask of humble politeness, hovering near the desk of the concierge for cables that do not come, going each day to the kiosk in the Kurfürstendamm for the English newspapers, scanning them for news; waiting, waiting, for word from Mitzke.

It never came. What came was news of exposure, of disaster. The time of anxious waiting for poor abandoned Itzke-Elliott was over. It was time to run.

But in Peking there was no waiting; there, it was all frenetic activity. Tisdall, the hard-bitten Old China Hand who was now collaborating with Henry in clearing up the mysteries, must have smelled that something was wrong. Henry, bogged down in a quicksand of deceit, was backing and filling, improvising and lying, to avoid the critical discovery that there never was a Chester James except in his own imagination. The first step was to try to convince others in the Peking office that they had actually met and talked with Chester James; this would create some verisimilitude. When this did not work, Henry prepared newspaper advertisements containing descriptions of both Chester James and his fictitious partner, Robert Hilliard, and offering a reward for information about their whereabouts. Tisdall and he searched every club and hotel, every resort frequented by Westerners; they even recruited the aid of the Chinese police, a delicate and expensive recourse, according to the knowledgeable Henry. Then Henry diverted suspicion from himself by suggesting that a fraud had been perpetrated by a former officer of the bank, a heavy drinker who had been dismissed for defalcation. At length, he led Tisdall to a dingy, obscure Chinese bank where they triumphantly "recovered" several thousand dollars that had allegedly been deposited by Chester James. (Later, Tisdall realized that it was not even a bank. He could not read the ideograms on the window, and only Henry could carry on the conversations.)

But at this point Henry's credibility sustained a hard blow. Tisdall received cable information from his head office that it had been discovered that Robert Werblow in New York had received a substantial part of the missing funds. Promptly, Tisdall suspended Henry from further duties at the bank, superseded him in the investigation with a new man hurriedly sent from Shanghai, and embarked on an intensive interrogation of Henry.

After a while, Henry told Tisdall he wanted to confess. Tisdall testified that Henry told him a man named Chester James had appeared in Peking, and tried to coerce Henry into joining the conspiracy. Tearfully, Henry said:

> He gave me proofs that my brother Robert was implicated in a conspiracy to defraud the Asia Banking Corporation. I begged of him to desist and even went so far as to offer him a sum of money, amounting to $30,000 if he would give it up. He told me he wanted me to join in. I refused. Whereupon, he informed me that the plot would go on whether I joined it or not. Therefore, in order to protect the bank and, if possible, to protect my brother and destroy all evidence against my brother, I consented to join in but, as far

as I am concerned, I want to take all the punishment
that is coming to me and I don't want my brother to
suffer in any way.

As to the yen drafts that had been sent to Robert, Henry
insisted they had nothing to do with Chester James, or with
Hankow; that in fact the money belonged to a Chinese
political refugee, a former Minister of Finance named
Chen Pan Fu. The money had been entrusted to Henry for
the benefit of Chen Pan Fu's little daughter who was in
hiding from assassins in America; it was sent to Robert
because he was the guardian of this exotic Oriental blos-
som, who of course existed only in Henry's imagination.
When Tisdall asked Henry for proof of his tale about Chen
Pan Fu, Henry said, "I have destroyed the proof. I do not
keep any letters or cablegrams or anything from Chen Pan
Fu, because he is a political refugee, and it would be to my
detriment and to the detriment of Chen Pan Fu if I did keep
such stuff."

Nothing more was ever heard of Mr. Chen or his
daughter until Henry returned to New York, when he
admitted to Dr. Holder and Mr. Nye, of Guaranty Trust,
that "the Chen Pan Fu story was a fake from beginning to
end."

When Tisdall suggested that the Asia Banking Corporation would be happy to hold this money for the little Chen
girl, Henry cabled to Robert suggesting he turn it over.
Tisdall testified that Henry then entreated him to let him
go to New York, "where he would very soon find out who
had stolen the check cipher." After consulting by cable
with his superiors in New York, Tisdall took Henry to
Shanghai, paid his passage to New York, and saw him off
on the steamer.

So much, for the moment, of Henry-Hotzke speeding

across the Pacific. What of Mitzke? What of Itzke?

Robert-Mitzke was enduring his own special ordeal in New York. On September 20 he received, at his apartment in Brooklyn, a cable from Henry:

> Communicate with the Asia Bank. Give them full details all private business especially Pan Fu account. Produce documents to support. Assign proceeds to Asia Bank Pan Fu last remittance yen 96,000. If necessary assign proceeds previous remittance. *Suggest you request his daughter to proceed to New York, support your testimony.*

In view of Henry's later admission that Chen Pan Fu and his daughter were entirely figments of his imagination, this last was a pretty tough assignment for Robert-Mitzke.

Reading this balderdash was no help to Robert, who was already running out of lies. Dr. Holder, who had made a hurried return to New York, and Mr. Nye grilled Robert mercilessly. Robert was evasive; he was "hazy." But he did inject some startling *new* confections into the tale. Confronted with documentary proof of his remittances to Itzke ("Icikas Verbelovas") in Berlin, he stoutly denied that Icikas Verbelovas was his brother Max Elliott or Elyot; he insisted that the recipient was a distant cousin whom he had never met and to whom he sent the money at Elyot's oral request (Elyot, by the way, seemed to have disappeared from the family abode). However, in humble compliance with Henry's telegram of September 20, on October 3 he did turn over to Asia Banking whatever was left (after secreting some of it with a brother-in-law in Brooklyn and sending several thousand dollars to the anguished Itzke in Berlin) of the proceeds of the yen drafts he had got from Henry. This amounted to about $45,000, and Dr. Holder gave him a formal receipt therefor. Nobody mentioned Chen Pan Fu or his daughter.

Primarily, Mitzke was stalling, fighting for time. He knew that Hotzke was on his way to New York "to clear things up," and he was determined to hold the line until they could coordinate. By now, Itzke has passed into the white mists of Eastern Europe, not to be heard from for years.

On October 28, 1922, Henry arrived in New York. The first public reference to the case was in *The New York Times* of October 29, 1922, which records that the shrewd and sagacious officials of the Asia Banking Corporation and the Guaranty Trust Company had detected the fraud and "lured" Henry into returning ten thousand miles to New York for arrest because "It was impossible to extradite him from China and difficult to try him there, so the plan of decoying him to this country was used successfully."

This must have been a press agent's invention. We know now from the later testimony of Dr. Holder himself and of Mr. Tisdall that it is completely untrue. Henry-Hotzke *wanted* to come back; he had so much self-confidence, such faith in his own ability to assuage every doubt with his special brand of malarkey, that his return was completely voluntary. The officials of Guaranty Trust had been so humiliated by the swindle that they may well have concocted the story about luring Henry back to the United States to make them look smarter. Dr. Holder laid this yarn to rest when he later testified:

I received a telegram from Henry Werblow saying, "will you not allow me to come to the United States to explain this whole thing?" Those were the words. Whereupon I cabled back to Tisdall to let him come and I cabled to Henry, "I have cabled Tisdall to allow you to come to New York. Hope you can explain and justify my appointment of you."

Henry's return to New York triggered some important events. From the moment he landed in Seattle, he was trailed across the country by detectives as he headed for a rendezvous with Robert in Brooklyn. By this time, of course, almost $100,000 had already been "voluntarily" repaid to the bank either by Henry in Peking or by Robert in New York. The difference of about $40,000 had either gone to Itzke, now disporting himself with the Guaranty Trust's *valuta* beneath the onion-topped domes of Muscovy, or was stashed away with relatives in Brooklyn.

When Henry arrived in New York, he took a taxicab from the railway station to the family apartment in Brooklyn, where he was to meet Robert. Dr. Holder, forewarned by the Guaranty Trust's gumshoes of Henry's imminent arrival there, had stationed himself across the street from the apartment house. When Henry emerged from the taxicab, Holder approached him and said, "Henry, I want to have a talk with you before you talk to anybody, and find out about this accusation that has been made against you." Whereupon Henry obediently deposited his baggage at the door of the familial residence and accompanied Holder back to his Park Avenue apartment in Manhattan. There then occurred a bizarre interview that was recounted in detail at the trial. Holder did not disclose that in the adjoining room, separated from them by a thin partition, were Joseph M. Nye, chief investigator for the Guaranty Trust Company, and a stenographer.

Holder complained that Henry had deceived him in Peking and exhorted him now to come clean. Henry explained that he could not have told Holder the truth in Peking: "I was afraid to tell you at that time because I did not know how deeply my brother was in this thing." He continued with a smooth-tongued fabrication, explaining that back in June, Chester James and Hilliard had come to him and said that they had bought the company's code and cipher from Robert in New York for $3,500, and that they asked him to join the conspiracy. He did not even try to explain how Robert could have obtained the code and cipher. He struck a poignant note: "I have always dominated my brother. He always was weak, and I was afraid he got himself into a snarl and probably I could get him out by pretending to go into this thing. Blood is thicker than water and I wanted to save him if I could. . . . I was convinced that he was probably taken hold of or influenced by a gang of crooks in New York."

After a few more exercises in romantic fiction, Henry came up with a startling solution to the whole problem. His proposition to Holder: "Well, if you will try to hush this thing up, I will make restitution." He explained that the remaining shortage was only about $30,000; that although he had only $15,000 in savings, he also had a $20,000 insurance policy on his life. He suggested to Holder that he would transfer the proceeds of his life-insurance policy to Holder and then commit suicide. Thereafter, Holder could tell the bank, " 'Why see, I appointed a man who is absolutely loyal to me. Here he turns this insurance policy over to me, kills himself . . . here's your money.' "

Holder rejected this desperate solution with a short expletive. Henry persisted in the request that he be permitted to perform hara-kiri for the benefit of the bank and his brother Robert, and to give his youngest brother James "a chance in the world," but Holder was not interested.

We hear no more of Hotzke's willingness to commit the honorable dispatch as an act of familial piety. He now

forsook any air of penitence or sorrow for the further pretense that he was a martyr to the greed and machinations
of his employers. From here on, the brothers elected, in the
words of Burke, "to die in the last dyke of prevarication."

Nye entered the room, questioned Henry, particularly
about all the cables. When the interview was over, Lieutenant Barney Flood of the New York City Police Department
appeared and arrested Henry, and at Police Headquarters
there was a touching fraternal reunion with Robert, whom
Flood had arrested earlier.* In those days, there was no
constitutional folderol about warnings against self-incrimination and the right to the presence of counsel. The two
brothers seem to have been subjected to on-the-spot grilling
by detectives, in the presence of the investigators of the
Guaranty Trust Company.

Robert and Henry were now established in the Tombs,
where they remained for a considerable time until bail was
furnished. Their lawyer, Samuel Markewich,† informed
the press that Robert "is absolutely innocent and doesn't
know what it is all about yet." As to Henry, Markewich
asserted that "instead of robbing the bank, Henry had, by
his vigilance, actually saved it about $100,000 so that the net
loss was only a few thousand dollars." Mr. Markewich by
this time had undoubtedly received the mythopoeic ministrations of the two brothers when they explained that they
had been victimized; that they "were played against each
other by a third relative who, in company with a gang of

---

*As reported in *The New York Times*, October 29, 1922.
†Markewich was a familiar figure to many generations of New York
lawyers. A skilled criminal lawyer, highly respected by the bench and
bar, he was an incomparable raconteur whose recollections at lunch in
Gasner's enriched our lives until he died a few years ago, at more than
ninety years old. He was survived by two gifted lawyer-sons, one of
them a Justice of the Appellate Division.

international bank crooks, had conceived the plan of swindling by means of forged telegrams passing between China, London and New York."

On October 30, 1922, Henry-Hotzke, Robert-Mitzke, and Isaac-Itzke were indicted by the Grand Jury of New York County for grand larceny in the first degree. For the people, the case was entrusted to Hugo Wintner, one of the most experienced of the assistants to Joab Banton, then District Attorney of New York County. The case did not come to trial for more than a year. During that time, commissions were issued to take testimony before the Extraterritorial United States Court in China. Many witnesses were examined by both sides and many interrogatories were propounded and answered. Itzke, of course, was a fugitive in Soviet Russia and was never brought to trial.

For some unexplained reason, the brothers elected to be tried separately. Henry's case came on before Judge Alfred J. Talley and a jury on January 7, 1924. It is not my purpose to recount all the details of the trial, but the brass-bound audacity of the defense makes it memorable. Henry's trial counsel was George Gordon Battle, generally regarded as one of the ablest and most eloquent criminal lawyers of his time, a Southerner with a magnificent command of the language, tremendous personal charm enhanced by a rich Confederate accent, and the highest technical abilities.*

Wintner's opening for the prosecution was thorough and circumstantial. He based his case on the telegrams. Battle conceded in *his* opening that the case "reads like an E. Phillips Oppenheim novel of international mystery."

---

*Battle is still remembered with affection and respect by many of New York's veteran lawyers. He died in 1949, but his name survives to this day in the title of an eminent New York law firm.

He waved in front of the jury all the red herrings that the fertile imaginations of Henry and Robert could devise, and strove laboriously to place the blame on poor "Elyot":

> He is not a full brother. He is only a half brother. He has been a wanderer and a black sheep. Henry, so it happens, has never even seen him. Elyot had been in the Russian army during the war. After the war, he became a Bolshevik and was in the Bolshevik army over there for a while and got in trouble there. He was imprisoned for grafting or profiteering.

The fatal cablegrams, claimed Battle with unparalleled audacity, were never sent by Henry, and although they were addressed to "Robwerblo," Robert never saw them or even knew of them. They were sent by some mysterious person whose identity would be revealed in the trial and were intended for that will-o'-the-wisp Elyot! (He ignored the fact that the originals bore Henry's handwriting.)

The reader must be gentle with Mr. Battle. He must not be condemned; he had only what his clients had given him, and what Henry and Robert had given him was one of the most outrageous, transparent, porous confections of *chutzpah* and mendacity ever flung in the face of an American jury.

The people's case was simply overwhelming. Every telegram that had passed among the conspirators was retrieved from the files in Peking, Hankow, London, Berlin, and New York. Witness after witness appeared and established the arrangements that were made for Elliott (or Robert) to go to London, Itzke's magnificent histrionics in London, what happened in Peking, and what happened in Hankow. Then came such witnesses as Tisdall, Holder, and Nye, to expose the fake "confessions," the fabrications and ludicrous explanations. When the prosecution rested its case, it was difficult to see how Mr. Battle could extricate his client from the avalanche of evidence under which he appeared to be buried.

Mr. Battle moved that the indictment should be dismissed because the "evidence clearly shows that all the substantive elements of the offenses were committed outside the jurisdiction of this country and outside the jurisdiction of this court." The trial judge then pointed out that the argument was somewhat vitiated if there were a conspiracy, for if the proof showed that part of the conspiracy were hatched in New York, then the New York court might have jurisdiction. But the indictment contained no count for conspiracy. The people's response was that the crime was covered by Section 930 (at the time) of the Penal Law, which provided that if *any* steps taken in preparation to commit the crime were taken in New York, the court's jurisdiction would attach. Mr. Battle's motion was denied, and the defendant proceeded to put in his defense.

The defense was an effort to create a "reasonable doubt." It is amusing that part of this effort was to establish that Elyot Werblow did not go to England but remained in New York throughout the summer of 1922. The suggestion was that the man who went to London and masqueraded as Max Elliott was not our Elyot, the Itzke of our tale, but by some fantastic coincidence was *another* man named Icikas Verbelovas, a distant cousin of the same name whom the Werblows did not even know.

The defense also introduced a number of depositions that Henry had accumulated in China, the thrust of which was that there was indeed a man named Chester James who was once in Peking, but nobody knew anything more than that about him. Depositions were offered from a number of

Caucasian expatriates in China who swore that they had once met a Chester James. They seem to have been barflies, picked up by Henry in Peking, who would have identified Beelzebub for a free whiskey and soda. Strangely, there was no effort to reincarnate Mr. Hilliard. Of him not even the susceptible alcoholics whom Henry had persuaded to "recall" Chester James could remember anything.

Robert Werblow took the stand for his beleaguered brother. He unashamedly recited the false pedigree he had concocted and, in substance, denied ever receiving or sending any of the fateful cablegrams. The substance of Robert's fable was that Elyot had told him he was engaged in importing and exporting flour in the Baltic states; that he "was receiving cables in connection with that business" and "arranged with Robert to use his cable address of Robwerblo." Thus, explained Robert, the cables sent and received in June, July, and August 1922 had nothing to do with him—it was all the work of the scamp Elyot. In brief, he was asking the jury to believe that he was not Mitzke! And since Henry-Hotzke was shortly to deny *sending* the cables and to suggest that they were sent by a faithless Chinese clerk (who was, of course, an adept in the Yiddish dialect), the jury was to accept the hypothesis that these intimate cables in code were exchanged between the treacherous Itzke-Elyot and a perfidious Yiddish-speaking Chinese who was really trying to incriminate the virtuous Henry!

Wintner did a first-class job of destroying Robert on cross-examination. He concentrated first on the false pedigree; so patent were Robert's lies about his past and his family that even the jurors joined in cross-examining him.*

---

*The active participation of several jurors in questioning witnesses is a curiosity in this trial. They frequently broke in with questions. There was no objection by counsel, and the trial judge permitted it.

Some of Robert's glib inventions were so preposterous as to be amusing: he admitted writing a letter dated September 11 to New York Trust directing the bank to send 300,-000 German marks (part of the swag from Hotzke) to "Icikas Verbelovas" in Berlin, but he insisted that he wrote it "under the instructions of Elyot." As to the documents that made such an overwhelming case against the brothers, he ascribed them to the sinister machinations of the investigators for Guaranty Trust, whom he actually charged with fabricating them.

We get the full flavor of Mitzke's testimony from a few gems. When his brother Itzke came to the United States in 1921, Mitzke explained:

> I asked him how he came to change his name *from* Elyot Werblow *to* Icikas Verbelovas. He told me at that time over in Europe, on account of the Bolshevik conditions, inasmuch as he ran away from the Bolshevik army and went to Latvia, the Latvia government tried to get hold of him because they were against the Bolsheviks and he could not come out in the open under the name of Elyot Werblow, and therefore had a friend of his, whom he said was a distant cousin of his, by the name of Icikas Verbelovas, who went to the American consul with his own passport to secure a visa for his entree to America. [*Emphasis supplied*]

Confronted with his own passport application, in which he said that from February to November 1918 he was absent from the United States, "in Paris, in the United States service, A.E.F.," Mitzke glibly admitted it was a lie, made simply "to expedite matters." Then he testified that his father "married my mother in Colorado about thirty years ago or thirty-one years ago."

One of the most amusing parts of his testimony came in

his explanation of his accent—obviously unsuited to a native American.

> _Q._ You realize the fact that you have a distinctive
> foreign accent?
> _A._ I have.
> _Q._ You did not get that in Colorado?
> _A._ No. I can explain it.
> _Q._ When did you get it?
> _A._ When I was born I was tongue-tied. After that I
> had an operation, but the operation was never perfect
> and that is the cause of it.

This explanation should be compared with Henry-
Hotzke's ingenious explanation for _his_ distinctive foreign
accent, which you will soon read.

The climax of the trial was, of course, the testimony of
Henry. If Robert had sounded the depths of mendacity,
Henry scaled the heights of audacity. Quite naturally, he
gave his birthplace as Fort Morgan, Colorado, where he
"lived until he was six." He worked for the Guaranty Trust
"in the foreign credit division," but "at night I used to
work with Captain Burke . . . of the United States Secret
Service." He described how he was sent to Siberia, where
he was "assigned to the Negative Intelligence Department
in the Cryptographic Division, that means deciphering
enemy messages." He then went to "the American Consu-
lar Service in Valdivostok." In September 1920 he began to
work for Asia Banking Corporation in Peking. According
to Henry, "everybody in the bank" knew the cipher; it was
available even to the native clerks.

In describing his meetings with Chester James, of Hilliard & James, Henry's imagination took off like a rocket.

Chester James' physical attributes were minutely described. Those qualities that made him a desirable customer of the bank followed next. All the circumstances
leading up to the opening of his account were recounted
with a rich profusion of detail. Carried away by his soaring
fancy, Henry even remembered a conversation with Hilliard.

Now Henry played his trump. He claimed that there
had been "irregularities" in the bank's dealings with the
Chinese government. He composed a tale alleging that Dr.
Holder had asked his help in covering up the bank's derel-
ictions in its graft dealings with the Chinese authorities.
He tried to intimate that in some way the charges against
him were connected with this rigmarole.

The Court: In what respect? I cannot see it.

Mr. Battle: In this respect, one of the contentions of
the defense is that these irregularities in the bank, in
its dealings there with the Chinese Government, was
one of the reasons why the bank officials were anxious
to pass this matter on this defendant. You will recall
I asked Dr. Holder and also Mr. Tisdall—

The Court: You mean trying to stick upon this defendant the theft of this amount of money to conceal
the irregularity?

Mr. Battle: That is the contention.

In fine, Henry's first line of defense was that Asia Banking had framed him because he had refused to accept the
responsibility for its fraudulent transactions with the Chinese government. He said Dr. Holder told him, "You are
a junior officer and I am going to make you a senior officer.
I will protect you if you will sign a statement saying those,
the graft transactions, were done on your account." And

then he told the court, "I refused to do it!"

He then described his efforts to trace the stolen funds after the fraud was discovered. He described how he and Tisdall had toiled shoulder to shoulder to find the malefactors. Then came a bombshell! Tisdall had told him that

> they had received information from New York that my brother had four drafts for 96,000—twenty-four thousand yen each, 96,000 total, and that my brother states that this draft was received by him from me. He further stated that my brother told them this draft belonged to a Chinese and gave the name. I told him I knew nothing about it. He said "Are you wrong or is your brother wrong?" I told him I didn't know anything about it. He said "Your brother is implicated in this affair," and in my brother's confession he also told him that I helped my brother in this affair, in this fraud. *And I told him I cannot see how my brother could say anything like that, because I had absolutely nothing to do. I had no knowledge of it. [Emphasis added]*

From that moment Hotzke would have had the jury believe he was a puppet in the hands of *Tisdall.* He did what he was told; he signed whatever they put in front of him. Anything, anything, to save his brother Robert. "I did not know anything about Elyot."

By this time, Henry's story was being received with complete incredulity by the judge and jurors.* It is plain from their questions that they were startled by a defense that, distilled, alleged an attack by the manifest malefactor on his victim.

---

*It was a remarkable jury; their questions throughout were direct, to the point, and amazingly perceptive. It must have been clear to Battle, if not to his deluded clients, that the quality of this jury spelled doom to the defense.

Wintner's cross-examination finished Hotzke. First he established that there never was a letter from Guaranty Trust to Asia Banking introducing the mythical Chester James. Next, after puncturing the fable that Henry was sacrificed by the bank to protect it from charges of illegal activities in China, Wintner confronted him with a cablegram dated September 9, 1922, addressed to one of the Asia Banking Corporation's officers, Emery. It read:

> For the sake of past relations and friendship I am appealing to you to persuade New York to hear my side of the incident before judgment passed. I swear to you I am not guilty of robbing the bank. The plot originated in New York. Tried very hard to stop. Discovered by me on evening of execution.

Henry insisted he never sent that cablegram, although under pressure he admitted that the *signature* on the original was his. He went through the same process with the other damning cables, including the Itzke-Mitzke-Hotzke series in Yiddish code. Yes, it was his signature—but he never sent the cables! He could not explain how it happened:

Q. How did it come that you signed it?
A. I would get a bunch of papers on my desk. Whether it was there and I signed it, or—

It was all a great mystery to him! No one in the Peking office could read or write Yiddish; *he* does not know Yiddish (he speaks "Russian, German, and Turkish" in addition to English, but not Yiddish).* How did he explain his

---

*There is something pathetic about the reluctance of the brothers Werblow to admit to a knowledge of Yiddish. We know now from Robert's

"distinctive" accent, so alien to the diction of an American from Colorado? Unlike Robert-Mitzke, he had no physical impairment. His phonetic problem was cultural. It seems that he spent only his first five years in Fort Morgan; then he was brought to Brooklyn. And then his mother's brother "wanted to adopt me and he took me along with him to Turkey and I spent from six years to twelve—I was in Turkey."

At length, the trial judge interrupted the cross-examination, exasperation breaking through the admirable professional restraint he showed during the entire trial.

The Court: Is this all in your handwriting (showing paper)—do you have to read it?

A. There has been some very grand fitters here and certainly I would like to read it.

The Court: I don't understand what you mean, explain to the jury what you mean by that language?

A. I mean that sometimes one cannot recognize one's handwriting and likes to read the letter in order to see what is in it, in order to help him to recollect.

The Court: That is not what you meant by the expression "grand fitters," is it?

A. In addition to that, I mean there has been so many things here that I know I have never written—I know myself I have never done, and also know the letters which I have written in April come up to me and say I have written them later on.

---

apologia in 1941 that Yiddish was their mother tongue. But in their minds an admission to a knowledge of the language would remove the keystone in their arch of geneological falsehood. German they would admit. This was consistent with their assumed Nordic lineage. But Yiddish—perish the thought!

The Court: What you mean is, somebody is substituting evidence in this case that has no place here or has been fabricating, making up evidence?

A. That is my opinion.

The Court: Is that what you want to convey to the jury?

A. That is my opinion.

The Court: Now, read it very carefully.

A. This is my letter, yes.

In desperation, Henry sought refuge in a fantastic invention.

Q. You did not send this cablegram signed by you to Robert, "Tell Isaac he must go away, they are after him"?

A. I did not.

Q. How do you account for it being signed by you, in your own handwriting, and written in Yiddish?

A. I did not—I did not know the telegram even existed.

Q. How do you account to these gentlemen that there is a cablegram here in Yiddish to Robert in which you say, "Tell Elyot that he must hide himself, they are after him," and they are signed in your name?

A. Mr. Koff, the accountant of the bank, told me just before leaving Peking some of these telegrams were sent through Mr. Ding and paid for. [Emphasis supplied]

Wintner pressed him on the cable of September 5, 1922.

Q. I ask you now to specifically direct your attention to what the juror has asked. Did you on September 5, 1922, send the following cable which appears in Mr.

Peterson's deposition, having been signed by you personally Hozke, "Isaac shall hide himself, they are looking for him bad. Henry. Love." Did you send that?

A. No.

Q. $310.80?

A. I don't know anything about that.

Q. You mean to tell these gentlemen that a cable in Yiddish of fifty-five words, that cost $310 to transmit, you inadvertently signed, not knowing its contents?

A. Many times I—

Q. Did you or did you not say that?

The Court: Is that what you mean to say?

A. It looks like it, yes, but that is what happened.

The Eighth Juror: You personally signed a cable addressed to Robwerblo costing the bank over $300, knowing that Robwerblo was the cable address of your brother in New York and did not know what was in it?

A. I did not know it went to Robwerblo.
It was addressed—I ask you if you did?

A. Evidently it looked like it.[Emphasis supplied]

At this point in the cross-examination, it appears that something snapped in Henry. Beset as he was by the prosecutor, the judge, and four jurors with a flair for inquisition, he exploded into his wildest indiscretion. He charged that Tisdall had written the cable; it "was a decoy cable to get my brother." Then came this story:

Q. Referring back to this cable, the Court asked you to tell this jury what your theory and what your contention was as to who sent it; why it was presented to you for your signature, which it bears, and how it happens that it says in Yiddish code, or German words, what in English means "Isaac must go away for five months." What do you want this jury to believe as to how this situation occurred, that you signed, as you admit, signed that cable without knowing its contents, it being addressed to your brother Robert, New York cable address. Now try it again, because you did not succeed the last time.

A. My basis for the belief that somebody, was Mr. Koff's statement to me that somebody in the Asia Banking Corporation, the bookkeeper Mr. Ding who ran the account, received cables from an outsider and received payment for them and they were sent through the bank by Mr. Ding.

Q. To your brother in New York?

A. To my brother.

Q. By Mr. Ding?

A. By Mr. Ding. He is the man that took the cable in the bank.

Q. He sent them to your brother without telling you about it?

A. I did not know they went to my brother.

Q. Did Ding send them?

A. I don't know if he—

Q. To your brother?

A. *Ding is the man—*

Q. Without telling you anything about it, is that your belief?

A. *Yes.**[Emphasis supplied]*

---

*My professional readers who recognize that the questioning at this stage owes more to Perry Mason than to Wigmore must be patient with Mr. Battle for not objecting to the prosecutor's queries. A reading of the full transcript convinces this writer that it was a reasoned professional judgment not to object. Henry's plight was so bad that it would have been worsened by invoking technical objections.

Battle's summation could do little to help the brothers. He resorted to that hoariest dodge among desperate defense lawyers: if you have no defense, attack the prosecutor. But Mr. Wintner had been a model of patience and decorum. The real oppressor of the brothers Werblow was the Guaranty Trust. So Battle rang the changes on the omnipotence of the Guaranty Trust Company:

> Every door at which the Guaranty Trust Company knocks flies open. They have had no difficulty in producing evidence here which would have been utterly impossible for us to have procured. You remember the old fairy story of the Fairy with the Wand; whenever the wand touched any door it flew open. That reminds me of what has been done here by the Guaranty Trust Company in preparing this case. The doors of the State Department stood open; the doors of the Post Office Department stood open; the doors of the Customs Department have stood opened; the doors of all the banks have stood open—at the touch of the magic wand of the Guaranty Trust Company—this wand of gold and of influence that has made it so easy for the prosecution to get the vast amount, the vast mass of evidence, which has been adduced here. I have never seen a case in which there was such a wealth of detail, in which there has been such a mass of evidence of every character brought in. It seems every paper these young men wrote in their lives has been hunted up and scrutinized and brought here. Application they made for positions when they were boys—applications for passports, applications of all kinds have been dug up and brought here before you.

But the sagacious Battle knew that no jury could swallow the yarn that this great bank was persecuting these insignificant boys from Brooklyn. He put on an all-court press. He next tried to convince the jury that his client was

the victim of a conspiracy between that Bolshevik scamp
Elyot and the Anglo-Chinese phantom Chester James.

> We believe he [Chester James] was an accomplice of
> Elyot. We believe that he went there pursuant to some
> conspiracy and arrangement with Elyot. We believe
> that he conducted this cable correspondence from the
> Asiatic city while Elyot conducted it from the Brook-
> lyn City.

While Battle was dragging this red herring across the
trail, the jury must have been wondering what happened
to that other conspiracy against the hapless Hotzke and
Mitzke—the one in which the great Asia Banking Corporation framed Henry in retaliation for his refusal to take the
blame for the graft transactions with the Chinese government; the one in which a Yiddish-speaking Chinese bank
clerk (or two such gifted polyglots) got Henry to sign cables
in Yiddish without reading them. Poor Mr. Battle! His
plight must evoke the compassion of every trial lawyer who
has found himself alone and afraid on the burning deck! He
was even driven to suggest that the people in the London
branch of the Guaranty Trust were in the plot against his
client. Imagine trying to incriminate those selfless drudges
who had appeared early in the trial to describe the dealings
with "Max Elliott," and who must have seemed to the jury
as characters out of a Dickens novel. But Battle tried everything. He cried:

> That would excite a suspicion in the mind of any
> man *that there was some collusion there in the London branch
> of the Guaranty Trust Company to permit such a thing.* It
> does not seem possible—it can be explained only by
> negligence—that the bank would allow a stranger to
> come in and open an account for 110 pounds, and then

on the receipt of two cabled advices, neither of them bearing with any distinctive signature, to credit him with 31,000 pounds, and then to allow him to draw it out again, all within a week or ten days. It seems to me too extraordinary to be attributed entirely to negligence. *It looks as if there was some collusion with someone.* Understand me, I do not mean to say that Mr. List [a clerk in the London bank] had anything to do with it. I do not think that for a minute. *But it does look to me as if there were someone in the bank there who had some collusion in this fraud;* otherwise, I do not see how it was possible to get them to pay out $150,000 to an unknown man, without any attempt made to identify him or verify the payments. [*Emphasis supplied*]

He wound up with a few bromides about circumstantial evidence and sat down to await the thud of the guillotine's blade. He did not sit for long. The record discloses that he left the courtroom when Wintner began to speak. Who can blame him?

Hugo Wintner had what Ring Lardner's baseball players call a "laffer." For him the score was 10–0 for the people, with two out in the ninth. Henry's handwriting on the fake cables sent from Hankow to London, and on the Itzke-Mitzke-Hotzke series, had been identified with surgical precision by Osborne (the most eminent handwriting expert of the time) and finally conceded by Henry; that was all he really needed. But the ardor of advocacy took over, and Wintner nailed down the coffin's lid with triple brass. He finished with a grand flourish of oratorical trumpets.

Gentlemen, this is a *cause celebre;* there are thousands in the far away Orient, up and down the coasts of the big Pacific Ocean where the pioneers of white people have gone and established commerce among a strange and alien people. *The Caucasian race in China is on trial here, gentlemen.* This story is known up and down in any of those port cities; there is not a banker or a merchant that is not listening for your verdict today. *The integrity of the white people, their traditions for honesty and faithfulness to a trust is at stake here.* Never let it be said, gentlemen, that in an American court twelve honorable men taken "from the walks of life in this great commercial and imperious [*sic*] City of New York, could on the show of such evidence that I have presented to you, honestly and humbly though it might have been, may it never be said that a man so disloyal, so untrue to his word, so unfaithful to his master, shall go unwhipped of justice. [*Emphasis supplied*]

As lawyers say, the trial judge went "down the middle" in his charge. He favored neither side; calmly, dispassionately, and objectively, he reviewed the events of the trial. With skill born of long experience, he avoided any suggestion of the disgust he must have felt with the defense. Why not? Why risk the inevitability of a well-deserved conviction with even the faintest deviation from the thrice-blessed middle of the road? The jury retired at noon, enjoyed a lunch at the expense of the State of New York, and, at 2:10 P.M. (about two hours for lunch *and* deliberation), returned a verdict that vindicated the morality of missionary Caucasians in the Orient. Henry was found guilty on all counts. Battle waived the two-day interval between verdict and sentence to which the defendants of that simple age were entitled by law. Hotzke asked to be heard by the court. His was a *cri de coeur* that was brief but prophetic.

I am innocent; I have been tried under difficulties because I could not bring my Chinese witnesses from China. *The crime was committed in China.* My acts were in China and I could not bring witnesses to prove anything in my behalf. [*Emphasis supplied*]

Battle had nothing to add, and the court sentenced Henry-Hotzke "to State's Prison for a term of not less than five nor more than ten years." *Finis* Hotzke? Not quite yet.

Now it was the turn of Robert, who had demanded a separate trial. He got it. On the Monday morning after Hotzke's conviction, Mitzke went to trial. One week later he was convicted after a trial that was all watered-down bathos. Again justice was meted out with dispatch. On February 22, 1924, Robert-Mitzke was sentenced to not less than five years nor more than ten years in Sing Sing.

There followed one year of silence, while the two brothers served their sentences in that grim, gray pile on the Hudson, and the lawyers worked on their appeals. From what we know of them, it can be safely assumed that Mitzke and Hotzke had little difficulty in adjusting to the social and commercial structure of Sing Sing.

On March 27, 1925, Henry's conviction was affirmed by the Appellate Division, First Department. All five judges of that Court concurred in an opinion by Judge Merrell* that left little doubt as to the propriety of the conviction. There was a lucid, succinct recital of the facts, ending with the voice of doom: "The record before us establishes beyond any question the commission of the crime of grand larceny and defendant's complicity therein. The evidence points irresistibly to the guilt of the defendant-appellant."

As to the two points urged by Battle at the trial and in the appellate court, they got the shortest of appellate shrifts: ". . . the jurisdiction of the New York Court was

*212 App. Div. 445.

complete; *there can be no question but that the proofs show the commission of this crime in part, in the State of New York. . . .*" As to the second point, that the defendant was deprived of the right to confront and cross-examine the witnesses whose testimony was taken by commission in China, there was nothing to it.

When the news of this disaster reached the brothers Werblow up in Ossining, there must have been cold despair in their hearts. One can imagine Henry looking up from the lunch he was sharing with Robert in the warden's private dining room and explaining to the warden that if he wanted them to run the prison for another few years, there would have to be some improvements in their creature comforts. They did not know that Battle was already engaged in preparing their appeals for consideration by one of the great jurist-philosophers of the age, and that before long those sage gray heads (including the sagest and grayest) in Albany would be nodding over the briefs and the record in *People* v. *Werblow*.

The appeal came on with great expedition. It was argued in Albany on June 11, 1925. Battle appeared for Hotzke, and for the people the district attorney sent *his* loudest trumpet, Felix C. Benvenga, Chief of his Appeals Bureau and soon to be a scholarly judge of the State Supreme Court. The only *real* point was jurisdictional. Did the facts demonstrate either that the crime was committed in part in the County of New York or that the acts committed outside of New York affected persons or property within the state, within the meaning of Section 19-3 of the Penal Law, as it then stood?

On July 15 Benjamin Cardozo spoke for a divided Court of Appeals. Not for him the urgent demand to justify the moral integrity of Caucasians engaged in carrying civilized commerce to the heathen Chinee; his only concern was with the hard, gemlike integrity of the law. In his inimitable style, the style that has made the name of Cardozo a synonym among lawyers for trenchant prose and lucidity, he rehearsed the statutory departure, embodied in the Penal Law, from the common-law concept that felonies belonged to the courts of the state where the felony was *completed*, that *there was no jurisdiction* elsewhere, however material or flagitious might be the earlier acts. In larceny, wrote Cardozo, under the rule of common law the crime is committed in the place where the money or other property was obtained by the offender. He rejected the doctrine that a conspiracy formed in New York gives jurisdiction under the statute to punish for a larceny abroad, unless some overt act can be found to be committed in New York in furtherance of the conspiracy. He invoked vast scholarship, including Stephen's *History of the Criminal Law*, Russell's *Crimes*, Halsbury's *Laws of England*, and he concluded that the crime was committed in *China*, not in New York. "Indeed," he said, "had the defendants been indicted for conspiracy instead of grand larceny, a single overt act in New York could sustain the conviction. But there was no conspiracy count." And he concluded that the defendant was aggrieved by the denial of his motions to dismiss the grand-larceny counts. "The defendant should answer for his crime to the courts of the sovereignty within whose territorial dominion it was committed in all its parts."

That meant Peking, not Manhattan, and with a single dissent, the court reversed the convictions and remanded for a new trial. Within days the defendants were released on bail, and on August 4, 1925, *The New York Times* carried a story that Acting District Attorney Ferdinand Pecora*

---

*Pecora's name will be more than familiar to readers over fifty. He became famous as the special counsel who conducted the Congressional

had decided not to retry the brothers Werblow, because of "jurisdictional problems." On October 16, 1925, the indictments against them were dismissed and bail was discharged. As far as the courts of New York were concerned, that was the end of *l'affaire* "Itzke, Mitzke, and Hotzke." But what of Itzke, the fugitive rascal?

We know now that sometime in the fall of 1922, Itzke-Elyot fled from London to Russia, with a brief stopover in Berlin. He had with him several thousand good solid American dollars skimmed by Mitzke from the yen drafts that came from Peking. It must have been a fortune in the inflationary chaos of Eastern Europe after World War I. Early in 1923, Robert, in New York, received a postal card from Itzke in Russia.

Dear Robert: If you had known everything now you would get crazy—I was led on a wrong way and awful abused. My talking herewith will be strange to you now. Well, well, more detail I will write to you by the next letter. But herewith another demand to you; If you have heard anything or if you will hear something at any case, for GOD sake don't say at home moreover don't write to Henry please, please, please. All the best your Itzok

In September 1923 there came another postal card to Robert from Itzke.

Dear Bob: This postel card I am sending with a friend of mine who is going to Germany for an operation—why don't you answer me on my letters and postel cards to you. What is the reason? All that was

---

hearings that led to the enactment of the Securities Act of 1933 and the ancillary legislation. Remember the midget who sat in J. P. Morgan's lap? Pecora was the lawyer in *that* hearing.

happened to me was not my fault; I was told grain
business as you know and it was a lie. What could I do?
—at any case if you have heard or will hear about my
misfortune, don't say nobody moreover don't write to
Henry for God sake. I was sick and at hospital. Next
week I hope to move. . . .

When Itzke was later confronted with these postcards,
his explanation of them was such a rich piece of typical
Werblowesque self-justification that I must interrupt the
narrative to set it out. He was shown these cards on cross-
examination in Robert's naturalization hearing in 1941,
when he appeared as a witness for the government in opposition to the granting of his brother's application. His testimony:

Q. Have you seen those postal cards before?

A. Yes, years ago.

Q. How many years ago?

A. Many years.

Q. Under what circumstances?

A. Let me explain it, please. Robert was most fortunate of all of us. He had a few sweethearts and
when investigation came up with the Guaranty
Trust Company, he wired a girl friend in Russia
and Germany. There were six cards. They were
written in Russia and he cabled to this party to
send blank cards. Blank cards. When the cards
came in, he himself wrote the cards. I wrote some
cards. There were six, see. I wrote some, he wrote
some, and we sent them back to the proper parties
and got them back by mail, to mislead the authorities in this country. That is a frame-up. It burns
me up. I want this to come out. Maybe one of the
cards now after years, maybe carries my writing.
There were six altogether.

Itzke finally came back to America. In 1928 he wrote to Robert that he was managing the Butler Hotel in Detroit, where he was living under the name of Albert Ternow. After a short time he came to New York, and he joined his brothers in managing the photographic-printing business in which they were then engaged. Now, he assumed the name of Albert Verner. In 1935 he testified (in litigation described below) that his name was bestowed on him by Robert.

It would be pleasant to recount how these brothers, who by the 1930s had emerged with comparatively few scars from the ordeal of the Guaranty Trust case, now lived on in fraternal amity and enjoyed the benefits of life in the United States, how they worked together to build themselves into respectability and affluence. It was not to be.

In the next few years after coming to New York, Isaac–Itzke–Elyot–Albert Verner–Albert Ternow–Michael Werblow, vice-president of the family's business and one of the managers in its plant, acquired a substantial stock interest in the company by gift from his brothers.

In 1929 Itzke–Elyot–Albert Ternow–Albert Verner filed an application for naturalization under the name of Michael Werblow, using the original entry of *Robert* Werblow in 1907 to document the fact that he had been lawfully admitted to the United States for permanent residence and was therefore entitled to naturalization. In the 1941 naturalization case, Robert explained that Itzke had no hesitation in using this entry:

Q. Can you conceive of any reason why he would adopt the name of Michael, your name?

A. Well, he knew of my trouble and the lies I began to tell in connection with naturalization. He knew all that, and he felt that I would never tell the truth and come clean and for that reason he thought he would adopt my name as I would never be trapped in a lie.

Q. He was lawfully admitted to the United States in 1921, wasn't he?

A. Yes.

Q. What possible advantage could come to him claiming your name?

A. Because he came back in 1926 or 1927 through Canada and he did not have an American passport to come back here, as at that time he was still a fugitive from the courts. . . .

Q. Nobody knew Max Elliott and Isaac were the same person?

A. Yes.

Q. Who knew it?

A. Everybody looking for him—The Guaranty Trust Company and the District Attorney.

But the rivalry and bitterness between Itzke and the other brothers persisted, and by 1935 this had erupted into a suit by Albert in which he charged that his three brothers (for James had now joined the company) were making improper withdrawals of the company's funds for their personal use. Robert, Henry, and James retaliated by trying to kick Albert out of the company, charging him with larceny from the corporation.* This fratricidal litigation was "resolved" temporarily by putting the stock of all of the brothers in a voting trust and appointing a distinguished New York lawyer, George W. Alger, as "arbitrator."

---

*It was for this litigation that Robert, Henry, and James retained Kaufman, and it was this accident that prevented the Special Unit from pursuing the criminal aspects of the Werblows' conduct.

During the negotiations that led to Alger's appointment as "arbitrator" (he was in fact a voting trustee) Itzke-Albert passed a paper to Mitzke-Robert that exemplifies the atmosphere of mutual blackmail in which these brothers lived.

Thought it over and decided to advise you for future reference. Next time Mr. Battle asks *who* I am, he will be furnished with a copy of a group-picture, illustrating papa, mama, and all of us (and you in a black shirt) with copy of family list and copies of everyone's birth certificates. Plus two more great *surprises*.

The joke is on you! I am asking again for a peaceful settlement before *we* go to court.

ALBERT

The truce lasted only a few months. Robert, Henry, and James now sued to set aside the voting-trust agreement as having been obtained by fraud and duress; they charged in substance that Albert had hornswoggled them into the agreement by threatening to make damaging disclosures about the old Guaranty Trust case. When they sued, Albert countersued, charging mismanagement and waste of corporate assets.

The action to set aside the voting-trust agreement came on for trial before Judge Bernard L. Shientag. Shientag was a distinguished jurist who was noted for his practical approach to litigative problems, and under his auspices this case was settled, after three or four days of reciprocal mudslinging, by an agreement under which Albert's stock (given to him by his brothers as a gift) was now sold to his three brothers for a considerable sum of money. The ink was hardly dry on this agreement before Albert struck again. This time he instigated a stockholder's suit against the brothers and even induced the oldest brother, Morris, to join in the suit as a coplaintiff. Morris, too, had received his Polygraphic stock as a free gift from Robert, Henry, and James. This case, too, was settled by a payment of money to the plaintiffs, some of it winding up with brother Morris, who sold to Robert the stock Robert had given to him.

As do most true stories, this one finally winds down into vapid anticlimax. The characters, having passed through the flame, settled down into prosaic, workaday lives. This writer knows not how Itzke-Elyot-Albert ended his days. We do know that Robert died in 1959 in New York. He left an estate of more than $1,000,000, most of it in securities. He had finally attained American citizenship in the U.S. District Court in Bennington, Vermont, in 1949. (The Polygraphic plant had been moved to Bennington in the late 1930s. Robert had established a home in that city, had become a leading citizen of the community and chairman of the board of a local bank.) His application was not contested by the government, and the court found that he was and had been for five years a person of good moral character. With citizenship had come apparent peace and respectability.

Henry Werblow died in 1958. He, too, left a considerable estate, and at the time of his death he lived the life of a country squire in Vermont. (He had moved to Bennington to supervise the plant.) Shortly after his death, in an affidavit in support of an application to the Surrogate's Court in New York to exempt the estate from New York estate taxes, his widow averred that he was born in Fort Morgan, Colorado, on June 5, 1896; that he moved to Brooklyn as a boy and spent his childhood there; that as a young man in his early twenties he left the United States and maintained no residence in this country for several years. He moved to Vermont in 1936 and he remained in business there until

1952. In Vermont, said his wife, "He specialized in the development of special Jersey cattle, many of which have been prize winners. This was Mr. Werblow's home, where he spent all his time that his other activities would permit. He thoroughly enjoyed his active participation in the management of the farm and riding horseback over his land."

A long road that started in Libau, way back in 1907, wound down to the bucolic tranquillity of Vermont.

INDEX

303